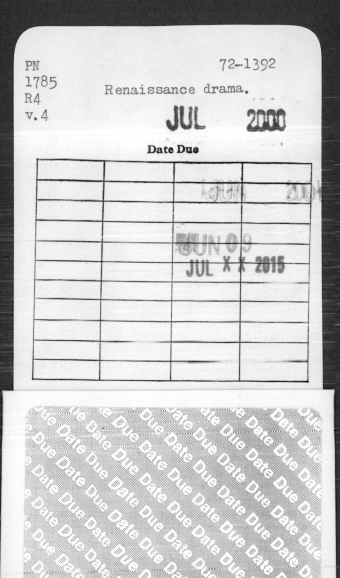

PN
1785
R4
v.4

72-1392

Renaissance drama.

JUL 2000

Date Due

		JUN	2004
		JUN 09	
		JUL X X 2015	

PRINTED IN U.S.A.

RENAISSANCE DRAMA
New Series IV ⁓ 1971

Renaissance Drama

NEW SERIES IV

*Essays Principally
on the Playhouse
and Staging*

Edited by S. Schoenbaum
Associate Editor: Alan C. Dessen

Northwestern University Press

EVANSTON 1971

THE COVER ILLUSTRATIONS are Inigo Jones's drawings for a private Elizabethan playhouse (see Plates 1 and 2). Reproduced by permission of the Provost and Fellows of Worcester College, Oxford.

Editorial Note

RENAISSANCE DRAMA, an annual publication, provides a forum for scholars in various parts of the globe: wherever the drama of the Renaissance is studied. Coverage, so far as subject matter is concerned, is not restricted to any single national theater. The chronological limits of the Renaissance are interpreted liberally, and space is available for essays on precursors, as well as on the utilization of Renaissance themes by later writers. Editorial policy favors articles of some scope. Essays that are exploratory in nature, that are concerned with critical or scholarly methodology, that raise new questions or embody fresh approaches to perennial problems are particularly appropriate for a publication which originated from the proceedings of the Modern Language Association Conference on Research Opportunities in Renaissance Drama.

For Volume V of this series our topic will be the theory and practice of comedy. Essays on Jonson are especially welcome. Manuscripts, for which the deadline is 15 February 1973, should be addressed to the Editor, RENAISSANCE DRAMA, Northwestern University, 617 Foster Street, Evanston, Illinois 60201. Prospective contributors are requested to follow the recommendations of the *MLA Style Sheet* (revised edition) in preparing manuscripts. For quotations from Shakespeare the Alexander edition is used.

Contents

RENAISSANCE DRAMA
New Series IV ❧ *1971*

The Question of
Harley Granville-Barker and
Shakespeare on Stage

MARION TROUSDALE

I

A NEW PLAY, *Orghast*, written in a newly invented language, Orghast, had its world *première* at Persepolis last September. It was written by the English poet Ted Hughes and directed by the English director Peter Brook. The intent was to return to the prelogical basis of drama; language in any conceptual sense must not be allowed to detract from the action of the play.[1] I cite it as an extreme example. Performance, I believe, has become one of the cults of our age, and it is with this cult as it affects Shakespearean studies that I am particularly concerned. Most recently, Ronald Watkins has reminded the readers of the London *Times* that "Shakespeare knew how to make a play," that "his plays cannot be fully experienced unless they are performed in the conditions they were written for."[2] John Russell Brown's pronouncements are even more indicative of a fashionable academic point of view.

1. This is based on the report of Irving Wardle, *The Times,* London, 10 September 1971, p. 11.
2. "Letters to the Editor," 9 October 1971.

3

"I think that becoming involved directly, at firsthand, with the process of a play in rehearsal and performance is an inevitable step that must be taken by the responsible critic of Shakespeare's plays." [3] Within this context Harley Granville-Barker provides some kind of center. He is a particular instance as well as the instigator of a now generally accepted view. I see him both as progenitor and chief advocate, a fact that at times may seem to cloud the issues with which I am principally concerned. When seen within a specific historical context, both his critical insights and his actual productions seem, in part at least, to belie his strongly expressed views. He provides in that sense counsel for the prosecution while serving as main witness for the defense. What I hope this investigation will provide, besides greater familiarity with that body of his writing that lies outside the *Prefaces,* is some insight into the origins of a literary fashion and some awareness of the kinds of questions that need to be addressed to what seems to me an increasingly entrenched Shakespeare-in-the-theater point of view.

I begin with his argument even though it is well known. It emerges in sharp outline, with its polemical overtones intact, in the first issue of the *Review of English Studies* in 1925, where, under the editorship of McKerrow and amidst such company as W. W. Greg, he suggested that had "Dr. Chambers hired an inn-yard and a mob (of medical students, shall we say, on holiday?), some boards and trestles and tapestry and faced his problem there, though he might have despaired of its solution, he would have sized it up correctly." Chambers is being taken to task for having remarked that there was "not much profit in attempting to investigate the method of staging in the inns as materials are lacking," and Granville-Barker in a characteristic way argues that, the theater being essentially a pragmatic concern, even historical problems can be solved in an essentially pragmatic way. [4] Even earlier he had complained to the Royal Society of Literature of the United Kingdom that, though

3. "The Theatrical Element of Shakespeare Criticism," *Reinterpretations of Elizabethan Drama,* ed. Norman Rabkin (New York, 1969), p. 188.

4. "A Note Upon Chapters XX and XXI of *The Elizabethan Stage," RES,* I (1925), 63. Granville-Barker observes of Chambers' two chapters on the staging of plays that "to those students . . . for whom the plays and their artistry are the heart of the whole matter—and it is at least arguable that they are—these chapters must be the most important in the book" (p. 60). See also his remarks on p. 70.

an overwhelming proportion of scholarly criticism was devoted to Elizabethan drama, a large part of it was "written by people who, you might suppose, could never have been inside a theatre in their lives."[5] The essential thing about *Othello* was not only the opportunity the part had offered to the talents of Burbage[6] but the vitality of its text when interpreted by properly trained actors, ideally before an enlightened audience on a properly constructed stage.[7] Without that, "with the breath out of its body, so to speak," a play text to this obviously talented producer was "nothing but a constricted if interesting form of literature, worthy, no doubt, of the learned footnotes that cling to line after line."[8] The technical demands of performance would solve pragmatically many apparent cruces in the plays. But performance was as well the only true reading of the text. Without that test "the scholar at best," he explained to the British Academy in 1925, "will be in the case of a man reading the score of a symphony, humming the themes."[9]

It is essentially this argument in various forms that Granville-Barker was to make again and again, and what it amounts to is an assertion, fundamental to any understanding of the position with which I am concerned, that a play's being, its *Dasein*, lies in performance. This is the tenor of his rather strong suggestion to Chambers which, as we have seen, is essentially the same suggestion as that delivered to the Royal Society of Literature some three years prior under the heading of "Some Tasks for Dramatic Scholarship." One can see its genesis in observations he made on his own first viewing of *King Lear* some twelve years before. Speaking to the Times Literary Club in the same year (9 June 1910), he pointed out that in twenty years of theater work it was the only

5. "Some Tasks for Dramatic Scholarship," 7 June 1922; *Essays by Divers Hands,* ed. F. S. Boas (London, 1923), III, 17. See also "Shakespeare and Modern Stagecraft," *YR,* XV (July 1926), 703.

6. "Elizabethan Stage," p. 62.

7. Presidential address to the Shakespeare Association, 25 November 1931, published as *Associating with Shakespeare* (London, 1932), pp. 22, 23, and *passim.*

8. *The Exemplary Theatre* (London, 1922), p. 74.

9. *From Henry V to Hamlet* (London, 1925), p. 28. See also "Some Tasks for Dramatic Scholarship," p. 37. "Reading a play, be it remembered, is comparable to reading the score of a symphony and asks as much skill" (*Exemplary Theatre,* p. 32). "About as many people can get at Shakespeare's plays by reading them as can appreciate Beethoven's Symphonies by fingering them out on the piano."

performance of *Lear* that he had had an opportunity to see. "I ask you," he said, in urging the creation of a National Theatre, "to appreciate the monstrosity of such a confession." "I had read *Lear* much and fondly," he went on to observe, "but I was electrified at things which actual performance threw into relief. I had hardly suspected the wonderful craftsmanship of the scene between blind Gloucester and mad Lear, when the dialogue only reinforces the poignancy of that perfectly devised meeting." [10] We have all had similar experiences, and we can only commend the rightness of Granville-Barker's position in urging more theater-going and nationally subsidized performances of Shakespeare's plays. But in addition to sniping quietly at the scholarly community locked away in their studies and disdaining the taint of the theater, Granville-Barker argues in his address to the Royal Society of Literature, with as much verve as he can muster while remaining polite, that the integrity of a play lies in its enactment. It is never fully alive until then. He makes his position even more explicit in his *Preface to Hamlet* (1937) when he maintains that Shakespeare was the genius of the workshop: "What he learned there was to think directly in terms of the medium in which he worked." [11] Although the experience of 1910 can easily lead to the position he takes in 1922, it is worth noting that the two views are not the same. In one, discoveries are made about dramaturgy, about how a text works on stage; in the other, these discoveries, or rather their possibility are taken as the defining element of the art of the play. What Granville-Barker is arguing in 1922 is essentially what John Russell Brown is arguing in 1969: "Shakespeare wrote for the theatre— that is his medium, the element in which his art is designed to live—and

10. "The Theatre: The Next Phase," *The English Review*, V (1910), 635, 636.

11. *Prefaces to Shakespeare,* with foreword, illustrations, and notes by M. St. Clare Byrne (London, 1963), I, 28. All references to the *Prefaces,* unless otherwise indicated, are to this edition. This belief is implicit in his early remarks on *Twelfth Night,* an Acting Edition with a Producer's Preface by Granville Barker (London, 1912; Boston, 1913), p. iv. "There is much to show that the play was designed for performance upon a bare platform stage without traverses or inner rooms or the like. It has the virtues of this method, swiftness and cleanness of writing and simple directness of arrangement even where the plot is least simple. It takes full advantage of the method's convenience. The scene changes constantly from anywhere suitable to anywhere else that is equally so. The time of the play's action is any time that suits the author as he goes along."

therefore, for all of its difficulties, theatrical reality is also *the* element of Shakespearean criticism." [12]

What is at once attractive and deceptive about such a view is its seeming simplicity. As with Iago's apt observations on jealousy, to disagree is to appear to put oneself in the wrong. Obviously the technical demands of performance must solve many cruces in a play text. Our only complaint might be that such a view can at times prove historically naïve. And as a play is by definition a text for performance, it seems self-evident that performance can constitute the only legitimate definition of the text. Any soundings may in such circumstances appear unwarranted, but they do, I think, give us some sense that the terrain is not quite as flat as it seems.

An opening observation is made inadvertently by Granville-Barker himself. In a mellow sexagenarian lecture in 1937 he pointed out the extent to which the Dryden reforms, as he called them, had led to a rift between literature and theater,[13] and it is useful, to begin with, to see that in this new orthodoxy there is suggested a similar if more insidious rift. What both Granville-Barker and John Russell Brown are saying is that the play in the theater is a totally different animal from the play as text (as a symphony is different from a musical score). A text meant to be spoken aloud, its nuances acted out, is as aesthetic object different not in degree but in kind from a text meant to be read. This means essentially that what is oral (and dramatic) belongs to an order of experience the dimensions of which require a response other than that required by what is literary—in its root sense, private, and, in any public sense, silent. A poem not intended for enactment and hence *not determined by it* cannot be judged in the same terms as a poem intended to be played. There is contingent upon this assertion another which may be thought logically to precede the first. In Granville-Barker's discussions of Shakespeare's stagecraft, as in his characterization of the nature of his genius and in his remarks on Chambers, it is assumed not only that Elizabethan plays (as all plays) were written with a particular stage in mind, but that the conditions for which they were written determined their form. The heavily descriptive verse is thus accounted for by the bare stage. We see

12. "The Theatrical Element," p. 189.

13. *On Poetry in Drama* (London, 1937), p. 9. The Romanes Lecture, 4 June 1937. He was actually 59 at the time that the lecture was delivered.

Harbage reaffirming this idea in his Alexander Lectures on Shakespeare's theater in 1955 when he remarks of Benedick's "Bring it hither to me in the orchard" at the opening of *Much Ado* that "in the orchard" would be superfluous if the orchard looked like an orchard.[14] "A particular sort of stagecraft must be rooted in the opportunities of its particular stage," Granville-Barker observed in his Clark Lectures *On Dramatic Method* at Trinity College, Cambridge, in 1930. "The whole fabric of a play's artistry will ultimately rest here."[15]

It follows from such beliefs that performance both conceptually precedes and predetermines the text. The design of a play and in turn of a play text is, in relation to the conditions of actual performance, seen more as result than cause, and the verbal structure exists essentially as gloss for action on stage. It is logical within such a context to hold that a play's true aesthetic significance lies only in its performance. A musical score that is not performed is of only academic interest, and it is essentially for the same reason that a play text is a dependent thing. "If Shakespeare, as I have contended, not only wrote but thought and felt dramatically, and has given us not merely plays in poetic form but something that is fundamentally and essentially poetic drama, it should follow that only in the theatre, and perhaps only in such a theatre as this for which he wrote them, will they be fully alive."[16] A play, though it uses poetry, is not—as the Elizabethans assumed—in the nature of a poem. It is rather closer in nature to the scenario, say, for *Last Year at Marienbad,* only an incomplete fragment once the film itself can no longer be viewed.

I do not mean to argue, at least not at this point, that this view of the nature of a play is wrong. I mean only to suggest that it is a view very closely allied to the sympathies of our own age. As a scholarly tool it is problematic, and if pursued as principle it produces strange bedfellows. In both Peter Brook's recent production of Ted Hughes's *Orghast* at

14. *Theatre for Shakespeare* (Toronto, 1955), p. 24.

15. (London, 1931), p. 15. He is discussing Greek tragedy.

16. "Shakespeare's Dramatic Art," in *A Companion to Shakespeare Studies,* ed. Harley Granville-Barker and G. B. Harrison (Cambridge, Eng., 1934; 2d ed., 1944) p. 83. Granville-Barker's argument in part is that Shakespeare's verse is an "enfranchised verse," especially in his later plays, and has "little validity apart from its dramatic purpose" ("Shakespeare and Modern Stagecraft," p. 703). See also *Prefaces,* III, 263 ff.

Persepolis, for instance, and in Granville-Barker's advocacy of Shakespeare-in-the-theater, it is taken for granted that performance defines, and indeed with Brook it supersedes, the text. Interestingly, both men look at theater as producers, and one must ask oneself whether this is not a point to be considered. Is the belief in the priority of performance with which we are concerned perhaps more a producer's than a scholar's view? The distinction may seem an arbitrary one, and I must leave it for the moment as such. Suffice it for now to suggest that though the two interests may overlap, they are not in their ultimate concerns consonant with one another, and when purposes are mistook, as Horatio notes, much may go awry.

Certainly the Granville-Barker who delivered the Shakespeare Lecture to the British Academy in the same year that he tangled with Chambers was at 47 an acknowledged *homme de théâtre*—an esteemed actor, playwright, and producer who, after recognized success, had decided for private and public reasons to quit the stage. In the most immediate sense the spectacular accomplishment of his London Shakespeare productions in 1912 and 1914 at the Savoy Theatre had been brought to an end by the war. But his break with the stage was even more decisively marked near the war's end by his divorce from the actress Lillah McCarthy, followed by his marriage to the American novelist Helen Huntington on 31 July 1918, a step which severed as well his personal friendships in the theatrical world. The shock of the news of his death in 1946 led Bernard Shaw to observe how he had for some twenty years "cherished a hope that our old intimate relation might revive." [17] Granville-Barker mounted two more plays in London after the war—Martinez Sierra's *The Romantic Young Lady* in 1920 and Maeterlinck's *The Betrothal* in 1921. With the publication of *The Exemplary Theatre* in 1922, he donned the mantle of writer-critic which he wore with apparent ease until his death. W. Bridges-Adams reports of him that he made a characteristically cool decision: "when he reached middle age he would retire from the theatre and write." [18] During the next two decades in numerous lectures

17. The only full-length biography of Granville-Barker is that of C. B. Purdom, *Harley Granville Barker* (London, 1955). Shaw's remark appeared in the 7 September 1946 *TLS* and is cited by Purdom on p. 276.

18. *The Lost Leader* (broadcast July 1953 in an abridged form; published London, 1954), p. 13.

of varying lengths and in his *Prefaces,* he developed the ideas on Shake-speare's stagecraft that as a producer had brought him most fame. His *Prefaces* he described in 1927, in a credo now familiar to most students, as an attempt to contribute to the new scholarship of Pollard and Chambers some research into Shakespeare's stagecraft. His plan was to examine the plays, one after another, "in the light of the interpreta-tion he designed for them, so far as this can be deduced; to discover, if possible, the production he would have desired for them, all merely in-cidental circumstances apart." [19] His concern until the end was with a working stage.

I would suggest, then, that his métier might impose a context on his critical judgments, and it is useful to keep that context in mind. What he sought to carry forward in the study was the work that the war, London audiences, and personal inclination had made impossible for him to carry forward on the stage; behind the often resonant phrases of the critic there remains a formidably imaginative but persistently prag-matic producer's mind. We can see this mind at work in all of its com-plexity in his use of the historical stage.

That use brings the question of the scholar-producer directly into view, and for a reason that should be clearly understood in all of its implications. If performance as determined by existing stage conditions of the period is the key to a sixteenth- or seventeenth-century dramatic text, we must then, in order to understand the text, know the stage conditions, and if one is to be rigorous, not only the general stage condi-tions but the stage conditions under which that particular text was per-formed. To understand Shakespeare's stagecraft in Granville-Barker's terms is necessarily to understand Shakespeare's stage. Granville-Barker was well aware of this fact, and it might be argued that he showed him-self not only a sensitive producer but a very acute stage historian in this regard. One of the things that he takes Chambers to task for is his unwitting imposition of the stagecraft of his day in his analysis of Elizabethan stage conditions, and one sees in Granville-Barker's re-marks that perspicuity which his own stage experience seems to have made possible in his reading of texts. He was later to remark of Acts III and IV of *Richard II* that "we are carried through the phases of

19. *Prefaces,* I, 4.

the three days' battle; and what other stage convention would allow us so varied a view of it, could so isolate the true drama of it," realizing sooner than anyone else the true glory of that Elizabethan freedom of place that the stage of Henry Irving and Herbert Beerbohm Tree could never know. "These scenes, in their kind," he continues, "show Shakespeare's stagecraft, not at its most reckless, but at its very best." [20] Of Chambers' definition of the Elizabethan dramatist's sense of place as localization by dialogue he asks, "Are [the instances] not themselves rather mere reinforcements for the actor in his task of capturing and enlarging the audience's imagination." [21] It is in this kind of historical theatrical perception that Granville-Barker is at his best, and at his best he is always acutely aware of the ways in which failure to recognize different dramatic conventions could result in failure to represent successfully the action of a play. His early producer's notes on *Twelfth Night* following its production in London at the Savoy in 1912 show just this kind of sensitive concern. Viola, he reminds his readers, was played and was meant to be played by a boy, and he shows in detail what this meant on stage to that original audience. "The strain of make-believe in the matter ended just where for us it most begins, at Viola's entrance as a page." Thus Shakespeare's audience saw "Cesario without effort as Orsino sees him; more importantly they saw him as Olivia sees him; indeed it was over Olivia they had most to make believe." And he adds the warning of the experienced producer bringing historical knowledge to bear upon his acting text: "The Viola who does not do her best, as far as the passages with Olivia are concerned, to make us believe, as Olivia believes, that she is a man, shows, to my mind, a lack of imagination and is guilty of dramatic bad manners." [22]

It is here, I think, that we must pause for a moment to note in more detail the kind of problem that Granville-Barker, in this instance as scholar rather than producer, brings into view. What he has given us, and we are grateful for it, is an illuminating gloss on a Renaissance text. We know better as scholars how to read its verbal nuances. But do we know better as producers how it should be played? The problem can be

20. Introduction to the *Prefaces*, I, 10, 11. See also "Elizabethan Stage," pp. 65–66; "Shakespeare's Dramatic Art," p. 58.

21. "Elizabethan Stage," p. 65. Cf. Harbage, *Theatre for Shakespeare*, p. 32.

22. *Twelfth Night*, An Acting Edition, p. vi. See n. 11 above.

seen in tne options that such knowledge allows to our scholar-producer. Should he: (1) use a boy to play Viola and make conspicuous what to the Elizabethans was commonplace; (2) instruct the actress playing Viola to play the part as though she were a boy playing the part of a girl and to play Cesario as though she were merely a boy; (3) play the part "straight," as Granville-Barker suggests, which will not make the Elizabethan reading possible but will at least save us from any further unnecessary distortion of the text? Such questions, I would argue, admit of no satisfactory answer. What they encourage is artful evasion. And what they reveal by virtue of that fact is essentially the dilemma of contemporary enactment which seeks for its interpretive definition the alien conventions (when known) of the seventeenth-century stage. The dilemma is not only that of the producer turned scholar but of anyone who argues that it is in such conventions, the deterministic conventions of an alien stage, that the true nature of the historical drama lies.

It is Granville-Barker himself, of course, in all of his engaging perspicuity, who first defined this problem, and he had his own solutions, none of which are easy ones. "It seems to me unquestionable," he told the Royal Society of Literature in 1922, "that we ought to go back as far as we can to meet the seventeenth century without sacrificing the spontaneity of our apprehension of the plays, and substituting for it a merely archaeological understanding." [23] What he has in mind is a particularly exacting distinction between what is accidental and what is essential in the craft of particular plays. The fact that Viola was played by a boy obviously affects the reading of the text, and some attempt must be made in the acting to account for that fact. Similarly the soliloquy is indicative to him of a particular kind of intimacy with the audience that is represented as well in the role of the fools, and he sees them as essential both to a play's economy and to its full emotional

23. "Some Tasks for Dramatic Scholarship," p. 30. See also Introduction, *A Midsommer Nights Dreame,* Players' Shakespeare (London, 1924), p. xii; *Associating with Shakespeare* (London, 1932), p. 18. His most carefully considered discussion of the problem occurs in the General Introduction to the Players' editions, *Macbeth* (London, 1923), pp. xiv–xv. It is this Introduction that appears in a revised form as the General Introduction to the *Prefaces.* As a producer he is particularly concerned that self-consciousness either of actors or of audience not be introduced into the theater.

effect.[24] But he is not one to urge boy actors, old methods of action, or reconstruction of the Globe. To do these obviously Elizabethan things would be to reproduce mainly the incidentals and accidentals which the Elizabethans accepted without question but which "we should find standing quite vexatiously between us and the *essentials* of the stage-craft." [25] It is here essentially that the producer reveals his hand. If what a scholar seeks is historically accurate knowledge about a particular event, whatever form that knowledge may take, then Granville-Barker at this point, though obviously a competent scholar, is not primarily in-volved with a scholar's concerns, nor does the original stage production really concern him *as such*. He was obviously a very gifted and a very conscientious producer, and what he is worried about in this instance is very much what any conscientious producer must worry about—the viability of a historical text on a contemporary stage. What he discovers in this context, and the distinction seems to me an important one, is not the performance that once defined the text, but rather readings that open up the continuing possibilities of the illusion-making apparatus of the play.

In insisting upon such distinctions I do not mean to suggest that we would wish it any other way. We owe to the consistently intelligent use of history by sensitive producers some of our best moments on the con-temporary Shakespearean stage. But if it seems true that the producer intent only upon the historical accuracy of his work is destined to produce bad plays, it seems equally questionable whether such a rich and obviously richly rewarding approach to Shakespearean production as Granville-Barker's can be as richly rewarding as a scholar's base. The scholar obviously must pursue his historical investigation without con-cern for a viable contemporary presentation. But given that obvious dis-tinction, is the belief that performance *defines* the dramatic text feasible as a postulate by means of which meaningful research can be done? I have no easy answers to that question. But I do think we should recog-nize that an insistence on the play *in the theater* which argues that the

24. Introduction to the *Prefaces*, I, 17. "There is no more important task for the producer of Shakespeare than to restore to the soliloquy its rightful place in a play's economy, and in particular to regain for it full emotional effect," p. 18. See also "Shakespeare's Dramatic Art," p. 69.

25. "Associating with Shakespeare," p. 16. Presidential Address to the Shake-speare Association, 25 November 1931.

essentials of any play are necessarily determined by the conditions of the particular theater for which it was written is necessarily an insistence on what is most ephemeral in the art of the stage, and one must feel that as such it is at best a quixotic scholar's tool. Professor Harbage argues that we should stage the plays of Shakespeare as they were staged in the first place "not because that necessarily is the best way to stage plays but because these particular plays were written to be staged in that way and we do not wish to change them" and then points out the impossibility of doing just that. What he feels is possible is to "stage the plays of Shakespeare as they were staged in the first place, but without seeming to do so." We can do this because "good acting is always the same, in that it employs persuasively the current conventions whatever they may be."[26] I ignore the logical difficulties of the argument, but what it brings to mind is the fact that if performance represents the essence of Shakespeare, performance being in and of its nature mutable, then that essence is mutable, and it will by performance be transformed again and again. We are told that Kemble said, "Sir my good FRIEND! I'll change *that* name with you," that he told Horatio and the rest, "We'll teach you to DRINK deep, ere you depart," that he asked, "Did YOU not speak to it."[27] Garrick was overcome by tears as he recited, "O that this too too solid flesh," and spoke "To be or not to be" with his hair disordered and one stocking ungartered—the Hamlet perhaps that Ophelia describes.[28] David Warner as the superior adolescent said, "How all occasions do inform against ME." To say that plays are only plays as played is, within a historical context, to say that plays are only plays as they *were* played. Something that is by nature changeable, performance, is attached as defining element to a text—something that being printed remains as record unchanged.

Similarly, it seems foolhardy to confuse historical with aesthetic concerns. Stanley Wells, who observes with some cogency that "our chances of arriving at a production which may be regarded as wholly authentic in its conditions—in methods of staging, in the very facts of what happens on the stage—let alone in its effect upon the audience, are so slim as to be almost negligible," argues in the same paragraph that the ef-

26. *Theatre for Shakespeare*, pp. 18, 44.
27. The New Variorum, ed. H. H. Furness (Philadelphia, Pa., 1877), II, 248.
28. *Ibid.*, II, 269.

fort must be made to present the texts that remain in a manner that will "reproduce for a modern audience the effect they may be supposed to have had upon their original audience." [29] I do not know whether such a thing is desirable. Will Kemp in his account of his nine-day dance to Norwich describes a cutpurse as "such a one as we tye to a poast on our stage, for all people to wonder at, when at a play they are taken pilfring."[30] To me that kind of activity seems unavoidably to be part of a play's effect. But whether or not it is desirable to reproduce the historical effect, honesty must force us to admit that such a thing is impossible, if only because it is impossible to know. Aesthetic response may be informed by a knowledge of history, a knowledge of the text, but it is impossible, given the nature of performance, for that response to be determined in any definitive aesthetic sense or defined by the original one. And one must add the more important point that what is deemed essential in Shakespeare's dramaturgy after 350 years can be deemed essential only by virtue of the text that remains. Aesthetically, even as scholars the text is all we can know. It is this text that we must necessarily exploit in our desire to render the true Shakespeare. To what extent, one wonders, does the literary nature of that text and our response to it not only logically precede but predetermine the desired presentation of that text on stage?

II

To ask this question is to ask a different kind of question from the one we have been considering, and it is to that question that we must now turn. Granville-Barker, as we have seen, argues that what is dramatic is basically different from what is poetic, that in effect the action of the play is what defines it, and that that action can only be realized fully upon the stage. We have talked about the extent to which this seems a useful distinction for the scholar, but there is a more important consideration. To what extent is it an accurate definition of the nature of a

29. "Shakespeare's Text on the Modern Stage," *Deutsche Shakespeare-Gesellschaft West Jahrbuch* (1967), p. 180. He does add that it is a task in which personal opinion must inevitably play a large part.

30. *Kemps Nine Daies Wonder: Performed in a Daunce from London to Norwich,* ed. Alexander Dyce (London, 1840), p. 6. I have not seen the original edition.

dramatic text? Ought the scholar as critic, as John Russell Brown suggests, assume that Shakespeare's text can be fully known only on the stage? Granville-Barker's own productions in this instance make us appreciate that the issues are not as clearly drawn as they may at first seem, at least not in Granville-Barker's case. His early innovative Shakespeare productions at the Savoy Theatre, 1912–1914, are a case in point. Their thrust seems directed essentially against the naturalistic theater of Irving and Pinero, and this must make us wonder to begin with whether a love of poetic drama as such and a belief that it can be performed is quite the same thing as an insistence that a play's integrity lies in its life on the stage.

The 1879 edition of *Hamlet* as arranged for the stage by Henry Irving and presented at the Lyceum Theatre in December 1878 gives us a very specific idea of the orthodoxy Barker was up against and a clearer idea of what he was about. In the graveyard scene, called significantly the "Church Yard Scene," the church is supposed to be built on the hill above the royal palace, and the procession is seen coming slowly up the ascent just as evening is changed into night. It was at this time, it is explained, that the "maimed rites" used to be performed over the dead, and our sympathy is evoked, as though by the shadow of Gray's *Elegy,* by the stars "beginning to shine faintly on the sad group gathered around the grave." Even more striking is the description of the play's concluding scene.

Through the arches at the back of the stage are seen the trees of what may be supposed to be the "orchard" in which the good king Hamlet met his death at his brother's hand.

Such a setting is felt to be especially fitting for the "execution of that vengeance so long deferred."

The contrast between the soft green foliage of early summer and the deepening gloom of the tragedy is not inconsistent with that terrible irony of fate which is one of the leading characteristics of the story of Hamlet.[31]

It is perhaps not surprising that in the face of such graphic delineation Granville-Barker chose to use the money that Lord Lucas took from

31. *Hamlet* . . . As Arranged for the Stage by Henry Irving and presented at The Lyceum Theatre, December 1878 (London, 1879), pp. viii, xi, xii.

the sale of his pig farm for the "Bard's pearls"[32] to present three of Shakespeare's plays that make no gesture toward realism. *The Winter's Tale* opened at the Savoy on 21 September 1912 for a run of six weeks, and was followed on 15 November by *Twelfth Night*. *A Midsummer Night's Dream* began the following season, running from 6 February 1914 until the middle of May. And it is not only the plays themselves which show us Granville-Barker's particular interest in the possibilities of an imaginative, poetic, even anti-naturalistic drama. His own published producer's notes on *The Winter's Tale* make it obvious that the play's attractions were precisely those characteristics which might have led other producers to reject it. The action is obviously contrived and its effectiveness entirely dependent upon the poet's and the producer's skill. The technique, as Granville-Barker observed, is that of a man "who knows he can do what he will, lets himself in for difficulties with apparent carelessness, and overcomes them at his ease."[33]

His sense of the stagecraft of such a play takes its cue from that sense of artifice which appears to have governed his original choice. Of Hermione as statue he remarks that "the crude stage effect is so good that hasty naked handling might have spoiled it." As playwright, however, Shakespeare has taken great care in his presentation.

The scene is elaborately held back by the preceding one, which though but preparation, actually equals it in length, and its poetry is heightened by such contrast with fantastic prose and fun. While from the moment the statue is disclosed, every device of changing colour and time, every minor contrast of voice and mood that can give the scene modelling and beauty of form, is brought into easy use. Then the final effect of the music, of the brisk stirring trumpet sentences in Paulina's speech. . . . And then the perfect sufficiency of Hermione's eight lines (oh, how a lesser dramatist might have overdone it with Noble Forgiveness and what not!).[34]

He shows an even more refined awareness of the possibilities of spoken verse in his discussion of *A Midsummer Night's Dream*. Discussing the structure of tone that the play calls for in the casting, he writes:

32. Purdom, *Harley Granville Barker*, p. 139.

33. *The Winter's Tale*, An Acting Edition with a Producer's Preface by Granville Barker (London, 1912; Boston, 1913), p. iii.

34. *Ibid.*, p. vii.

Take the first scene. It opens with the formal serenity of Theseus' and Hippolyta's speeches, mellow-toned—note the sound of the vowels in "Now, fair Hippolyta, our nuptial hour Draws on apace." Impinging on this comes the shrill rattle of Egeus with his "rings, gawds, conceits, Knacks, trifles, nosegays, sweet-meats"; Next, Hermia's meek obstinacy, rhythmical, distinct, low: "I do entreat your grace to pardon me" . . . Then Demetrius and Lysander strike each his note. Demetrius, slow, hard-bitten, positive, pleasantly surly. . . . And Lysander, glib and impertinent, melodious, light.

It is remarkable, he notes, "how much sheer sound, in quality, contrast, change, is made to contribute." [35] One sees a similar marked concern with the essentially technical poetic effects of Shakespeare's text in Granville-Barker's followers. Thus John Russell Brown notes as an example of theatrical criticism (as distinguished from literary criticism) how in Polonius' discourse on plays (II.ii.392), after the "first long sentence of Polonius' speech, the structure and rhythms then shorten; after an antithesis that is comparatively brisk, the last sentence starts with an adverbial phrase and then a short statement." [36] These are useful observations about the way in which poetic drama should be played. One hears behind them the voice of Samuel Daniel, who admits in his *Defence of Ryme* that to his ear "those continuall cadences of couplets used in long and continued Poemes are verie tyresome," and adds that "sometimes to beguile the eare with a running out, and passing over the Ryme, as no bound to stay us in the line where the violence of the matter will breake thorow, is rather gracefull then otherwise." [37] Such spoken verse is obviously effective on stage. But we must ask ourselves in what sense its techniques show a dramatic rather than a literary concern. Granville-

35. Players' edition (London, 1924), pp. xxvii–xxviii; xxx. See also p. xxxi: "When a particular effect is wanted we are more likely to find it made by purely poetic means. We have the change to a tenser metre for Puck and Oberon when the magic of the love juice is in question, or when Puck is dancing with suppressed excitement. We have the pretty use of a quatrain to emphasize the drowsy happiness in which Hermia and Lysander wander through the wood; the use of quatrain and couplet and a four times repeated rhyme when there is need to stress the increasing delusion of the lovers—this sudden pleasant artificiality does somehow help to."

36. "The Theatrical Element," p. 191. See also the textual analyses of J. L. Styan, *Shakespeare's Stagecraft* (Cambridge, Eng., 1967), pp. 141, 142, 144, 150, and *passim*.

37. G. G. Smith, *Elizabethan Critical Essays* (London, 1904), II, 382.

Barker describes Shakespeare's stagecraft in *Antony and Cleopatra* as something that one might liken to the skill of a musician:

master of an instrument, who takes a theme and, by generally recognized rules, improvises on it; or to an orator, so accomplished that he can carry a complex subject through a two-hour speech (III.5).

"Clarity of statement," he adds, "a sense of proportion, of the value of contrast, justness of emphasis—in these lie the technique involved." One is forced to ask, if only for the sake of clarity of statement, in what sense this skill *as skill* is essentially dramatic, however effective it may be when enacted. Does Granville-Barker establish the *innately* dramatic nature of Shakespeare's text? Or does he show us how a poetic text should be played?

T. S. Eliot in his essay *Dialogue on Dramatic Poetry,* first published interestingly enough in 1928, has B say apropos of William Archer that the greatest drama is poetic drama. C asks, "Do you mean that Shakespeare is a greater dramatist then Ibsen, not by being a greater dramatist, but by being a greater poet," and B replies, "That is precisely what I mean." It is a question, surprisingly, that Granville-Barker's own commentary brings to mind, and one that must ultimately be raised in any attempt to determine the validity of our belief that plays are dramatic rather than literary in conception and dramatic rather than literary in effect. Does *dramatic* mean something determined by the conditions of performance, as Granville-Barker elsewhere suggests, or something effective when played? We can see in support of the first premise, for instance, how the opening of *Hamlet* was obviously envisioned in terms of enactment. There is very little explicit exposition to help the inexperienced reader along, and a student who does not closely plot the sequence of events may lose track of who is relieving whom. We can similarly see how Polonius' "Will you walk out of the air, my lord?" depends for its reference on a particular kind of stage. But taken in and of themselves such theatrical glosses seem incidental in any consideration of Shakespeare's text as a whole. What they define essentially is occasion, and one must ask to what extent occasion can be taken as the definition of a literary text, or of a work of art. Chartres in that sense is defined by the cult of the Virgin; *Lycidas,* by the death of Edward King. But this is in part to misrepresent the issue. A dramatic text is written *to be* performed. What Granville-Barker has in mind in his insistence on action is something that the Elizabethan audience seems to have responded to more passionately than any modern audience could. It is what Heywood is talking about in his *Apology* when he observes that "a Description is only a shadow received by the eare but not perceived by the eye" and then goes on to laud the moving effects of the realization of such "description" on stage. His account conveys in a marvelously graphic way the whole sense of excitement that must have been part of seeing at least the first production of a play. "To see a souldier," he remarks, "shap'd like a souldier, walke, speake, act like a souldier":

to see a *Hector* all besmered in blood, trampling upon the bulkes of Kinges . . . To see as I have seene *Hercules* in his own shape hunting the Boare. . . , taming the Hart, fighting with Hydra, murdering *Gerion,* slaughtring *Diomed* . . . Oh these were sights to make an *Alexander*.[38]

It is very precisely this kind of realization that Lamb objected to, remarking on how "cruelly" such enactment operates upon the mind's free conceptions, cramping them and pressing them down to "the measure of a strait-laced actuality," but there are few today who would not grant Heywood his point. There is something undeniably more immediate, more moving, more exciting about a play effectively acted on stage. Can we not thereby allow that that pleasure created by enactment defines the essential nature of the text?

Eliot suggests not. He suggests that, though the effect may be dramatic, the skill is not, and he adds to that the observation that the better play is created by the greater skill. The question thus raised is whether the purely verbal effects with which *Hamlet,* for instance, abounds and which have been amply documented can accurately be called dramatic in nature. I am thinking of the parallel plots, the verbal play on appearance and reality, the attention to the concept of "play"—in short the whole elaborate skein of metaphor so eloquently explored by such scholars as Maynard Mack. It is not sufficient to argue that such metaphoric overtones are more effective or affecting when spoken on stage. Obviously the text is brought to life, as it is given live embodiment. One can make the same observation about a non-dramatic text such as *The*

38. *An Apology for Actors* (1612) in Scholars' Facsimiles edition, with an Introduction by Richard H. Perkinson (New York, 1941), B3ᵛ–B4.

Canterbury Tales. And it is obvious that any reading of the text oral or printed, if it is a well-considered reading, opens up new insights into the play. But to what extent are the verbal effects dramatic rather than poetic in origin and dramatic rather than poetic in *essential* effect?

Granville-Barker himself certainly does not restrict his definition of Shakespeare's dramaturgy to his poetry. Following his discussion of the statue scene in *The Winter's Tale,* he remarks of Hermione, "I seem to see an exquisitely sensitive woman, high-minded, witty too, and tactful. . . . one can tell that she knows the danger of the man." [39] And it is significant that to him Bradley was a critic for whom the plays never ceased to be plays.[40] But his true genius is with the language and the delivery of the lines. "This speech must be like a polka," John Gielgud reports Granville-Barker saying of Lear's "Come, let's away to prison" in Act V, "sung in every possible range and variety of tone, but lightly, like a boy of nine telling a story to a child of six." [41] Much earlier, writing to Gielgud of his Richard II, Granville-Barker complains of his delivery of the verse. Shakespeare, he points out, "has not yet learned to express anything except in speech" and therefore "everything the actor does must be done *within the frame* of the verse." These are profound perceptions about the nature of Shakespeare's text, and it is obviously this kind of linguistic awareness that is oral as well as literary which made it possible to put Lamb's *Lear* on stage. But consciously or unconsciously the shape of the argument changes. He is not arguing that performance is primary or that stage conventions are basic to an understanding of a play text. He is telling us only what T. S. Eliot was to rediscover and what the Elizabethans never questioned—that it is the language that determines on stage or off the worth of a play.[42] His penchant for

39. (London, 1912), p. viii.

40. "Some Tasks for Dramatic Scholarship," p. 20. Granville-Barker argues that both the concept of character and the ability to express it developed by virtue of enactment. See *From Henry V to Hamlet* and Introduction, *Prefaces.* The same argument has most recently been made by M. C. Bradbrook in *Shakespeare the Craftsman* (London, 1969).

41. Hallam Fordham, *Player in Action* (unpublished MS, Folger MSS Collection T.b.17). The commentary follows the description of V.iii. The manuscript is without pagination.

42. This point of view seems to me to become increasingly explicit in his work. See particularly his discussion of verse and speech in *Coriolanus,* published posthu-

poetical drama is especially evident, I think, in remarks that he made in 1910 on Maeterlinck in which he pointed out that the theater that was needed for his plays was one specially created for them, "far other than the one he could then step into for a franc or two, far other than any he has found since, in this country at least."[43] This in effect contradicts his postulate about the historical Shakespeare. He knows of the existing stage at the time that Maeterlinck wrote, and he knows that what his plays demanded, if they were to be produced, was a very different kind of stage. Similarly, in an essay on "Tennyson, Swinburne, Meredith— and the Theatre," published in 1929, he says of Swinburne's *Bothwell*: "This last scene is true drama; it will answer to any test," and he then adds, "If it seems not to fit the work-a-day theatre, a theatre can be moulded for it."[44] In such a view, the literary text precedes and pre-determines performance. It was essentially in the same way that he worked on the staging of Shakespeare's plays.

Such remarks may seem to call in question those views of Granville-Barker's with which we began, and it is perhaps only my analysis of them that is at fault. I do not mean to say that Granville-Barker in either instance is wrong, but it does seem on occasion that because of a particular historical situation, the evidence, if not misstated, has perhaps been misread. What Granville-Barker was principally concerned with, as we can see from his early remarks on *Lear* and his repeated efforts to create a National Theatre, was to see Shakespeare unadulterated on stage. But this fact should not keep us from realizing in retrospect that the means by which he justified that wish, his polemic, if you will, proves weak if not factitious as a working critical postulate, even in his own work. He is obviously not only principally a producer. Herbert Beerbohm Tree, after all, was also a producer. Granville-Barker's importance is precisely his response to Shakespeare's dramatic poems and his ability to see how they might as poems be played.

mously in *RES*, XXIII, no. 89 (January 1947), pp. 1–15, and now included as part of the *Preface*. The letter to Gielgud is dated 15 October 1937, and is cited in Purdom, *Harley Granville Barker*, p. 253.

43. Maurice Maeterlinck, *Three Plays*, trans. Alfred Sutro and William Archer (London, 1911), p. vi.

44. *The Eighteen-Seventies: Essays by Fellows of the Royal Society of Literature*, ed. Harley Granville-Barker (New York, 1929), p. 184.

It is just such a profound Coleridgean sense of Shakespeare the poet, I feel, that explains a very basic confusion that emerges in his views—between the nature of performance and the nature of the text.[45] Texts, as we have come to view them, are the closest things we have, apart from standing monuments, to permanent record; they remain as tangible artifacts when the person, the performance, and even the culture are gone, and unstable as they now appear even as artifacts, what with the vagaries of the compositors and the wayward scribes, they are at least authentic memorabilia of the age. It is not surprising, then, that a producer interested in the historical Shakespeare should share the scholar's respect for his text. Granville-Barker's mentor, William Poel, had admonished stage managers to "produce this play as it is written or leave it alone," although he himself did otherwise.[46] Granville-Barker commends the work of Pollard and, both in his own productions and in his critical comments, follows Poel's advice.[47] He took the Folio text for his three productions, as he did for the luxuriously bound and illustrated Players' edition, and he played the entire text. Stanley Wells reports some twenty lines cut from *The Winter's Tale*.[48] In that sense he restored the authentic Shakespeare to the stage.

But did he? And in what sense were his productions authentic? If a play text is but a score for performance and if performance is at best a mutable thing, in what sense can one argue in terms of performance for the integrity of the text?

There are many possible answers to these questions. The titles of the early Quartos provide us with the most immediate one. *The Tragedie of Gorboduc* is set forth, we are told "as the same was shewed before the Quenes most excellent Majestie, in her highnes Court of Whitehall, the xviii. day of January," 1562. *Fedele and Fortunio* is "set downe according as it hath beene presented before the Queenes moste excellent Majestie," 1585. *The Most Lamentable Romaine Tragedie of Titus Andronicus* is "as it was Plaide by the Right Honourable the Earle of Darbie, Earle of

---

45. Coleridge, he observes in his address to the Shakespeare Association, 25 November 1931, rescued Shakespeare the poet and set us all stargazing (*Associating with Shakespeare,* p. 10).

46. *Shakespeare in the Theatre* (London, 1913), p. 180.

47. Introduction to the *Prefaces,* I, 4.

48. "Shakespeare's Text on the Modern Stage," p. 177.

Pembrooke and Earle of Sussex their Servants," 1594. Of *The Misfortunes of Arthur* we are told more precisely that it is "set downe as it past from under his [Thomas Hughes] handes and as it was presented, excepting certaine wordes and lines, where some of the Actors either helped their memories by brief omission: or fitted their acting by some alteration," 1587. Whether or not we believe the obviously promotional descriptions, there is a sense in which the texts of the Quartos, unlike the texts of the interludes that Bevington discusses, are at least as much record of performance as text to be played. They are close in that sense, at least in intent, to the accounts of the triumphs or the Lord Mayor's shows—Dekker's *The Magnificent Entertainment Given to King James* (1604), for instance, or Thomas Churchyard's *Discourse of the Queenes Majesties entertainement in Suffolk and Norffolk* (ca. 1578). The 1590 Quarto of *Tamburlaine* is explicitly addressed to those "that take pleasure in reading Histories." But even when explicitly intended for play texts, their authority remains that of a record of an event. *Damon and Pithias* (1571) has a prologue "somewhat altered for the proper use of them that hereafter shall have occasion to plaie it," but is otherwise claimed as the text of an actual performance before the queen by the children of the chapel.[49]

If transcript of performance can be equated with authentic text, then in those instances in which the Quarto claim can be substantiated, it might be argued that we have a text that might prove satisfactory for an authentically historical-modern version of a play. One's thoughts turn inevitably to the good and bad quartos of *Hamlet*—perhaps too exceptional a case to prove a point. But what it brings to mind is the very obvious point that the exigencies of acting have always made of the play text less a dependent than an expendable thing. Granville-Barker in 1922 observed that the professional actor may cut the play's fabric and suggested that a play might "often be heard in fuller integrity shouted through whole-heartedly and unself-consciously by a band of school-children,"[50] giving away his persistently literary point of view.

49. Ben Jonson scrupulously distinguishes between the common practice and his own in *Every Man Out of His Humour* (1600), published "As it was first composed by the Author B. J. Containing more than hath been Publickely Spoken or Acted."

50. *Exemplary Theatre*, p. 75.

More accurately, one must admit, by the measure of dramatic performance, texts have rarely been sacrosanct. Garrick writes of *Hamlet,* "I had sworn I would not leave the stage till I had rescued that noble play from all the rubbish of the fifth act." [51] One can hear Shakespeare making the same judicious observation about the early *Leir.* Hamlet himself adds a speech to *The Murder of Gonzago.* The only essential difference is that unlike Garrick, he has no intimations of guilt for tampering with the text. Rather it is the means by which the play is made to render the very shape and body of the times. It is what Shakespeare with far deeper implications did to the texts of other men's plays.

It is, then, not consistent and certainly not historically accurate, if one's criteria really are those of performance, to apply what are essentially literary standards to the staging of a play text. Granville-Barker's point as producer is that of Kenneth Muir as editor when he notes in the Arden edition of *Lear* that a modern editor, whether he follows the Folio or the Quarto, will restore the omitted lines, and adds that in following the Folio he will use the Quarto not only in cases of corruption but also "where [the Q] seems palpably superior." [52] "If an editor's judgement is worth anything at all," Greg remarks, "it should enable him to approach nearer to the author's original than does either of the transmitted texts." [53] It is the elusive authority of the Coleridgean poet more than the mutable authority of performance which underlies our difficult pursuit of the true text. [54] This is not to say that literary texts should not be sacrosanct or should not be played. It is only to suggest that as one cannot at the same time be both scholar and producer, so a similar conflict of interest exists between author and actor, between text and enactment as it did in Shakespeare's day. The first edition of *Hamlet,* McManaway points out, "seems to show

51. To Dr. Hoadly, January 1773. See Percy Fitzgerald, " 'Hamlet' with Alterations," *The Theatre,* 1 May 1886, p. 252. Garrick remarks of his production, "It was the most imprudent thing I ever did in all my life."

52. (London, 1952), pp. xvi, xix.

53. *The Editorial Problem in Shakespeare* (London, 1951), p. xxvii.

54. Malone's point in 1790 was that the "genuine text" of the poet must be the first concern of any responsible editor. It is this view that leads Greg to prefer foul copy to prompt-book even if both are autograph (*Editorial Problem in Shakespeare,* p. 47).

that from the outset the acting versions had an abbreviated text with possibly some irregularities in the order of the scenes." [55] One can argue convincingly that the full text was never meant to be played. Similarly actors were suspect even in the eyes of the dramatists who worked most closely with the stage. Quiller-Couch in 1921 pointed out, almost as though in response to Granville-Barker, that it is to do Shakespeare an injustice to view his verse primarily as "material for an actor to juggle with and use to the best advantage of the drama." [56] We have long since outgrown that point of view. But Hamlet, who alters another man's text with impunity, admonishes the players to stick to their lines, and Dekker complains to the *Lectori* in putting into print *The Whore of Babylon* (1607), "Let the Poet set the note of his Nombers, even to Apolloes owne Lyre, the Player will have his owne Crochets and sing false notes, in dispite of all the rules of Musick." This view of the actors is well known but perhaps too little regarded. If we are to see Shakespeare in the theater for which he wrote, as we are more and more admonished to do,[57] it

55. "The Two Earliest Prompt Books of *Hamlet," Studies in Shakespeare, Bibliography, and Theater* (New York, 1969), p. 93. See also p. 95.

56. Introduction to the Cambridge Shakespeare, published in the first volume, *The Tempest*, p. xxiv.

57. This is Granville-Barker's definition of the new scholarship of Pollard and Chambers. See the Introduction to the *Prefaces*, I, 4. There is a strange sidelight on Granville-Barker's own views of acting in an interview reported by the Oxford Drama Commission during a visit to the United States in 1945, at which time the Granville-Barkers were residing in New York. The commission had raised the question as to whether a student's understanding of drama might be increased by participation in actual productions. They describe Granville-Barker's point of view as "clearly that of a scholar interested first and foremost in the scholarly study of the drama" and report that "he was inclined to press the view that dramatic activities on the part of students so far from increasing their understanding of a particular play, tended to diminish it. He made the point that a student who is required to act a part in a play immediately becomes engaged in the method of presenting his part and ceases to let his mind turn on the significance of the play as a whole. Mr. Granville Barker said that it was a valuable lesson to watch the way in which a preoccupation with acting began to divert attention from the meaning of the play, and he thought that the point at which this came was different in different types of plays; it came early, for example, in Shakespeare, and late in Ibsen." The commission adds, "It almost seemed that Mr. Granville Barker was so much afraid of the seductive effect of dramatic activity that he would prefer to keep students at a University from acting altogether." *Report of the Oxford*

would seem worth taking into account the Elizabethans' own attitude toward enactment on stage.

There is evidence enough that before the days when drama was rediscovered as ritual (and Granville-Barker's close and long friendship with Gilbert Murray seems important in this regard) acting lacked the conceptual importance that it has since acquired. There were in sixteenth-century England no "ideas of theater" in our sense. Playing, however moving it might be, was a game (even if a morally dangerous one), a nobleman's pastime, a rustic's part-time job, a professional venture, a mechanical skill. "Why *Roscius* . . . proud with *Esops* Crow, being praукt with the glorie of others feathers?" Greene jibes. "Of thy selfe thou canst say nothing." The commonplace finds its way into Donne and Jonson. "If hee pen for thee once," Tucca says to the player Histrio of Crispinus, "thou shalt not need to travell with thy pumps full of gravell, any more, after a blinde jade and a hamper: and stalke upon boords, and barrell heads, to an old cract trumpet." [58] And Gulch in *Histrio-Mastix* observes sadly that the gentlemen see into their trade. "We cannot gull them with browne-paper stuffe. And the best Poets growne so envious They'le starve rather then we get store of mony." [59] A good poet could make a player as a good poet could make a play. This is essentially Sidney's point even though his judgment seems awry, and it is significant that to him the very shape of a play is "tied to the lawes of Poesie." [60] It is language again that commands the attention of Nashe when he remarks on how eloquent their gowned age has grown, and he lays the blame, as we all know, at the feet of the "vain-glorious tragoedians, who contend not so seriouslie to excell in action as to embowell the clowdes in a speach of comparison." [61] And it is the "high astounding tearms" of Tamburlaine that seemed, to whoever penned the prologue for the Quarto of 1590, to shed glory on

---

Drama Commission (Oxford, 1945), pp. 9–10. See also *Exemplary Theatre*, p. 23.

58. Jonson, *Poetaster*, III.iv.167 (*Ben Jonson*, ed. C. H. Herford and Percy and Evelyn Simpson [Oxford, 1925–1952], IV, 250). Jonson's remark is, of course, meant ironically. Donne, *Satyre II*, 11–16.

59. IV.i. H. Harvey Wood, *The Plays of John Marston* (London, 1939), III, 282–283.

60. Smith, *Elizabethan Critical Essays*, I, 198, 201.

61. *Ibid.*, pp. 307–308.

Marlowe's hero. Elizabethan plays were acted and were written to be acted, and we should never forget that fact. But to the Elizabethans, Heywood notwithstanding, the acting seems to have meant essentially a heightening of the effects, and particularly of the moral or immoral effects, of the text. At its best it gave life to "dead poesie." [62] It was a livelier image. But plays were by definition "excelling parts of Poesie." [63] They were always seen as verbal compositions, and enactment never took precedence, in our sense, over the text.[64] There is little recorded memory of stage action. It was rather, as in any poem, the text that mattered, even when played upon the stage. The lines, if they were worthy, would be taken down in commonplace books, savored in conversation, imitated, parodied, remembered—and, if deemed worthy, published for those that "take pleasure in reading Histories" or collected in a first Folio for the "great Variety of Readers" who, those two experienced theater men assumed, would stand for their privileges "wee know: to read and censure." They are admonished, we should remember if only as corrective, to "reade him, therefore; and againe and againe."

III

There are other questions that seem to need asking once one begins to try to match our concepts of theater with the Elizabethan point of view. They are questions too complex to do justice to here. But it does seem hazardous to assume of an age so conscious in its pursuit of artistic mastery as the Elizabethan that the form of the play is determined, so to speak, by the form of the stage. And it is difficult to believe that stage conditions as such are any more important as the stuff from which art must be made than the inherited plot, the narrative

62. Thomas Gainsford, *The Rich Cabinet* (London, 1616), fol. 116.

63. This is Sidney's phrase: "But I have lavished out too many wordes of this play matter. I doe it because as they are excelling parts of Poesie, so is there none so much used in England, and none can be more pittifully abused. . . . Other sorts of Poetry almost have we none . . . (Smith, *Elizabethan Critical Essays*, I, 201).

64. See, however, Marston's well-known remarks in his address "To my equall Reader" in the 1606 Quarto of *The Fawne*.

source, the latest literary gossip, the metaphoric fashion, the humor of the queen. All contribute to our understanding of the text. What the Elizabethans did with their theater they did, it would seem, consciously.[65] To them it was not ritual but created art. Similarly we must be wary of seeing in the verbal exploitation of stage conventions something endemic to the stage (any more than Michelangelo's *David* is endemic to the marble from which it is made). The conventions of time and place, for instance, seem as closely allied to the stage's early use of prose romances as to the conditions of performance, and given the Elizabethans' ability to produce elaborate scenic devices when desired, one must wonder whether the stage conditions determined the artistic concern, or the artistic concern determined the use of the stage. Granville-Barker's observations on Cesario and Viola in *Twelfth Night,* as we have noted, illumine the verbal nuances of the text. But the *use* that Shakespeare makes of a stage convention is no more determined by the stage convention than it is by the rhetorical and artistic conventions of the time in which situations, hypothetical or actual, were taken as subject and enlarged.

We can see quite clearly what Shakespeare actually does in a famous example from *Antony and Cleopatra.* It occurs in Act IV, when Cleopatra with the help of her maids draws the dying Antony aloft so that he may die in her arms on the upper stage. Her words both literally and metaphorically describe the action on stage.

> Here's sport indeed! How heavy weighs my lord!
> Our strength is all gone into heaviness;
> That makes the weight. Had I great Juno's power
> The strong-wing'd Mercury should fetch thee up
> And set thee by Jove's side. Yet come a little.
> Wishers were ever fools. O come, come, come,

65. See, for instance, Webster's remarks to the Reader of *The White Devil* (1612): "If it be objected this is no true Drammaticke Poem I shall easily confess it . . . willingly, and not ignorantly, in this kind have I faulted," or Dekker's own description of his attempt in *The Whore of Babylon* (1607): "The Generall scope of this Drammaticall Poem, is to set forth (in Tropicall and shadowed collours) the Greatness . . . of our late Queene." He goes on to justify what may appear to some readers a failure by explaining his technique, and reminds his readers that he writes as poet, not as historian (*The Dramatic Works of Thomas Dekker,* ed. Fredson Bowers [Cambridge, Eng., 1953–1961], II, 497).

And welcome, welcome! Die where thou hast liv'd.
Quicken with kissing.

(IV.xv.33)

The choral response is "A heavy sight!" What Shakespeare has done
is to take what must transpire in performance and use that verbally
as his vehicle. We see a similar artistic use made of the music with
which *Twelfth Night* obviously begins, in Orsino's opening line, "If
music be the food of love, play on." One could argue that such passages,
and the plays are full of them, establish the essentially dramatic nature
of the text. But in so arguing one needs to take cognizance of the
fact that the device *artistically* is the same device that one sees, for
instance, in the first of Elizabeth's coronation pageants. "The uniting
of the two howses of Lancaster and Yorke," we are told by the
commentator, "was grounded upon the Quenes majesties name," and
in another she saw "one personage, whose name was Tyme, apparaylled
as an olde man, with a sythe in his hande, havynge wynges artificiallye
made" leading his daughter Truth, meant to be embraced by the young
queen.[66] The occasion, as in *Antony and Cleopatra,* has provided the
matter of the artistic elaboration. The same kind of rhetorical use of
occasion is common to Elizabethan sonnets. Thus Shakespeare ends one
sonnet with "That in black ink my love may still shine bright" (Sonnet LXV). In this sense it would seem that Cleopatra's "Come, come,
Antony" is at least as much determined by an artistic mode as it is
by the existence of an upper stage.

But as the boy actor playing Viola playing Cesario speaks in fact of
himself and of Shakespeare when he tells Olivia he would be loath to
waste his speech on the wrong lady, for, "besides that it is excellently
well penned, I have taken great pains to con it" (I.v.164), so the
upper stage provides the occasion for Cleopatra's words and visually,
physically supports the text. This is perhaps all that we mean when
we proclaim the essentiality to Shakespeare's art of Shakespeare's stage.
And perhaps there lies in this essentially rhetorical device one of the
secrets of a good play.[67] But to the Elizabethans, as to T. S. Eliot,

66. John Nichols, *The Progresses and Public Processions of Queen Elizabeth*
(London, 1788), I, 5, 16.

67. This is essentially Raymond Williams' argument in *Drama as Performance*
(London, 1954; rev. ed., 1968).

the ability to transmute such dross to gold seemed less the prerogative of the theater than of the poet. Some sense of their point comes through, I think, even in a short passage from *The Death of Robert, Earl of Huntingdon* (1601). Robin Hood is dead. Friar Tuck has come on stage to give the epilogue and is interrupted by Chester, who pleads on behalf of the audience that the play go on. They are to show "Matildaes Tragedie." Chester and evidently the Chorus are sent away to change to clothing befitting a tragedy, and during their absence the Friar invokes the aid of the Muse that he might "thunder out wrong, compast in clowdy teares." It is the Chorus, now dressed in black, who help both him and the audience remember the story of King John, and at his use of the word "vision" they recall, by the simple verbal device of association, that King John was said to have had three visions. It is at this point that the Friar decides to begin the action. He draws the curtain to show the King sleeping in his chair, and he provides the commentary for the pageant that ensues (D2ᵛ–D3). There is in this short passage much evidence of the most deeply rooted and per-vasive conventions of the Elizabethan stage. Neither time nor place is of any immediate concern. The illusion of reality is approached with all leisure and all frankness. An intimacy with the audience is taken for granted and used dramatically on stage. And at the end of the pageant, as the third vision, Matilda appears, played by a boy and pursued by the King. What have these conventions to do with the integrity of the play? One is tempted, after admitting that it is ob-viously more effective played than read, to respond very little. The scene is too loose-jointed and too lazily contrived. The invocation, the narrative summary, the pretense of authorial concern do not create that variety of dramatic perspectives which may illumine a central action. They seem rather redundant if not irrelevant in their design. The Friar, in a huffing part, exclaims, "O what is he, thats sworne affections slave, / That will not violate all lawes, all oathes?" The most significant thing about the passage is, in short, that it is poorly penned. It is in this sense that the poet seemed more important than the dramatist and that the players were but the poet's "factors, who put away the stuff, and make the best of it they possibly can, as indeed 'tis their part so to do." It is in this sense, too, that the theater itself was but "your poets Royal Exchange, upon which their muses that are now turned to merchants, meeting, barter away that light commodity of words for a lighter ware than words—plaudities, and the breath of the great beast." [68]

This kind of concern with language makes Granville-Barker very much an Elizabethan, and, in those terms at least, it is Shakespeare the Elizabethan poet whom he put on stage. The true nature of his genius emerges in the reports we have in a Folger manuscript by Hallam Fordham which includes notes by John Gielgud of the staging in 1940 of *King Lear,* a performance by Gielgud which brought the producer out of his study for only the second time since his retirement almost twenty years before.[69] Granville-Barker set forth his conception of the play both in the Players' edition of 1927 and in the revised *Preface* (1927). He defines in strong terms near the beginning of the *Preface* the basis of Shakespeare's stagecraft in the crucial storm scenes: it is essentially to make Lear and the storm as one, and he observes "any actor who should try to speak the lines realistically in the character of a feeble old man would be a fool. There is no realism about it. No real man could or would talk so." [70] He reiterates, in other words, Lamb's *Lear* while maintaining that it can indeed be played.[71] This

68. Thomas Dekker, *The Gull's Hornbook* (1609), ed. R. B. McKerrow (London, 1905), p. 49.

69. Fordham, *Player in Action.* See n. 41 above.

70. *Prefaces,* II, 7. The quotation is from the Players' edition, xvi. The phrasing in the *Preface* is "What actor in his senses, however, would attempt to act the scene 'realistically.' "

71. Lamb argues that "the greatness of Lear is not in corporal dimension, but in intellectual." Granville-Barker answers him not by disagreeing about Lear but by pointing out that he has an erroneous conception of the stage—"and this is the Lear, great not in corporal but in intellectual dimensions, the Lear of Lamb's demand" (Players' Edition, xvii). He sees in Lamb's view a failure to understand Elizabethan stagecraft, but what Lamb specifically objects to is the imposition of concrete embodiment upon his own imaginative realizations. One sees a similar scruple by Harbage, though his response to it is to plead for a theater in which actors are trained to recite rather than interpret. See *Theatre for Shakespeare,* p. 17, and *passim.* John Russell Brown, "The Theatrical Element of Shakespeare Criticism," makes an admirable attempt to come to terms with this problem which seems to be a recurring one for literary scholars. It is interesting to note in connection with Granville-Barker's *Preface* his remarks in a letter to Gielgud while the performance was in progress: "*Lear* really is difficult, next door to impossible,

impression is reinforced by his other observations on producing the play. The actor of the part of the Fool "must sing like a lark, juggle his words so that the mere skill delights us, and tumble around with all the grace in the world."[72] He gives even more specific advice about the crucial opening scene, where he feels "the producer should observe and even see stressed the scene's characteristics":

> . . . the strength of such single lines as "The bow is bent and drawn, make from the shaft"—with its hammering monosyllables; and the hard-bitten "Nothing; I have sworn; I am firm"—together with the loosening of the tension in changes to rhymed couplets, and the final drop into prose by that businesslike couple, Goneril and Regan. Then follows, with a lift into lively verse for a start, as a contrast, and as the right medium for Edmund's youthful optimism . . . the development of the Gloucester theme.[73]

In the actual production, inspired by Granville-Barker's *Preface* and directed by him for two weeks prior to the opening—Purdom reports that he returned to Paris after the first dress rehearsal—the first scene at his expressed desire was presented as a "straightforward formal ceremonial, setting forth in the broadest possible lines the argument and the fable on which the rest of the play depends."[74] Gielgud adds that Granville-Barker emphasized continually in this scene the rhythmic, measured sweep of the verse and the importance of style and grandeur in the acting. Hallam Fordham, who took notes at rehearsal, remarks that ceremonial staging was used throughout the production; such staging was obviously meant to reinforce what the *Times* review (16 April 1940) marked as the production's strength—"the bold recognition from the first that in this tragedy we are borne through realms of fantasy in which cold reason cannot find satisfaction."[75] In the movement and

---

and perhaps I did lessen its impossibilities a little. . . . But with *Othello* there are no such fundamental difficulties." Cited in Purdom, *Harley Granville Barker*, p. 263.

72. *Prefaces*, II, 58; Players' edition, pp. lxi–lxii.

73. Players' edition, pp. xviii–xix; *Prefaces*, II, 12. Granville-Barker has changed "Edmund's youthful optimism" to "Edmund's sanguine conceit."

74. This comes directly from the *Preface:* "It has a proper formality, and there is a certain megalithic grandeur about it," p. 12. The statement differs slightly in the Players' edition, xviii. Gielgud reports Granville-Barker's desire and the result in his notes on the opening scene in Fordham, *Player in Action*.

75. A transcript of this review is included in Fordham, *Player in Action*, as an appendix. The original review is on p. 4 of the *Times* (16 April 1940).

grouping of the actors, Fordham notes, Granville-Barker used a "simple, classic shape, employing broad right-angled and diagonal crosses for the actors," making it possible to weld them "into pyramidal or triangular shapes with the central characters at the peak." In the triangular grouping of Lear, Goneril, and Regan, for instance, the two side arches could suddenly "be brought into importance, like flanking attacks, upon which the grouping suddenly converges, in a sensational but simple way, at the moments when they add significance to the action." [76]

The same kind of concern with the stage embodiment of a dramatic poem marks much of Granville-Barker's advice. Gielgud, Fordham reports, presented Lear in the opening of the first storm scene "more as a symbol than as an actual man, deliberately treating the first great storm speeches in a detached and unrealistic manner both in gesture and vocal delivery." The verse was spoken with "the full sweep of elevated speech," with postures "statuesque and broad." [77] Gielgud, responding to the criticism of the scene as being neither "completely stylised nor treated realistically," states that Granville-Barker's purpose was "to allow the voice to convey the main feeling of the storm." His direction to Gielgud was to "use the full range—like an organ in oratorio." In the scene between blind Gloucester and mad Lear (IV.vi.) he reports that at first he had attempted realistically doddering movements, twitching hands, staring eyes, and so on, but had been admonished by Granville-Barker that the prevailing note must be kingly dignity, "the entrance to be a caricature of the first entrance in the play, combined with a feeling of lightness and freedom: speaking aloud to the trees and birds." He found particularly helpful to his realization Granville-Barker's direction that "the imagined and real characters are of equal importance and must be created completely in Lear's imagination." [78] "Mr. Gielgud," the *Times* reviewer wrote, "concerns himself little with the corporal infirmities of the old King. . . . He trusts the verse and his power to speak it, as a solitary silver figure in the dark loneliness, he speaks the storm, and his trust is never at any vital point betrayed." [79]

76. These remarks by Fordham occur in his description of II.ii.
77. *Player in Action*, III.iii.iv, vi (discussed as a unit).
78. *Ibid.*, IV.vi (Gielgud's notes).
79. 16 April 1940, p. 4.

We do not know if that is how the Elizabethans presented their plays, and that remains an important, if obvious, point. But it is hopefully no more than a caution on the road ahead. This essay began, long before pen was put to paper, as an appreciation of Harley Granville-Barker, and, if anything, that appreciation has deepened with the realization of how close in many ways he was in his deepest sympathies to that love of pleasurable embellishment with which the Elizabethans made playing an art. He wrote as early as 1912, in a letter to *The Play Pictorial,* that "we shall not save our souls by being Elizabethan. It is an easy way out." It was not an easy way for him. It was rather a sustained, intelligent, conscious effort to restore to the stage the innately dramatic excitement of seeing a Hector "all besmered in blood, trampling upon the bulkes of Kinges." It was an excitement that, almost since the time of Heywood, the stage seemed to have lost.

Its art he himself described in words that anticipate the *Times* reviewer in his evocative description of Gielgud's Lear. He is talking of the Elizabethan actor, and he remarks that he had "to step out on the bare boards, in shine or cold, wind or calm, and, with little but the poetry in his mouth for a weapon, to quell his audience and keep it his own." [80] I think that with only that observation to go by, we might begin again to try to define in a more usable way what were partisan issues in 1925 and remain partisan issues today—the relation of text to performance, of enactment to verbal art.

Raymond Williams points out in *Drama in Performance,* a book that deserves to be better known,[81] that Shakespeare, unlike Ibsen, expresses the essential action or pattern of a play in its poetry. That seems a possible point from which to start. We have seen an example of what Williams means in the speech that Cleopatra makes to the dying Antony. What this suggests to me is not that the literary cannot be separated from the dramatic, although that is one way that it might be read, but that the dramatic cannot be separated from the literary. It has been imaginatively made part of the poetic text. That means in Granville-Barker's terms that the essential action is part of the poetic

80. "Elizabethan Stage," p. 63.
81. (London, 1968). The book first appeared in 1954. The new edition is revised.

structure. But it means as well, at least in Elizabethan terms, that such dramatic texts are fully alive when read. If this is true, it would seem that what blurs our vision and raises such apparently intractable problems about the nature of drama as such, is a modern separation between a written and an oral culture which makes a distinction between a written and a spoken text. We cannot do away with that distinction. But we can appreciate, I think to our own advantage, that such a distinction is not Elizabethan, and as it did not exist in the sixteenth century, so it does not exist in any substantive way in the texts of that period. The conscious accomplishment of the Elizabethans was to make their drama literary, and one must add that to them poetry was an oral art.

In an essay concerned only with definitions, Armado's "sweet smoke of rhetoric," any attempt at final answers would be out of place. My only conclusion is a personal one, in the form of a linguistic metaphor, perhaps an appropriate closing to put beside the images of ritual at Persepolis with which we began. I imagine the two ages, set end to end, as a kind of historical palindrome. Shakespeare, following in the footsteps of Marlowe, must have shown the Elizabethans what Granville-Barker showed the descendants of Charles Lamb—that poesy as speaking picture is not out of place on a stage. Their points of departure lie at opposite ends of a spectrum which at times seems spatial as well as chronological. But, were the smoke to clear, one is not quite sure whether, read backwards, they might not mean the same thing. Certainly neither one would think *Orghast* a step forward in the arts of the stage.

The English Playhouse:
1595-1630

D. F. ROWAN

To MANY, the assumptions implicit in my title will be questionable, and to still others the possibility of dealing successfully with so complex and protean a problem in so modest a compass will appear remote. I have, in fact, rigorously restricted my chronological range to the limits imposed by the primary pictorial evidence of the DeWitt sketch of the Swan in 1595, and the Jones / Webb drawings of the Cockpit-in-Court in 1630, although it is my belief that the evidence warrants extrapolation to the conventional limits of the Elizabethan theater, 1576 and 1642. I do not, however, attempt to divide the subject into "public" and "private" theaters, as it is my thesis that such a distinction is illusory and ill-founded. It is, in fact, my belief that the "public," "private," and "court" theaters together constitute a continuum loosely bounded by the Swan drawing at one end of a social and chronological spectrum, and by the Cockpit-in-Court drawings at the other. I am driven to this contentious position by the converging pressures of the work of a number of theatrical scholars, and by the new pictorial evidence of the recently discovered drawings of an Elizabethan private playhouse in the Jones / Webb collection at Worcester College, Oxford (Plates 1 and 2). I view these drawings as a theatrical missing-link between the Swan and the Cockpit-in-Court; as a keystone which, when dropped into place, locks firmly the slow-built and laboriously constructed arch of the modern concept of the Elizabethan theater, a variegated arch built of single bricks and stones brought from afar by many individual workers. Although I shall not attempt to weigh or test each of these bricks and stones, it is against this fabric of Elizabethan theater scholarship as a whole that I wish to study in detail the primary pictorial evidence which we now have.

With regard to the famous, or infamous, Swan drawing, the center of so much debate in the past, and in Richard Southern's apt phrase "the rock on which research workers are split,"[1] it is now possible to content ourselves by simply reiterating "that DeWitt's sketch is accepted by most modern scholars as an accurate reproduction of at least one Elizabethan theatre,"[2] and, as such, evidence of primary importance and authority. As the advocates of the "inner stage" have withdrawn from the field, the need to discredit DeWitt or VanBuchell, or the drawing itself, has disappeared, and the attitude pungently epitomized by John Dover Wilson when he dismissed the evidence as "one Dutchman's copy of another Dutchman's sketch"[3] is happily part of the past history of theatrical scholarship.

A similar progress toward "relevance" and respectability has marked the recent history of the Cockpit-in-Court drawings. Although the drawings are probably in John Webb's hand, and although certain features such as the railing around the stage may represent Restoration alterations, the plans essentially reflect a design of the King's Surveyor, Inigo Jones, and accurately represent a "court" theater built at Whitehall in 1629/30. Most important of all is the recognition that this theater was not a "playtoy" for elegant amateurs, but a working theater for that most professional of companies, the King's Men, which only happened to be located at court.[4] The evidence of the drawings is

1. "Current Controversies about the Elizabethan Stage," *World Theatre,* XIII, Nos. 1 & 2 (1964), 76.

2. D. F. Rowan, "The 'Swan' Revisited," *RORD,* X (1967), 33–48.

3. *"Titus Andronicus* on the Stage in 1595," *ShS,* I (1948), 21.

4. D. F. Rowan, "The Cockpit-in-Court," *The Elizabethan Theatre* [I], ed.

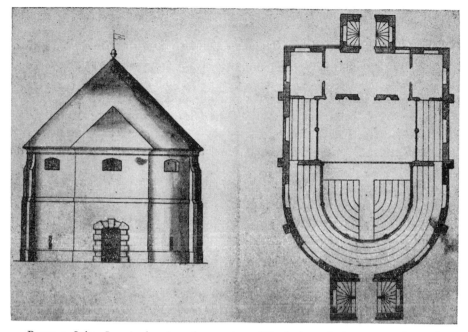

PLATE I. Inigo Jones's drawings for a private Elizabethan playhouse: exterior and floor plan. From the Jones/Webb collection at Worcester College, Oxford. Reproduced by permission of the Provost and Fellows of Worcester College, Oxford.

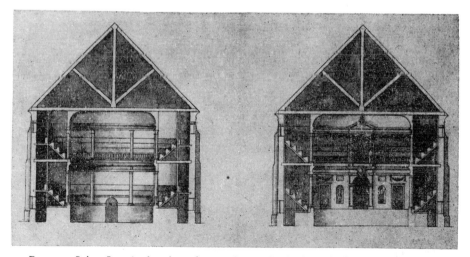

PLATE 2. Inigo Jones's drawings for a private Elizabethan playhouse: the interior. From the Jones/Webb collection at Worcester College, Oxford. Reproduced by permission of the Provost and Fellows of Worcester College, Oxford.

therefore, like that of the Swan, of the first order of importance to any study of the Elizabethan professional theater, whether "public" or "private."

As noted earlier, the recently discovered theater drawings in the Jones / Webb collection at Worcester College, Oxford, are central to my argument. I have discussed fully the provenance of these drawings in earlier work, and have, as well, touched tentatively on their ultimate significance.[5] From time to time I must of necessity repeat or draw upon this earlier work, but I should like to begin by proposing that these drawings be identified as "Inigo Jones's Drawings for a Private Elizabethan Playhouse." I am happy to abandon the cumbersome working title of my first article, "A Neglected Jones / Webb Theatre Project: Barber-Surgeons' Hall Writ Large," as I am now convinced that the drawings are by Inigo Jones, and that they have nothing to do with Barber-Surgeons' Hall. When I published the drawings I expressed a hope that someone would come forward to identify them, as W. J. Lawrence did for Hamilton Bell's drawings of the Cockpit-in-Court. Unfortunately this has not as yet happened, but two distinguished scholars in private correspondence have emboldened me to propose my new title. Professor Rudolf Wittkower in a letter of 11 January 1970 is able to write that "after looking carefully at the photographs of 7B and 7C, I think that it is not at all unlikely that they were made by Inigo Jones himself." The testimony of so eminent an art historian, combined with the certain provenance of the drawings as part of a known Jones / Webb collection, points unmistakably to Jones himself as the draughtsman.

I was led to suggest an association of the two unknown drawings with Barber-Surgeons' Hall by the anonymous compiler of the Worcester College collection, who associated them with two other drawings of

---

David Galloway (Toronto, 1969), 89–102; Glynne Wickham, "The Cockpit Reconstructed," *NTM*, VII, no. 2 (1967), 26–36; reprinted in *Shakespeare's Dramatic Heritage* (London, 1969), pp. 151–162.

5. "A Neglected Jones / Webb Theatre Project: 'Barber-Surgeons' Hall Writ Large,' " *NTM*, IX, No. 3 (1969), 6–15. A redaction of this article appeared in *ShS*, XXIII (1970), 125–129. See also "A Neglected Jones/Webb Theatre Project, Part II: A Theatrical Missing Link," *The Elizabethan Theatre II*, ed. David Galloway (Toronto, 1970), 60–73.

the "Theatre of Anatomie" of the Barber-Surgeons' Company of London. While it was immediately clear that such a private theater was not built for the Barber-Surgeons, I did suggest "that Jones was intrigued by the unusual shape of the first Barber-Surgeons' Hall, which he certainly viewed no later than early 1636, and that in response to the stimulus to his imagination he designed this playhouse." In this I was totally wrong, and I am most grateful to Professor Glynne Wickham who has privately pointed out to me as a result of his own research that "the eighteenth century survey of the Company's property certainly shows a rectangular Hall with an apse in the Western end; but the buildings surveyed then were those built after 1666 to replace those lost in the Great Fire of London, and the apse was only incorporated into the Livery Hall when it was rebuilt in 1668." The albatross of the Barber-Surgeons' Hall falls away with relief, and it is with some confidence that I suggest "Inigo Jones's Drawings for a Private Elizabethan Playhouse."

The link with Barber-Surgeons' Hall not only made for a cumbersome title, but also tended to push the date of the drawings to the outer limits of our period, as Jones is known to have been closely associated with the Barber Surgeons only in the years from 1635 to 1637 when he built their theater of anatomy. The divorce of the drawings from the Barber-Surgeons' Hall reinforces other evidence pointing to an earlier date. 7B and 7C carry a watermark of a family whose known range is from 1592 to 1616, and this fact, combined with the relationship of these drawings to the Cockpit-In-Court drawings—a relationship which I shall explore more fully in a moment—strongly suggests a date in the twenty-five year period between the attachment of Jones to the Court (1605) and the building of the Cockpit-in-Court (1630). Such a date anchors Jones's drawings firmly in the midstream of the development of the Elizabethan theater, and it is for this reason that I use the adjective "Elizabethan" in its generic and conventionally accepted sense in my proposed title. While it is part of my general thesis that the stages of the "public" and "private" theaters of the period were basically or essentially the same, the term "private" remains useful in distinguishing a roofed or "private" theater from the open or "public" theater of the time.

By way of introduction to a discussion of specific points raised by the drawings, I should like to draw a summary from my earlier work. If we accept the scales at the bottom right hand corner of the drawings as representing 5 feet and 1 foot,—a common scale of the time—we have a small, unusually shaped "private" playhouse with a maximum interior width of 37 feet and a length of 52 feet. A fine sense of proportion places the front edge of the 4-foot-high stage precisely at the midpoint —26 feet from the back wall of a tiring house just slightly over 10 feet in depth and stretching the width of the theater. On each side of the stage, galleries measuring 6 feet 9 inches leave a stage 23 feet 6 inches wide, and 15 feet deep. The front wall of the tiring house is broken by an arched central door 8 feet high and 4 feet wide, and flanked on either side by rectangular doors 6 feet high and 2 feet 6 inches wide. From the floor of the pit to the curved ceiling is a distance of 26 feet 9 inches. In this height the architect has placed two galleries, the first of which rises 11 feet above the level of the stage, and the second, an additional 7 feet. These galleries are broken at the midpoint of the playhouse: both the upper and lower galleries of the "house end" of the building have four degrees and space for a walkway behind the last row. These galleries are approximately 7 feet 6 inches in depth. The lower galleries of the "stage end" appear to butt against the tiring-house wall, and also have four degrees but no walkway behind. The upper galleries at this same end also have four degrees and no walkway, and may (the drawing is not clear on this point) continue unbroken around the upper stage corner. There are, however, only three degrees of seats above the stage and they are interrupted by a classically ornamented "window" 4 feet wide. In the pit, as shown on drawing 7B, are oval degrees which gracefully reflect the curve of the playhouse wall. Divided by a central gangway, I believe that they probably rise at the back to the 4-foot level of both the stage and the floor of the first gallery; 7C does not show these degrees. The floor of the pit itself is unraked, but this is not unexpected, as it is much simpler and more economical to construct raised degrees than to rake an entire floor.

Let us consider first the unusual shape of this playhouse. We know that the octagonal shape of the Cockpit-in-Court was forced upon Jones by the limitations of the existing structure which he was to remodel and refurbish. "Forced" is perhaps too strong a word to apply to the semicircular seating arrangements, for both neoclassical precedent and native example supported a semicircular auditorium, and I suspect that Jones was glad to make a virtue of necessity. The influence of the Teatro Olympico is apparent in the seating arrangements proposed in Jones's own plan for a perspective theater found in his copy of Palladio, and the example of the success of such circular seating in the public theaters of England could not go unnoted. Italian theater designers had long grappled with the problem of placing semicircular degrees in rectangular buildings, and, although evidence is lacking, it is not impossible that the proprietors of the premier private theaters, the Second Blackfriars, the Phoenix, and the Salisbury Court—"all three built almost exactly alike, for Form and Bigness" according to Wright —may have built semicircular galleries within their rectangular buildings. So too with the Fortune, although here again clear evidence is lacking. When Jones undertook to design a private professional playhouse from scratch, the advantages of a building combining semicircular seating in the "house-end" with the capaciousness of a rectangular tiring house would be obvious, and such was the playhouse which he proposed: an economical marriage of the classical with the contemporary, of the aesthetic with the practicable. Deprived of the corners provided by a rectangular building, Jones placed his main public entrance in the center of the apse and flanked it with exterior double staircases leading to the upper galleries. A single doorkeeper or gatherer would presumably be required at each level, although the drawings are confused on this point. The elevation of the "house end" on 7C does not show the entrance door on the second floor which is indicated on the plan view of 7B. Indeed, this is part of a general confusion of levels which is apparent in this plan view—the "stage end" is at ground level while the "house end" delineates the second story. Confusions of this nature reinforce my belief that the theater was never built; although the drawings are carefully finished in many respects, they cannot be working drawings. A careful search of available maps has revealed no building with this distinctive shape, and, while such negative evidence can never be conclusive, I believe the drawings to body forth only a theater of the mind, but one which is nevertheless firmly grounded on Inigo Jones's knowledge of the working theaters of his age.

The gracefully curved degrees in the pit, shown in the plan view on 7B, although aesthetically satisfying, leave much to be desired as theater seats. The fact that they do not appear in the elevation on 7C may reflect Jones's inability to solve the problem presented by the central corner seats flanking the gangway, where the unfortunate spectator must either sit side-saddle or view the play at right angles over his shoulder. In the Cockpit-in-Court, Jones sidestepped the problem by doing away with the awkward corner seats—one of the many straws in the wind suggesting that this theater antedates the Cockpit and that much of the court theater is a development out of and a refinement on the plans for this earlier theater.

I have remarked elsewhere that I should be far less certain of my line of argument were it not for the striking independent corroboration of the main features of the drawings by Richard Hosley's recent theoretical reconstruction of the stage of the Second Blackfriars.[6] It is hardly an exaggeration to say that drawing 7C could serve as an illustration for this provocative study, and it is a tribute to Hosley's brilliant pioneering in this field that his independent theoretical conclusions are so strongly supported by this new concrete pictorial evidence. There is agreement on many important points: a gallery over the stage for actors, musicians, and spectators; an unrailed, unraked stage of a little over four feet in height running across the width of the playhouse; a flat tiring-house façade with three doors; and seats for spectators along the sides of a stage with almost precisely the expected 8:5 ratio. Such remarkable agreement, arising from totally independent sources, must support my contention that the drawings are closely related to the actual stage of the Elizabethan playhouse. On one major point only do the two theaters diverge, that of the arrangement of the galleries. I do not regard Hosley's stepped galleries as either likely or proved. As I pursue this point in some detail elsewhere,[7] I must here content myself by noting that Jones avoids the stepped galleries of Hosley's reconstruction by placing the floor of the lower gallery at approximately the level of the stage floor. This solution of the problem is architecturally sounder and gives, as well, better sight lines to the spectators in the lower galleries. I regard the

6. "A Reconstruction of the Second Blackfriars," *Elizabethan Theatre* [I], pp. 74–88.

7. In a forthcoming article in *Theatre Notebook*.

number of galleries as essentially a function of the height of the theater, but I think it not unlikely that the example of the public theaters would invite imitation, particularly in a hall as high as the great Parliament Chamber.[8] Nevertheless, while staying firmly in the established theatrical tradition of vertical galleries, Jones chose to seek intimacy and excellent sight lines for all by gracing his private playhouse with only two galleries.

There can be no doubt that stage-sitting was an established custom in the Elizabethan private theater, and Jones's theater elegantly caters to the "Magistrate of wit" who sits in daily judgment "on the Stage at Black-Friars, or the Cock-pit." At the same time the railing shown in the plan view on 7B might be of some service in keeping the spectators out of the way of the actors, although it appears that the more ostentatious patrons might still insist on sitting or standing on the stage proper.[9] Hosley's reconstruction of the Second Blackfriars has boxes in the same position as Jones's degrees, but the solution proposed in both theaters is essentially the same. Had Jones wished to provide privacy at the expense of sight lines, a simple partition or two could have been added. Whether degrees or boxes, the effect is the same; in the Swan, in the Blackfriars, in Jones's private playhouse, and even in the Cockpit-in-Court, the audience presses in on the actors from at least three sides, just as they had done for centuries in the most primitive of early theaters.

Did not the audience range itself along the fourth side as well? The vexing question of the use of the "upper area" above the stage may well be answered finally by Jones's drawings, in which a multipurpose gallery is shown. The ornamental "window" in the elevation on 7C is clearly for actors or musicians, but the degrees on either side are just as clearly for spectators. Leslie Hotson's instincts may have been right when he argued that the Elizabethan theater was "theatre in the round." Although modern scholars reject his canvas houses, the "people" above the stage in the Swan drawing are almost certainly spectators, and the most recent work of Herbert Berry has proved that

8. See Irwin Smith, *Shakespeare's Blackfriars Playhouse* (New York, 1964), pp. 290–292.

9. Herbert Berry, "The Stage and Boxes at Blackfriars," *SP*, LXIII (1966), 163–186.

the "gallaryes over the stage" in the Boar's Head Inn were a major source of income.[10] Because of the special nature of the Cockpit-in-Court the use of this area for spectators was out of the question, but the evidence now available to us forces the conclusion that in Elizabethan theaters, both "public" and "private," the upper area above the stage was used by spectators, actors, and musicians as circumstance permitted or occasion demanded.

The presence and use of a multipurpose upper area clearly binds all these theaters together, but it is when we turn to an examination and comparison of the tiring-house walls in the three sets of drawings that we must be struck most forcibly by a sense of unity and continuity of development in the Elizabethan playhouse, whether "public," "private," or "courtly." The curved tiring-house wall at the Cockpit-in-Court was forced upon Jones by the need to build his theater within an existing octagonal building; there was no precedent, either classical or native, for a curved tiring-house wall, as there was for a curved auditorium. Jones embraced it reluctantly, rejecting the opportunity of placing above the angled side doors the window / balconies which some scholars believe to have been a regular feature of the Elizabethan theater. Instead he provided a single window—totally without any classical precedent—because all the Elizabethan theaters had such an upper area, and both the plays and the players demanded it. He rejected, as well, the opportunity of creating a much larger central opening—it was structurally easily possible—because none of the professional theaters had an "inner stage," and neither the plays nor the players needed or wanted it. The curved tiring-house façade cannot disguise the fact that this is a professional theater firmly rooted in a flourishing popular professional tradition—superficial decoration must not deceive us, for "the Colonel's Lady an' Judy O'Grady are sisters under their skins!"

If one compares the Cockpit-in-Court elevation with the elevation of Jones's private playhouse stage on 7C, two facts are immediately apparent. Both façades are the work of the same man—although the drawings are in different hands—and the Cockpit-in-Court façade is

10. "The Playhouse in the Boar's Head Inn," *Elizabethan Theatre* [I], pp. 45-73.

simply a somewhat more elegant elaboration of Jones's earlier theater. Some neoclassical bric-a-brac has been added, but the bones of the structure are the same. The curved façade of the Cockpit presented Jones with the opportunity of providing the conventional five doors of the classical theater. I believe that the three central doors would have answered all the actors' requirements, but the actors made no objection to the additional doors, which satisfied the architect's classical instincts without interfering with their own needs. Jones's skill was such that he succeeded in creating a superficially classical theater elegantly reflecting both the glory of a Renaissance prince and his own interests in Neo-Vitruvian theory, without straying in any essential way from the well-trodden path of the professional theater, as represented by the Swan drawing and the drawings of his private playhouse.

In the Swan is the expected flat, unrailed stage thrust well forward into the auditorium; probably to the middle, for it is more than coincidence that the fore edges of the stages of both the Fortune Theater and Jones's private theatre bisect the playhouse. Behind this stage rises the flat tiring-house wall, broken by a number of doors, and topped with a multipurpose upper area. There is no "inner stage," and I once again respectfully state that in the face of such hard negative evidence, scholars must abandon this dubious thesis until equally convincing positive evidence can be discovered or adduced.

The question of the number of doors in the tiring-house wall is fascinating, unavoidable, and of great import. In the Swan there are two; in Jones's private playhouse, three; in the Cockpit-in-Court, five. What is the explanation? Briefly, I believe that the earlier Swan stage draws its lineaments from its origins, and here the fine work of Glynne Wickham and Richard Hosley is of most pertinence. Wickham in the first two volumes of his monumental study, *Early English Stages,* demonstrates the influence of the temporary, curtained booth stage on the first permanent theaters, and Hosley in a series of lucid and incisive articles has insisted, both directly and obliquely, on the traditional Tudor hall screen, with its two doors and musicians' gallery above, as a model which the builders of the first playhouses could not or would not have ignored. Both lines of argument converge in an early theater with the expected two doors, although I should not be surprised to discover that other early theaters might have had three doors instead of two. Lest I be accused of backtracking on my argument, I might simply point out that the curtain at the back of a booth stage can be split in a number of places and the convenience of three entrances simply achieved when required. Similarly, the existence of hall screens with three doors, or the use of a split curtain hung between the normal two doors, would quickly point the way to a three-door façade as a most desirable theatrical resource.

Jones's private playhouse has three doors and basically reflects what I believe to have been the normal number of doors in the Elizabethan tiring-house wall. Some classical influence may be at work in the decorated and arched central door, larger and more impressive than its rectangular and smaller neighbors, but such a "royal door" would serve equally well for some of the more elaborate and spectacular discovery scenes which were part of the professional repertoire. It would seem to be a natural dramatic development from either two or three doors of equal size in the earlier theaters. I have already discussed the five doors which are found in the Cockpit-in-Court, and I can only repeat that their origins are in the classical theater, and the players simply accepted them as being perhaps occasionally useful, without interfering with their traditional repertoires. I must take direct issue here with Robert M. Wren who writes in his article, "The Five-entry Stage of Blackfriars," that, "The discussion will show that the Blackfriars theatre had a five-entry, architectonically-segmented facade stage, markedly unlike the Swan or any reconstruction based on the Swan."[11] I remain totally unconvinced by the arguments advanced, believing them to be based on a fundamental misconception of the nature of the Elizabethan stage—doors do not automatically retain their topographical identity from scene to scene—and maintain on the basis of the pictorial evidence that the Elizabethan theater normally had no more than three stage doors. In this belief I draw support from T. J. King's recently published major work *Shakespearean Staging, 1599–1642*. I shall return to this important book later in this article, but, of plays acted by professionals in the period under discussion, King writes that "only one text that may depend on prompt copy

11. *ThR*, VIII (1966), 130–138.

carries directions to suggest the need for a third entrance"[12]—let alone a fourth, or a fifth!

While I am satisfied with the general question of the size and number of openings onto the Elizabethan stage, I should welcome further evidence as to just what went into these openings. The Swan drawing is clear on this point, but both of Jones's theaters reveal nothing more than openings. Curtains, of course, could be and were hung, but serviceable doors appear to be required in a number of plays. Perhaps Jones is influenced by the classical or perspective theaters in leaving off the doors, but it seems more likely that he chose not to concern himself with such detail. No doors at all are shown in the Cockpit-in-Court drawings, and, with the possible exception of the pit door, perhaps indicated in the elevation on 7C, no doors—not even an outer door on the main entrance—are shown in the earlier drawings. As noted before, the drawings are confused or unfinished at some points—note the ragged openings in the lateral walls of the tiring house shown in the plan view on 7B—and we are left with no choice but to speculate. Neither lights nor traps nor flying machinery is shown in either of the two sets of drawings, and yet we know that all three existed at the Cockpit-in-Court. While I should have preferred some graphic indication, I believe we are justified in presuming that Jones's private theater was similarly equipped.

The implications and assumptions underlining the title of my article must by now be obvious. I believe that on the basis of the primary pictorial evidence one can justifiably speak of *the* English playhouse from 1595 to 1630, and in the absence of evidence to the contrary, I further believe that one can now speak with some measure of confidence of *the* Elizabethan theater, whether "public," "private," or "courtly." Where these theaters differed, they differed as ball parks and football stadiums of today differ; the players do not play a different game any more than the actors played a different play in each new venue. As always they were flexible, as King's recent book has once again clearly demonstrated, ready to improvise in the provinces and private halls, and equally ready to exploit whatever additional resources, such as artificial lighting, they found in a closed theatre, or the additional set

12. T. J. King, *Shakespearean Staging, 1599–1642* (Cambridge, Mass., 1971).

of doors they found in the Cockpit-in-Court. But such things were not essential, and their working theater consisted of a large flat thrust stage, backed by a flat tiring-house wall with two or three doors, and topped by a multipurpose upper area. This, with a trap or traps and sometimes simple flying machinery, was what they needed and expected, and this they found in their professional theaters, as they moved from the open playhouses on the Bankside to the closed playhouses of the City, and even to the royal playhouse at Whitehall.

Although I have deliberately centered my arguments on what I consider to be the primary graphic evidence, I have gratefully drawn support from other scholars whose approach to the question of the Elizabethan theater has been from other directions. I view the newly discovered drawings of Jones's private playhouse as important new evidence; in fact, as the keystone in an arch of scholarship laboriously raised over the past seventy years or so. However, without the supporting arch the keystone must fall to the ground. It strikes me as most appropriate that this volume of *Renaissance Drama* should focus on playhouses and players, for I believe that Elizabethan theatrical scholarship can and must move forward now to occupy new territory. It is seventy years since George F. Reynolds' first published work and thirty years since the publication of his seminal *The Staging of Elizabethan Plays at the Red Bull Theatre,* with its plea for a careful methodology to deal with the treacherous evidence of the texts. Regrettably, his work was overshadowed by John Cranford Adams' more spectacular, and unfortunately more influential, theoretical reconstruction of the Globe playhouse. The time was not right, and Reynolds' seed fell on barren soil, germinating only in the last decade, and finally blossoming in 1971 in King's fine new book. It is over a decade since the first volume of Glynne Wickham's *Early English Stages* appeared, but this expansive study of the roots of the English theater is soon to be completed with the publication of Volume II, part II. Richard Hosley has for something over a decade, in a flood of provocative articles and papers, led a cadre of pioneers against the "forts of folly," and although some walls still stand, their foundations are mined, and the dungeon of the "inner stage" at least has been blown sky-high. Herbert Berry's work, meticulously documented with material in the Public Record Office, has led to a number of carefully argued articles, most recently throwing welcome light on the innyard theaters. G. E. Bentley's great compendium is now complete, and there are, of course, many others, as well, who have contributed smaller bricks and stones to a foundation on which we can now build. In short, I believe the way is clear to build with studies of the ways in which individual dramatists exploited the known resources of their theater, to move from speculation on the statics of theater buildings to the dynamics of theatrical production.

In closing I must once again return to the work of King, who writes in the Introduction to his book:

During the period 1599–1642 the royal and courtly influence on the drama increased and, as G. E. Bentley observes, a social cleavage developed in the London audiences. The gentry and professional classes went to enclosed private playhouses such as Blackfriars and the Phoenix, while the lower classes went to open-air public playhouses such as the Globe and the Red Bull. Although these two kinds of playhouses differed in outward appearance, analysis of 276 plays probably first acted by professionals in this period shows that there were no significant differences in the staging requirements of the various companies and that the stage equipment needed was much simpler than has been thought.[13]

And again, with reference to the visual evidence which King divides into two basic designs, that with which I have concerned myself, "doorways and an open space above" and "a gallery above with curtains hanging from its lower edge," as in the *Roxanna, Messalina,* and *Wits* drawings: "Either of these basic designs can, with minor adjustments, provide a suitable facade in front of which to act all of the texts that may depend on prompt copy from an English professional company in the years 1599–1642."[14]

The evidence, both graphic and textual, is as conclusive as scholars can hope for, and we may now speak with a degree of assurance, not possible before, of the physical resources of the Elizabethan playhouse, open or closed, "public" or "private."

13. *Ibid.,* p. 2.
14. *Ibid.,* p. 4.

"Neere the Playe Howse": The Swan Theater and Community Blight

WILLIAM INGRAM

THE HAZARDS OF PLAYGOING in Elizabeth's reign were not different from the common hazards of large assemblies: the risk of infection or of contact with disorderly persons, the chance of having one's pocket picked, and the rare but possible danger of finding oneself in the midst of an affray. These disorders were endemic: cases of drunkenness and riot, of purse cutting, and of other disturbances of the peace in various places around London fill the records of the Middlesex and Surrey Sessions in this period, and the playhouses had their reasonable share of such happenings.[1] Their frequency eventually blunted the public sense of outrage. By the end of Elizabeth's reign the scuffles of apprentices at playhouses had become commonplace; in 1611 a cutpurse's victim at the Swan was spoken of with ridicule rather than

---

1. Perhaps one example will suffice, from an available source (*Middlesex County Records,* ed. J. C. Jeaffreson, 4 vols., [London, 1889–92]). On the evidence of these volumes, pockets were picked in locales ranging from whorehouses to "the wrastling ground in Moore Feildes"; one pickpocket out of seven was apprehended in a playhouse.

sympathy in *The Roaring Girl,* and in 1614 a pickpocket was shown in triumphant action in *Bartholomew Fair.*[2]

Faced with these hazards, Elizabethan playgoers continued to go to plays. They were perhaps more sanguine about such occasional disruptions than we give them credit for. The reputation of a playhouse might suffer in their eyes if incidents became too frequent, but their censure seems not to have passed beyond the bounds of the immediate occasion. The surrounding community would not necessarily suffer their disfavor. Notions about the social pervasiveness and contagion of lawless behavior are more the product of our own times than of Elizabeth's. Indeed, in the 1590s playhouses might have been bad for the soul, as the Puritans would have it, but they were not on the whole bad for the neighborhood. Yet consider this view, from a recent and valuable study of the Bankside:

> [Francis Langley] built the Swan Playhouse [in Paris Garden in 1595-6] and also some tenements nearby and in Upper Ground close to the mill. The playhouse brought actors and hangers-on to the neighborhood and in October, 1596 householders were ordered not to take lodgers into their houses without permission from the constable, and Langley was instructed to mend the cage, the cucking-stool, the pound, and the stocks.[3]

The assumptions underlying this paragraph are all too familiar. The import of the statement is that orders about not taking in lodgers, and about repairing the local instruments of justice, were a result of the arrival in the area of certain theatrical types whose presence is suggested to have been undesirable. This state of affairs resulted in turn from the first cause, the erection of a playhouse. Parts of these assumptions are of course inescapable; a playhouse when in operation would bring actors and their retinue—and perhaps pickpockets—into the neighborhood whenever a play was to be performed. Such actors—and the pickpockets as well—presumably went home again at the end of the day, like tradesmen of other callings in other parts of the city. There are scant grounds for assuming that these people would proceed to settle themselves in the vicinity of their playhouse, and in fact most of the actors about whom we know very much seem to have lived

2. E. K. Chambers, *The Elizabethan Stage* (Oxford, 1923), II, 105, 413.
3. *The Survey of London* (London, 1950), XXII, 97, "Bankside."

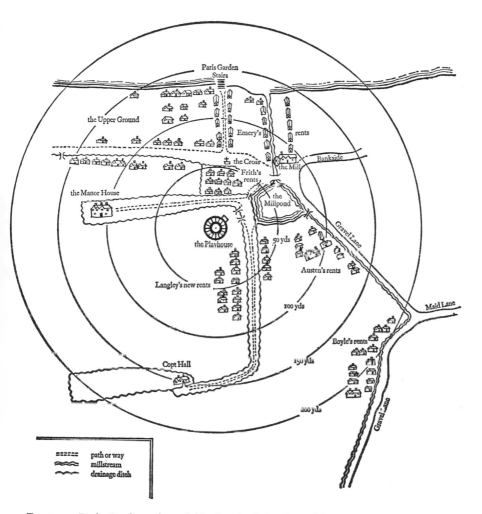

Figure 1. Paris Garden—the neighborhood of the Swan Theater. Drawing by the author.

in neighborhoods of their own choosing regardless of where they were playing. Richard Burbage continued to live in Shoreditch long after his company was installed in Southwark and at Blackfriars; so did Nicholas Tooley. John Heminges and Henry Condell lived in the parish of St. Mary Aldermanbury, where Condell was a churchwarden and Heminges a sidesman; Robert Armin lived in St. Botolph's parish outside Aldgate; and so on. The living habits of Elizabethan pickpockets are, of course, lost to us; but we may assume that those who worked the playhouses also worked elsewhere, and that they would not wish to live in the public eye in any event.

Those players who did live near the Bankside playhouses divide along interesting lines. While few of Shakespeare's fellows lived near the Globe, a surprising number of Admiral's players lived near Philip Henslowe and the Rose. I do not yet know why these two groups should have had such different living habits, but it bears investigating and may tell us yet more about Henslowe's methods. Of the ill-fated Pembroke's company that played the *Isle of Dogs* at the Swan in 1597, four—Robert Shaa, Richard Jones, William Borne, and Thomas Dounton—lived near the Bankside, Jones and Dounton having been with Henslowe at the Rose before 1597 and all of them signing on with Henslowe after that year. The other two named players from Pembroke's, Gabriel Spencer and Ben Jonson, lived in Middlesex. None of these six men moved over to Paris Garden for his season at the Swan.

Some players did live in Paris Garden; John Lowin and Joseph Taylor, for example, bulwarks of the King's Players from the latter half of James's reign, lived virtually in the shadow of the Swan, though they never played there. (This last is not strictly true, for Taylor joined Lady Elizabeth's Men in 1611 and probably played at the Swan for a year or two with them; but as he had already been living by the playhouse for several years before that time, and continued long after, such a coincidence has little value as evidence.)

At the outset, then, we must query the relationship implied in the above quotation between the erection of the playhouse, the prohibition of lodgers, and the readying of cage, stocks, and cucking stool. The quotation implies that the deterioration set in quickly, for by October 1596, the date of the orders about lodgers and stocks, the Swan could hardly have been in operation for more than a few months. If we look again at the source of this information, we will find that the directions about stocks and lodgers formed a part of the business of the annual view of frankpledge held at the manor that October. The latter direction states that no one with lodgings available should admit any person to those lodgings without permission from the constable or some other officer.[4] The penalty for violation was to be 3*s*. 4*d*. per night. But at this same session ten persons were cited and fined for having—or having had—lodgers or "inmates," their fines ranging from the specified 3*s*. 4*d*. up to 10*s*.[5] It is clear from these citations alone that the direction about lodgers was a reiteration and not a first formulation of the rule. A closer look at the language of the document shows that those who were presented for having "extranior*um*, anglice Inmates" were described simply as having acted "contra Statut*um*"; and by looking a bit farther afield we find that the relevant statute against lodgers was not a contrivance of the steward of the manor, or of his representatives, but was one of the accomplishments of the Parliament of 1592: "Noe p*er*son or p*er*sons inhabitinge & dwelling within [three miles of London] shall . . . receyve or take into his or their House or Houses any Inmate or Undersitter or Inmates or Undersitters; vpon payne to forfeyte for everie monethe," etc.[6] Thus, though some desirable purpose

4. "Item preceptum est cuilibet inhabitantum qui custodit sive custodiunt hospiti*um* anglic*e* lodginge infra libertatem pr*e*dictam quod non recipiunt aliqua persona vel p*er*sonas in domibus suis sine Consens*us* Constabular*ii* vel alterius officiar*is* sub pena forisfacere pro qualibet nocte in contrar*ium* 3*s* 4*d*." From the Paris Garden Court Minute Book at the Minet Library, London, VI.237, fol. 3.

5. Those cited were John Aston, Isaac Towell, John Brooker, John Keyllock, John Cockett, Thomas Boddam, John Buckett, Thomas Ridley, William Bowles, and one Heard. John Bromfield was cited for dividing his house into tenements ("quia dividit domu*m* su*um* et recipit extran*eos* anglic*e* Inmat*es*"). In 1598 only four persons were presented for having lodgers, but they were fined £5 each, a sharp increase.

6. *Statutes of the Realm* (1819). This Statute is 35 Eliz. cap. 6, "An Acte again*ste* newe Buyldinges." For an earlier source see *A Collection in English of the Statutes Now in Force* (London, 1945) (*S.T.C.* 9319), fols. 78 and 272[v] The statute concludes: "Be it further enacted, That for auoidinge of colourable contynuyng of Inmates again*ste* thintenc*ion* of this Acte by p*re*tence of any Leases or Estates made to them, the saide Inmat*es* pretending anye Leases shall at the next Leete or Courte to be held in the Man*n*or or Place where the Houses inhabited by Inmates are

was perhaps being served by attempting to explain the no-lodgers order at Paris Garden as resulting from the erection of the Swan playhouse, a full view of the evidence will not allow this supposition to stand.

One would want to go further, of course, for a single refutation hardly makes a case. Fortunately, there is additional information available. The Swan, like the Rose and the Globe, was in St. Saviour's parish, and the fullness of the surviving records of that parish makes possible many lines of inquiry for a Bankside playhouse which would be utterly impractical for, say, the Curtain or Newington Butts. And the Swan is a convenient place to begin: where the Globe, and especially the Rose, were built in neighborhoods already "transitional" (as we might say today), the Swan was circumstanced somewhat differently, lying further west, past the end of the Bankside and on the edge of the open fields of Paris Garden manor. It was built in what might be described as a comparatively "nice" neighborhood, and therefore one more susceptible to (and sensitive to) the possibility of decline. The copyhold lands of the manor, consisting mostly of "tenements" or lodgings, lay to the east and north of the playhouse; the manor house itself stood to the west, and the demesne lands of the manor, some fifty acres of meadow and pasture, stretched to the west and south. The environs of the Swan were therefore unlike those of the Rose or Globe, and more like the surroundings of the Newington Butts playhouse.

Paris Garden had only recently become residential, even along the Thames. Some fifteen years before Langley's decision to build the Swan, the riverside portion of the manor was described as "so darke" even on a moonlit night "being shadowed with trees that one man can not se an other," and in places along the Thames "virgulta or eightes of willows" had grown "exceeding thick" and "are a notable covert for confederattes to shrowd in."[7] This is William Fleetwood,

---

scituate, shall produce his or her lease, and therof make good proofe before the Stewarde of the Leete or Courte & the Jurie, which if he shall not doe, then the said Inmate to be forthwith remooued as aboue is mencioned."

7. P.R.O., SP12/125, fol. 42 (13 July 1578). He must have meant that the willows were in clusters or clumps; a *virgultum* is a thicket, and by *eight* he probably meant *ait* or *eyot,* an islet.

describing to Lord Burghley the site of some clandestine political meetings between the Bishop of Ross and the French ambassador in 1578. Fleetwood concluded that the grounds of the manor were "the boowre of conspirac*es*" and "the College of male cou*n*sell." The building of new dwellings along the river in the 1580s helped to alter this Spenserian landscape, and the new residents of Paris Garden soon found the ordinary variety of community difficulties more immediate than any threat of lurking conspirators.

One of the most persistent problems in the immediate area where the Swan was to be built was the daily overflowing of the neighboring millstream and millpond. Paris Garden manor was from earlier times surrounded by a drainage ditch which was also a tidal stream, opening onto the Thames at the northwest corner of the manor by Bargehouse Stairs, and running thence in a southerly, then an easterly, and then a northerly direction, tracing the boundary of Paris Garden on those three sides until it returned to the river in the northeast corner of the manor near the playhouse site. A mill, called Pudding Mill, was built on this stream on the Upper Ground at its eastern end, functioning as a tide mill with the rising and falling of the river; that is, its wheel turned in one direction as the tide rose and the millstream filled, and in the other as the millstream emptied. There was a large pond behind the mill, less than a hundred feet from where Langley was to build his playhouse, in which the miller was able to store extra water at each high tide; but it regularly overfilled, and its faulty embankments and inadequate floodgates caused daily inundation of the surrounding area. Successive sewer commissions ordered the lord of the manor, or his tenant the miller, to board, pile, and cope the banks, especially "att the southend of meadelane [Maid Lane] where the water floweth over," or more precisely "att the farther end of Maidelane close vnto the raile w*h*ich parteth the highewaie and theire wall." The miller was ordered not to "take anie more water in att the said Mill from the river of Thames but onlie to the Nayle w*h*ich is fixed in the Cuckingstoole there in the millpond," because the floodgates and groundwork of the mill were "verie lowe" and the tidal water "oftentimes floweth over the same"; when this happened, the neighboring "land*es* houses & groundes and likewise the highewaies are overflowed

and surrounded to the greate annoyaunce and dam*m*age of the land-
holders." [8]

So soggy a spot would seem an unlikely locale for such a public
enterprise as a playhouse; yet despite the hazards of muddy feet or
damp rot which the millpond presented, the area where the playhouse
was to be built was reasonably well populated by the early 1590s. Most
of the people who held copyhold lands of the manor in the vicinity
of the playhouse—William Hobson, James Austen, Richard Ryder,
Thomas Iremonger, Richard Frith, William Emery, and others—had
built or developed tenements on their lands and leased them out. As
early as 1588 some one hundred families, averaging three adult members
and probably as many children in each, lived within two hundred yards
or so of the playhouse site.[9] We know a fair amount about them
because they were visited and enumerated by the churchwardens of
the parish church in February or March of each year when money
was collected for the communion tokens. (Attendance at Easter communion was mandatory, under penalty of law, for all persons over
sixteen years; admission to Easter communion at St. Saviour's was
by token only, purchasable in advance from the collectors at 3*d.*
each.) [10]

The itinerary of the token collectors was the same from year to
year. It brought them to Paris Garden on the completion of their
rounds in Clink liberty. Passing beyond the western end of the Bankside, they entered the grounds of the manor just east of the millpond.
Turning from Bankside south onto Gravel Lane, they collected from
the tenants in Austen's rents, and then from those in Boyle's rents;

8. British Museum, MS. Add 34,112A. Greater London Council, SKCS 22, memb.
3; SKCS 28, memb. 5ᵛ.

9. An extract from the Court Baron roll of 13 Feb 1595 (memb. 12) will give an
indication of the density of such dwellings. In one of the transactions recorded on
that date, Thomas Boddam surrendered to Florence Caldwell five messuages or
tenements newly built, in the tenure or occupation of Robert Turner, Gabriel North,
Roger Mayot, Christopher Fawset, and John Cocket, with their families. The five
tenements stood on a parcel of land measuring 47 feet east to west and 33 feet
north to south, or a little over 300 square feet of ground for each family.

10. G.L.C., P92 / SAV / 240 / 4.

then westward to the tenants at Copt Hall, and north again across the playhouse lot to Frith's rents; then past the west side of the millpond into the Upper Ground, beginning at the mill and proceeding westward to Bargehouse Stairs. All the inhabitants were listed in a book, prepared in advance by the parish clerk from the previous year's book; the wardens made additions, deletions, and changes in this book as warranted, and it then became the basis of the following year's book. The number of adults in each family was recorded, as well as the number of tokens purchased.

By reading through these books in sequence for several years, one can see if changes were introduced by (or at least were concurrent with) the erection of the Swan. If the playhouse did indeed affect the neighborhood sufficiently to require stocks and cucking stools to be put in order, then one ought to be able to notice changes beginning in about 1596 which are different from the normal patterns of change before then. Let me examine these areas briefly.

The tenements known as Austen's rents, directly east of the playhouse site, began to grow in 1593 when James Austen bought William Hobson's eight messuages just below the millpond and began building more beside them. Austen had thirteen householders by 1594, sixteen by 1595, and twenty early in 1596, by which time the playhouse was certainly under construction and perhaps completed. Thereafter his tenants held steady at twenty or so families over the next decade. Austen seems to have stopped building at about the time Langley began. Turnover was moderately low in these rents; in this period Austen's average tenant stayed with him for seven years, and, of the twenty families living in his rents in 1603, four had been there since before the playhouse was begun.

The tenants in Boyle's rents, just south of Austen's, were more transient. Henry Boyle had sixteen tenants as early as 1589, and about the same number seven years later, but only eight of them had been there for the whole span. By absorbing Richard Ryder's six tenements in 1596, Boyle raised his total to twenty-four by 1597, but his rentals fluctuated thereafter between twenty and twenty-six, with rapid turnover. An average of nine tenants moved out of Boyle's rents every year during this period; nevertheless in 1603, as in Austen's rents, four families could be found who had been there since before the playhouse was begun.[11]

Frith's rents, immediately north of the playhouse, were a contrast to Boyle's. Richard Frith had built his tenements by the beginning of the 1590s, and held steady at ten householders throughout the next dozen years. Turnover was remarkably low; of the ten families living there in 1603, fully eight had been there since before the playhouse was built, and five had been there since 1588.

William Emery's tenements, sometimes called Emery's rents but more often simply "the upper ground by the mill" in the token books, held steady at eight or nine families, with moderate turnover, during the same period.

Copt Hall, south of the playhouse, had no tenements in 1589; it was then a single messuage in the tenure of William Dyos. By 1593 the property had changed hands several times, and there were five tenements in the area, with families moving in and out each year. For five years after that there was little change; if anything, tenancy seemed to be declining in the middle of the decade. But suddenly in 1598 there were ten families listed in the token book, in 1600 fourteen, in 1601 eighteen. At that juncture the parish clerk, who made up the token book each year by copying the previous year's book with modifications, must have recognized that there were far too many names under "Copped Hall," that the new tenements were in fact elsewhere, and that a new heading was necessary.[12] As result, in the token book for 1602 one finds the first appearance of "mr langlyes newe

12. The token books were always slow to reflect changes of this sort. Robert and William Emery bought Thomas Skinner's rents in 1583, but the heading "Skinner's rents" still appears in the token books as late as 1588. James Austen bought William Hobson's rents in 1593, but "Hobson's rents" still appears in the 1595 token book. As a matter of interest, the heading "near the playhouse" disappears after 1629, and the names of the residents continue as under Copt Hall. But in Nicholas Goodman's *Hollands Leaguer* (1632) the playhouse is spoken of as still standing, though decayed.

11. Included in the business of the view of frankpledge on 8 October 1596 was the presentment of both Austen and Boyle to mend various bridges on the common way, and Boyle to repair bridges at his tenements. Boyle may have suffered more than Austen from the overflowing of the millpond, and this might account for his greater turnover in tenancy.

rent*es* neare the playhouse"; nine names appear under that heading in 1602, eight of them from the former Copt Hall list, including Langley himself and one William Kempe. The remaining Copt Hall list returned to its size of ten years earlier, where it stayed for many years.

A few simple patterns emerge from all this. Emery's rents, Frith's rents, Boyle's rents (combined with Ryder's), and even Copt Hall when separated from Langley's buildings, show no development or increase in size throughout the 1590s. Their patterns of tenancy differed from one another, but those differences, like the patterns themselves, remained constant throughout the decade. Austen's rents showed a marked expansion, but it was finished after 1595. Thereafter building ceased in these areas, and in 1621, when the playhouse was last mentioned as being used for plays, their population was no higher, or higher by only a few families, than it had been in 1595.

The only development which came after 1595 was the erection of Langley's new rents near the playhouse. When occupied, these playhouse tenements increased the size of the neighborhood (and it must be remembered that by "neighborhood" I mean a small area, lying within two hundred yards of the playhouse) by thirteen families in the four years between 1597 and 1601. This is in fact a slower rate of growth than James Austen produced in the three years between 1593 and 1596, when he brought the same number of new families more rapidly into a community whose base was smaller. The growth of the neighborhood was, if anything, retarded after the building of the Swan, though it is a moot point whether people like James Austen would have built more tenements if they had had more land. Perhaps we may safely say that whatever the entrepreneurial copyholders could do to develop the area around the playhouse had already been done by the time the playhouse itself went up. Langley had no competition in building after that date, for he alone still had open ground in the area.

Nor were Langley's tenements an afterthought, built as a consequence of the appearance of the playhouse. They were a part of his original scheme for developing the property, and in fact Langley was concurrently building tenements elsewhere on the manor grounds. But let us suppose for a moment that the playhouse tenements *were* a sudden late idea of Langley's, and see what the implications might be. The sudden development of a demand for lodgings near the Swan would be a healthy sign if those who wanted to live there were a representative cross section of the ordinary Bankside citizenry. It would be a sign of deterioration only if those seeking lodging were the "actors and hangers-on" so disapprovingly cited in my opening quotation. Had Langley capitalized on a demand of this latter sort he would have been undercutting the value of his own investment, and it is unlikely that the tenements would have gone up under those conditions. And in fact the token books negate any such prospect. The occupants of Langley's new rents were, like the other tenants in the area, long-term residents and family groups; the nine householders listed in the 1602 token book bought twenty-three tokens among them, and if we estimate an equal number of children under sixteen we arrive at an average family size of five persons. Langley himself lived there all his life, and his widow stayed on with their four children for some years after his death.[13] The only tenants whose names might suggest playhouse connections were the aforementioned William Kempe, who may have been the actor, and one Thomas Hayward, who appears several times in the St. Saviour's parish register as "a player" and who may have been Thomas Heywood.[14]

Francis Langley was at the height of his career in the mid-1590s, a speculator of moderately wealthy means whose chief desire was to become even more wealthy. He was careful to protect his own investments, but was not the sort of man to be constrained by the niceties of social awareness where his interests were not involved. He invested a fair amount of money in and near the Swan (it was the finest playhouse in London, according to one contemporary account), and there is no evidence that his money-making projects in the area failed to make money. Where there was no possibility of profit there was

13. She married George Delahay in 1606, but in 1608 a widow Delahay is back in the playhouse rents with four children.

14. In 1599 Langley was sued for debt in the Court of Kings Bench by one William Kympe, gentleman, who was probably his neighbor. For Hayward, see the parish register for baptisms of his children on 5 October 1600, 5 June 1603, 16 September 1604, and 5 September 1605; also Edwin Nungezer's *Dictionary of Actors* (New Haven, Conn., 1929).

little incentive for his concern, however, and since the copyholders of Paris Garden were outside his authority as lord of the manor (they had been running their own affairs since 1580) he was little likely to be interested in their welfare, though in fact he did have certain responsibilities toward them of a custodial nature. Indeed, when he succeeded Thomas Cure as lord of the manor in 1589 it must have seemed to the copyholders to be a change for the worse. Cure had done little to improve the manor during his nine years' tenure, but he had apparently performed the ordinary chores of maintenance. After 1589, however, there is evidence of general neglect in the common areas of the manor, which traditionally had been the lord's responsibility. Paris Garden wharf was soon found to be in need of repair; Mill Bridge, on the main road through the Upper Ground, was shortly in a decayed state; the drainage sewers were blocked, and in need of casting and cleaning. By 1593 the banks of the millstream were collapsing, and legal action was initiated:

we present ffrauncis Langley or Mathewe dawson the miller to fill Cope and make higher vj pole more or Lesse of the wall from John Wrenches garden house to Robert ffaces sluce by *our* Lady daie next vpon payne of eue*r*ie pole then vndone xvj*d*.[15]

Langley neglected to comply, and was cited at the following court and at several subsequent courts. By 1599 his fine for not maintaining the millstream had risen from 16*d*. to £30. He responded that year by furnishing a conciliatory supper for the sewer commissioners, but still declined to do the necessary work. They in turn declined to modify their judgment; despite his hospitality they fined him again when next they sat. That same year the bridge by the mill was found to be so decayed that it needed to be made new:

and we doe fynd that ffrauncis Langlay ought to make the same, in respect he is owner of the manor of pa*r*ishe garden, wh*i*ch hath allwayes repayred the same bridge.

In the margin opposite this entry, the clerk of the court has written "not done." At a subsequent court the commissioners ordered

15. Court records of the Surrey and Kent Commissions of Sewers, court of 5 December 1593 (G.L.C., SKCS 18, fol. 194ᵛ).

a warrant to be made to sommon ffrauncis Langlay gent to appeare here the next Courte day to shewe cause why he doth not new make parishe garden bridge according to the order made the last court and why he should not paye xx*li* which he hath incured for not making the same bridge, and further to stand to the order of the same Courte.[16]

There is no evidence that Langley complied with this order either. Such conduct by the lord of the manor would not inspire confidence, or be conducive of good will. Langley may have profited from those who dwelt near the playhouse, but he surely exasperated them as well. In similar fashion Langley had kept up a running disagreement with the elders of the parish church. His extensive building, and his profits, had not escaped attention, and in 1598 the vestry of St. Saviour's decided to take notice:

Item it is Ordered that a viewe shalbe made by the Churchwardens howe manye newe tenem*entes* m*r* Langlye hath builded since the Order sett downe for his Tythes And that they shall speak to m*r* Langley & m*r* Henslowe & Jacob Meade for monie for the pore, in Regarde of theire plaies.[17]

The churchwardens were treated with the same respect accorded the sewer commissioners, and similarly given no money. Unlike Philip Henslowe, who was later a vestryman and churchwarden himself at St. Saviour's (as was Edward Alleyn), Langley was not receptive to the idea of tithes, or of money for the poor. After the wardens had taken their "view" of Langley's property they told him what reasonable amount he ought to pay; he then countered with his own offer of considerably less; they held to their original figure and further resolved that "if he refuse, then the wardens to proceede by lawe against him"; but they fared little better than the sewer commissioners, Langley paying them only 20*s.* for their pains.

Given such attitudes on Langley's part, it is not surprising that the instruments of manorial justice should also be found in need of mending—not, as implied in the opening quotation, because of any marked increase in the number of punishable persons, but simply because they were deteriorating. Langley was cited at the court-leet of the manor on

16. Courts of 29 June 1599 (fol. 293ᵛ), 5 October 1599 (fol. 300ᵛ), and 17 Dec 1599 (fols. 310 and 317).

17. Vestry Minutes of St. Saviour's, 20 April 1598 (G.L.C., P92/SAV/450, p. 323).

8 October 1596 by a copyholders' jury to repair the cage and the cucking stool. The stool, in the millpond by the playhouse, seems to have been mended; but two years later, on 6 October 1598, Langley was again cited to repair the cage, and this time the pound and the stocks as well. How long these items continued in need of repair is unknown, for the presentments at these two courts-leet are the only ones which have survived.[18] It is likely that this second order was not obeyed. Langley need not have interested himself in the manorial pound, and given his record of noncompliance in other such matters one might reasonably assume that he continued to be cited by subsequent juries to make repairs, and continued to ignore them.

Langley's success in flouting the decrees of manor court, parish church, sewer commission, and other duly constituted bodies, and in ignoring the minor functionaries of the law with whom he occasionally came in contact, was ultimately one of the causes of his undoing, for these local successes emboldened him to use the same tactics on the Lord Mayor and Aldermen of the City, and even on Sir Robert Cecil and the Privy Council. Needless to say, with these men he had met his match.[19] When his bubble finally burst in 1601, he lost everything—money, prestige, respect—and died shortly after, not even leaving a will. The lordship of Paris Garden was sold to Hugh Browker, one of the prothonotaries of the Court of Common Pleas, and a respected member of the community. In 1592 he had been a member for Southwark in the Parliament that passed the statute restraining lodgers. Browker had known Langley for many years, but had not liked him. As a sewer commissioner he had fined Langley for the decayed bridge, and as a churchwarden of St. Saviour's he had confronted him about the tithes. Browker, as might be expected, became a conscientious manorial lord: the sewers

18. The records of these two courts-leet are joined with views of frankpledge for the appropriate years. They are in a manuscript book which also contains the records of various courts-baron and views of frankpledge for other years in the 1590s and early 1600s. The book seems to be a permanent record; and, as no leaves are missing, it is possible that no other courts-leet were held during Langley's tenure as lord. Strictly speaking, this was illegal—a manorial lord was required to hold his courts at least once a year—but this would not have constrained Langley.

19. See my "The Closing of the Theaters in 1597," MP, LXIX (1971), 505–15, for Langley's encounters with the Privy Council.

were cleaned, the wharves repaired, the millstream banked, the tithes paid, money given to the poor—but, equally to the point, more tenements were built by the playhouse, and the Swan itself was let to players. By 1604, two years after Langley's death, Browker had increased to twenty the number of tenements "near the playhouse," and in subsequent years the records of the collectors for the poor show payments from "the players in the Swan" for poor relief. Browker's show of responsibility toward the manor as a whole, and his concurrent continuation of Langley's program of building despite his distaste for Langley, suggest that Langley's playhouse and tenements were not the community blight implied in my opening quotation. I think the evidence makes fairly clear what was wrong with Paris Garden in the latter half of the 1590s; the decline of the neighborhood, if such there was, was not due to the presence of the Swan playhouse, but to the neglectful and exploitative attitudes of the man who built it.[20]

20. This study resulted in part from the support of the Faculty Research Fund of the Horace H. Rackham School of Graduate Studies, the University of Michigan.

Tree Properties and Tree Scenes in Elizabethan Theater

WERNER HABICHT

THEATER HISTORIANS and literary critics alike have increasingly made us aware of the considerable extent to which meaningful visual and "emblematic" elements must have contributed to dramatic performances on the Elizabethan public stage.[1] In this general context it seems useful to reconsider the dramaturgic function of large stage properties. The present essay, which concentrates on trees in particular, is an attempt to point out the use to which a constantly recurring type of property was put in an important phase of the history of the theater. It is also intended to plead for a combined consideration of the physical presence of these properties on the stage on the one hand, and of their part in the drama-tists' scenic vision on the other. For even if it were possible to determine definitely how, when, and in what shape tree (or any other) properties were practicable on Elizabethan stages—and there is a considerable lack of certainty in these matters—such information would not tell us much

---

1. See especially G. R. Kernodle, *From Art to Theatre* (Chicago, 1944), which includes an extensive bibliography; John McDowell, "Conventions of Medieval Art in Shakespearian Staging," *JEGP*, XLVII (1948), 215–229; Glynne Wickham, *Early English Stages,* Vol. II, pt. I (London, 1963), pp. 210 ff.

about the impact original performances owed to their use. Nor is justice done to Elizabethan theater practice if, conversely, a study of the plays themselves leads one to recreate imaginatively scenic panoramas by indiscriminately piecing together the impressions conveyed by descriptive passages in the dialogue, or even by the poetic imagery, and to imagine what could actually be seen on the stage.[2] It is the interaction between the scene qua set and the scene qua literary unit with which we ought to be concerned. The question to be raised, then, is what the visual presence of stage properties "meant" in the total context of a performance and in what sense the use of properties on the "open stage" of the Elizabethan playhouse constituted an integral element of dramatic form.

Elizabethan properties were single set pieces which obviously could not by themselves provide, or even suggest, anything like an illusionistic scene locality; nor were they intended to do so. Certain standard properties, whose availability need not be doubted, may have helped to "mark" corresponding typical scenes of the plays. But such conventional scene types were defined by the property itself and its iconographic associations rather than by a suggested scene locality. For example, a throne would have marked court scenes—not, however, in the sense that it suggested the splendors of a royal palace, but because it visually emphasized the presence of royal power; "throne scene" would in fact be the adequate designation, at least from the point of view of the drama-in-performance. Similarly, one may recognize such recurring scene types as the bed scene, the monument (or tomb) scene, the banquet scene,[3] perhaps also the gate scene,[4] and, indeed, the tree scene. All of these, typified as they are both by the use of one or several conventional properties on the stage and by the observance of equally conventional literary patterns by the dramatist,

2. This, of course, is the method of many literary critics (and also of illustrators). For example, D. W. Rannie in *Scenery in Shakespeare's Plays,* 2d ed. (Oxford, 1931) is explicitly "not thinking of stage scenery, which, as everybody knows, was in Shakespeare's day practically non-existent" (p. 127). Even more recent and more theatrically minded studies like Rudolf Stamm's essays on "word scenery" in *The Shaping Powers at Work* (Heidelberg, 1967), or Dieter Mehl's "Schaubild und Sprachfigur in Shakespeares Dramen," *SJ* (*West*), 1970, pp. 7–29, have relatively little to say about the actual contribution of stage setting and stage properties.

3. For the properties involved, cf. G. F. Reynolds, *On Shakespeare's Stage* (Boulder, Colo., 1967), pp. 29 ff.

4. Cf. Irwin Smith, " 'Gates' on Shakespeare's Stage," *SQ,* VII (1956), 159–182.

lend themselves most readily to an examination of the evocative dramaturgic relationship of the sister arts realized in a play's performance.

I

The more general problems involved are, of course, not limited to the Elizabethan period alone; and different explanations will be required in different historical contexts. The ways in which dramatists and scene designers cooperate (or quarrel with each other like Ben Jonson and Inigo Jones) are subject to changes in conceptions of the theater, literary standards, and tastes in scene *décor*. Dissimilar are the inspirations that emanate from, for instance, the classical principle of the unity of place, the Wagnerian idea of a scenic *Gesamtkunstwerk,* the Victorian predilection for spectacular effects, or the naturalistic emphasis on environment. And yet some basic types of scene and scenery have always been such omnipresent forms of theatrical expression that they can be regarded as scenic *topoi.* Tree scenes most certainly belong to this category.

Trees, set pieces made up of tree and foliage elements, entire sets composed of trees, and dramatic scenes with a tree or trees as a point of reference of action and dialogue can easily be traced throughout the history of drama and theater. The tree may be a single but dominating item, solidly present and yet strangely disturbing, appearing in various stages of growth or decay. Or it may help to constitute scene localities such as the forest or the garden, which in turn occur over and over again as scene sets and set scenes, whether they be presented in symbolical stylization or in decorative profusion. And since, moreover, the tree motif has an extremely rich iconographic tradition, the property tree on the stage stands ready to attract and to release mythical, symbolical, and emblematic meanings of many a derivation.

The dominating single tree was required in medieval productions of mystery plays; a Tree of Life may have been all that was necessary to represent the Garden of Eden (it is the only piece of scenery explicitly referred to in English creation plays); but even when, as in the French *Mistère du Vieux Testament,* it was surrounded by a more picturesque *décor* made up of natural and artificial plants and painted canvas, it was still "l'arbre de vie plus excellent que tous les autres" that occupied the central position.[5] Some of the trees of later drama are no less impressively tied up with one's recollection of the plays to which they belong, such as, to name but a few obvious examples, Herne's oak in *The Merry Wives of Windsor,* the *Weltesche* in Richard Wagner's *Valkyrie,* the shattered apple tree which in Arthur Miller's *All My Sons* foreshadows a tragic revelation, the rudimentary tree where Didi and Gogo wait for Godot, or the "big tree on mound" which in John Arden's *Armstrong's Last Goodnight* indicates the central section of a tripartite stage modeled on the medieval example. Stage design has established stereotyped patterns of placing the dominating tree, patterns which can be descried in both nineteenth-century illusionism and twentieth-century stylization, and which are so persistent that their implementation is sometimes a purely formal one. The tree may massively stress one side of the stage—a frequent pattern of nineteenth-century sets, whether for melodrama or for productions of Shakespeare, the latter including Kean's *King Lear* (1858), where a leafless tree at the right-hand border of the heath set is in the reconciliation scene replaced by a leafy oak overshadowing the French tent; and an *Othello* of the Comédie Française (1899), where a big cedar is set against the right-hand half of the Cyprian palace on the back perspective.[6] Or a tree may be firmly planted (or painted on the backcloth) in the center, its branches encompassing the entire stage or an important part of it; a more recent design for *Love's Labour's Lost*[7] and some sets for American musicals such as *Oklahoma!* or *The Golden Apple*[8] are equally striking examples. Again, the tree element may grow out of one or several pairs of wings and form an arch across the top, a

---

5. G. Cohen, *Histoire de la mise en scène dans le théâtre réligieux français du moyen-âge,* 3d ed. (Paris, 1951), p. 91. For trees in the mystery plays, see also Mc-Dowell, "Conventions of Medieval Art in Shakespearian Staging," p. 226; M. D. Anderson, *Drama and Imagery in English Mediaeval Churches* (Cambridge, Eng., 1963), pp. 64, 124.

6. Designs reproduced in Richard Southern, *The Victorian Theatre* (New York, 1970), pp. 49–50; Denis Bablet, *Esthétique générale du décor de théâtre de 1870 à 1914* (Paris, 1965), fig. 9.

7. Stratford Festival, 1934; reproduced in R. Mander and J. Mitchenson, *A Picture History of the British Theatre* (London, 1957).

8. Scene photographs reproduced in Cecil Smith, *Musical Comedy in America* (New York, 1950), fig. 59; Barnard Hewitt, *Theatre U.S.A., 1665 to 1957* (New York, 1959), p. 466.

device that can be traced from the foliage arcades of the seventeenth- and eighteenth-century theater down to some effective modernizations as, for example, in Gorelik's design for O'Neill's *Desire under the Elms.*[9] Or else, there is the more diffuse way of suggesting the omnipresence of trees by means of transparencies; Arthur Miller in *Death of a Salesman* and Robert Bolt in *The Flowering Cherry* rely on gauze curtains or cycloramas depicting leaves and blossoms respectively in order to visualize their heroes' hidden dreaming. Stylistic and technical details and symbolical implications apart, we may, then, recognize the dominating tree as a scenic *topos* established in dramatic literature and in the art of scenic *décor,* respected by the playwright and by the designer—and by the actors as well; for the stage tree has its equally conventional and recurring dramatic functions as a spot for hiding, eavesdropping, or appointments, or else as an instrument for climbing and hanging.

A similar standardization has affected the scenes whose main visual elements are trees—outdoor scenery of various kinds such as garden, park, grove, wood, wilderness, idyllic landscape, seashore, etc., and divers combinations and mixtures of these. The three Vitruvian types of scenery already include a tree scene—the *scena satyrica,* whose description was elaborated in Serlio's illustrated account.[10] As the well-known drawing in *D'Archittetura* shows, suggestions of wood, grove, and garden, of natural and artificial elements, coalesce theatrically, thus setting a type of Renaissance outdoor scenery which influenced many a perspective set for pastoral plays in particular. For it is an adequate visual counterpart of the eclectic arcadian landscape which in the tradition of poetry is nature in artificial combination.[11] Renaissance plays themselves suggest a juxtaposition of forest and pasture, which in the anonymous Elizabethan play *The Maid's Metamorphosis* is formalized in verbal debates between the forester and the shepherd,[12] and which is also harped upon in Shake-

9. Design reproduced in John Gassner, *Producing the Play,* rev. ed. (New York, 1953), p. 253.

10. Reproduced in E. K. Chambers, *The Elizabethan Stage* (Oxford, 1923), IV, 362, and elsewhere. See also L. B. Campbell, *Scenes and Machines on the English Stage During the Renaissance* (Cambridge, Eng., 1923), pp. 35 ff.

11. Cf. E. R. Curtius, *Europäische Literatur und lateinisches Mittelalter,* 2d ed. (Berne, 1954), pp. 191 ff.

12. In R. W. Bond's edition of *The Complete Works of John Lyly* (Oxford, 1902), Vol. III; see especially I.i.

speare's Forest of Arden. Renaissance pageantry of medieval derivation
and multiple-stage arrangements in courtly halls provided comparable
combinations; for in these the garden, the bower, and the grove were
standardized scenic structures. In the changeable landscape sets of
Jacobean masques classical and native traditions converged; the multiple-
stage elements were absorbed by the perspective panorama. Its trees and
foliage could concurrently be implemented in localizing, symbolic and
spectacular functions, as Campion's *Description of a Masque* (1607)
testifies: painted "shrubbes and trees" furnished the general background;
the dominating Tree of Diana on top of the mountain set a symbolical
stress; and there was the movement of further trees, which sank, cleft
apart, and emitted the dancing masquers.[13] After the Restoration, when
directions for scenery and indications of locality at the heads of the
scenes became a regular feature of the printed editions of stage plays, the
distinction of separate kinds of outdoor scenery was made more explicit,[14]
although, in accordance with contemporary tendencies in the arts, a
predilection for the theatrical elements of the garden and the park, even
in what were called wood or forest scenes, is as obvious in late
seventeenth- and eighteenth-century plays and decorations as is the popularity of the illusion of wild and fantastical woods in nineteenth-century
productions, especially of opera and melodrama. But both dramatists and
designers did come to recognize at least the garden and the forest as
distinct standard sets; and both figure among the five prefabricated stock
sets advertised by the Samuel French company in 1821.[15] Arthur Kopit in
his recent play *Indians* may well be making use of such degenerations of
the art of stage design by having "a painted forest of the worst melodramatic order" evoke the sentimentality of fictionalized history in order
to confront it with the harsher historical realities.[16]

If one considers them in the context of the plays which originally re-

13. Thomas Campion, *The Description of a Maske* [. . .] (London, 1607),
sig. A 4.

14. Cf. Montague Summers, *The Restoration Theatre* (London, 1934), pp. 223
ff.; see also A. S. Jackson, "Restoration Scenery 1656–1680," *RECTR,* III, no. 2
(1964), 25 ff.

15. Cf. G. A. Leverton, *The Production of Later Nineteenth Century American
Drama* (New York, 1936), p. 21.

16. Methuen ed. (London, 1970), p. 39.

quire them, both the wood and the garden type of scenery, and the dominating single tree as well, almost invariably have some kind of ambiguity about them, which, according to a greater or lesser degree of theatrical competence, affects the dramatic situation, the characters, or the thematic implications of the scenes in question. Stage trees and tree sets tend to be associated with deception, error, uncertainty, disguise, dueling, betrayal, mystery, dream, magic, or the goddess Fortune. Even if nineteenth-century *décor* may at times have obscured or leveled the dramatic impact of such ambiguity, its full force has been expressively revived by more than one twentieth-century playwright. Eugene O'Neill for one has repeatedly done so; the forest in *Emperor Jones,* in which the main character seeks refuge only to be overcome by the guilty visions of his life in civilization, is as central to that expressionistic play as, say, Mrs. Harford's garden, the symbol of her escapist dreams of the past, is to *More Stately Mansions;* and the dominating trees in *Desire under the Elms* are to give the impression that they "protect and at the same time subdue."

II

It would be a tempting enterprise to study the continuity and the ramified variations of the stage tree in particular, and of outdoor scenery in general, in the changing contexts of theater conditions, literary styles, and cultural associations.[17] Our immediate concern, however, is with the significance of the Elizabethan contribution to these developments. On the Elizabethan public stage—and it is only the public stage which is to be dealt with here—the single tree property and the tree scenery must have been practically identical. There is sufficient evidence for the assumption that tree properties were in fact available, in spite of J. C. Adams' more austere assertion that the stage posts were all that was needed.[18] What exactly these stage trees looked like, how they

17. For a special point, see my article "Becketts Baum und Shakespeares Wälder," *SJ* (*West*), 1970, 77–98. Some of its material is included in the context of this section.

18. *The Globe Playhouse,* 2d ed. (New York, 1961), p. 111. See also Bernard Beckerman, *Shakespeare at the Globe* (New York, 1962), p. 75. For a different view, cf. G. F. Reynolds, "'Trees' on the Stage of Shakespeare," *MP,* V (1907),

were manufactured and dealt with, we have no safe way of knowing; besides, there is no reason to assume uniformity in these matters. But it is fairly obvious that only one or a few single trees or tree elements were possible, and that their function was therefore symbolical and evocative rather than localizing and decorative. The property trees listed in Henslowe's inventories—"j tree of gowlden apelles; Tantelouse tre"—are indeed symbolical ones.[19] On the other hand, scenes and scene sequences ostensibly associated with trees are fairly frequent in Elizabethan plays; they are readily identifiable, even if one disregards the localizing scene headings introduced by later editors. For although the stage was in principle a nonrepresentational and "placeless" one, and although it gained temporary localization through the dialogue and the acting only where needed and relevant, it is still worth noting that localization of the latter kind occurs with particularly striking regularity and intensity where gardens, orchards, forests, groves, wildernesses, etc., are to be imagined; such scenes are clearly set off against the more neutral scenes that surround them. The wood scenes in the middle acts of *A Midsummer Night's Dream,* for example, are carefully prepared for, and their text contains numerous references to phenomena of nature both onstage and offstage, whereas in Acts I and V, where all we get by way of spoken localization is an occasional reference to "Athens," the place is left unspecified; editorial scene headings like "A room in Theseus' palace," for all the picturesque stage traditions they have subsequently given rise to, are, of course, entirely arbitrary. If, then, wood, garden, and similar tree scenes are more distinctly localized than others by direct and indirect references to scenery, it seems difficult not to suppose that they were also marked visually; and trees would have been the obvious properties to do the marking with. The argument to the contrary, which uses the very frequency of these textual references as proof that the performance took place on an empty stage, on which outdoor scenes were in special need of being equipped with a "word scenery" to make up for the lack of visual *décor,* overlooks the demonstrative quality of such

---

153–168; and *The Staging of Elizabethan Plays at the Red Bull Theatre* (New York, 1940), p. 72. See also Richard Southern, *The Seven Ages of the Theatre* (New York, 1961), p. 183.

19. *Henslowe's Diary,* ed. R. A. Foakes and R. T. Rickert (Cambridge, Eng., 1961), p. 320.

references (*"this* wood," *"this* garden," *"this* tree," etc.), which surely implies gestures that establish a relationship between the spoken words and the visual impressions.

One may indeed assume that there was in Elizabethan performances something like a general type of scene with the visual and dramaturgic use of the stage tree as its salient characteristic. Visually, the difference between, say, the wood scenes in *A Midsummer Night's Dream,* the heath scenes in *King Lear,* and the garden scene in *Richard II* need not at all have been great; explicit references to the presence of a tree, at any rate, are contained in each of them.[20] The basic type may have permitted individual variations; but these were only to some extent variations of actual stage setting. Additional properties would have supplied further emblematic details rather than localization. A tree scene may be specified as representing a garden by suggestions of gates or walls (if only by the actors' drawing the audience's attention to natural resources of the stage such as the door or the façade); for these, along with the fountain, are age-old iconographic signs of the garden.[21] The gate which in *Twelfth Night*[22] admits "Cesario" to the garden of Olivia (whose very name is associated with the tree), or else the walls which Romeo or Jack Cade (in *2 Henry VI*) have to climb to get into a "garden,"[23] may evoke the image of the enclosed garden and the range of its associations,[24] which is also made to surround Friar Lawrence's first appearance in *Romeo and Juliet* (II.iii). Wood scenery may have included properties equally traditional, such as banks, bushes, caves, rocks (these are referred to in *The Birth of Merlin*); moreover, the stage trap was used to represent ditches and holes in the forests of *The Merry Wives of Windsor* and *Titus Andronicus.*[25] But even combinations of properties in tree scenes would by themselves hardly have sufficed to establish specific and

20. *A Midsummer Night's Dream,* I.ii.97 (the mechanicals meet "at the Duke's oak"). *King Lear,* II.iii.2; III.iv.45; V.ii.1. *Richard II,* III.iv.25.

21. Cf. Kernodle, *From Art to Theatre,* pp. 15, 95.

22. III.i.89.

23. Cf. *Romeo and Juliet,* II.i.5 (and, for the tree, II.i.30, 34); *2 Henry VI,* IV.x.9.

24. Cf. Stanley Stewart, *The Enclosed Garden* (Madison, Wis., 1966).

25. *The Birth of Merlin,* in *The Shakespeare Apocrypha,* ed. C. F. T. Brooke (Oxford, 1908); see especially V.i.61. See also *Titus Andronicus,* II.iii.186, 198, 277, 249; *Merry Wives of Windsor,* V.iv.3.

visually recognizable types of outdoor locality. Mixtures of garden and forest items in fact seem to have been common enough. An arbor or bower—another standard tree element—may well be expected to stand for a garden, as it probably did in *Much Ado About Nothing* in Benedick's eavesdropping scene.[26] In Kyd's *The Spanish Tragedy,* too, a "leafy bower"—as illustrated on the 1615 title page—served to mark "this garden," where both the lovers' meeting and Horatio's hanging take place;[27] but when Hieronimo enters the garden in his mad search for Horatio, the scenery his soliloquy refers to seems to be rather more like a forest—"[I] look on each tree, and search through every brake, / Beat at the bushes, stamp on grandam earth."[28] In fact bowers were also used for forests; Sherwood Forest in Munday's *The Downfall of Robert Earl of Huntington* is, as the dialogue repeatedly affirms, at least partly represented by one, which serves as a lovers' retreat.[29] Or else such a property was introduced into an otherwise nonrepresentational (courtly) episode, as in *A Looking Glass for London and England,* where "an Arbour," intended to gratify the sinful pleasures of Rasni's mistress, was conjured up (probably via the trap) by the magicians and then destroyed (from above) through divine intercession.[30]

If there is anything like a special local atmosphere of a particular tree scene, it is the result of a combined poetry of words, gestures, and sounds which is unsteadily woven around the stage and its properties. For such a poetry creates varying, evanescent, many-layered, not, however, permanent, impressions. At the very beginning of a tree scene the dialogue is often quite explicit in specifying the place in a general way: "Well, this is the forest of Arden," or: "The garden here is more convenient."[31] But descriptive elaborations of statements like these tend to point beyond the visible stage; hence, they are not simply verbal substitutes for the absence of picturesque settings, but they expand the scene imaginatively.

26. Cf. II.iii.33.

27. Cf. II.iv.269; II.v.314, 318.

28. III.xiiA, 915 ff.

29. In Malone Society Reprints (Oxford, 1965); see ll. 1363, 1372, 1381, 1574, etc. For the bower see also Wickham, *Early English Stages,* II.i.210 ff.

30. *The Plays and Poems of Robert Greene,* ed. J. C. Collins (Oxford, 1905), Vol. I, ll. 491 ff.

31. *As You Like It,* II.iv.11; *1 Henry VI,* II.iv.4; cf. also *2 Henry IV,* IV.i.1 f.

Elizabethan wood scenes are neither locally delimited nor fragmented into well-defined sections; editorial scene headings like "Another part of the forest" are therefore particularly misleading. The wood, or the garden, is as it were present as a totality, fraught with heterogeneous, ironical, and paradoxical associations which are evoked by words, images, sounds, and by the acting. It is this heterogeneous totality which the tree property unifyingly stands for. Poetic fallacy is at work when in *As You Like It* the Forest of Arden is felt to be a paradise by some characters and a desert by others, or when the forest in *Titus Andronicus* is described, in one and the same scene by one and the same character, as a blissful bower and as a "barren detested vale," [32] though the tree, mentioned several times in both cases, visually guarantees a general unity of the place.

Gesture and movement, too, contribute to identify, and at the same time to explore expansively, the scenes signaled by the tree. The very tone of the verbal references to either "this forest" or "the garden here" might well imply different gestures. Garden scenes are sometimes suggested by movements of leisurely walking on imaginary paths, as when Iden in his garden is pleased to "enjoy such quiet walks as these"; [33] or else there is playful movement, sportive action, or handling and strewing of flowers. The acting in wood scenes, on the other hand, usually suggests a sense of distance. We are shown in advance the setting out of the characters for their journey toward a forest, and sometimes at the beginning of a wood scene mention is made of horses that have just been disposed of. [34] In the course of these scenes uncertain movements prevail. "We've lost our way in the woods," is the repeated exclamation of the three servants at the beginning of Peele's *The Old Wives' Tale*, and they display fittingly grotesque behavior, which seems to include climbing a

32. II.iii. For a recent discussion, see Clifford Leech, "The Function of Locality in the Plays of Shakespeare and His Contemporaries," in *The Elizabethan Theatre* [1], ed. D. Galloway (Toronto, 1969), p. 114.

33. *2 Henry VI*, IV.x.17.

34. See, for example, Beaumont and Fletcher, (*Works,* ed. A. Dyce [London, 1843–46]), *The Lover's Progress,* Act IV; *Love's Pilgrimage,* II.ii; Shakespeare, *3 Henry VI*, IV.v.19. The same device can still be found in Restoration drama; see for example Aphra Behn, *The Widow Ranter* (*Works,* ed. M. Summers [London, 1915], IV, 256.

tree. In *A Midsummer Night's Dream* the lovers no sooner appear in the wood, than they "have forgot our way." [35] In *The Birth of Merlin* Joan, pursuing her seducer who has disappeared in a forest, is directed in a deliberately casual manner—"This way, that way, through the bushes there"—and yet storms on, "winged with sweet desire." [36] In Massinger's *The Bashful Lover* one character, because he fails to see his way, gets desperately trapped in a forest full of his enemies—"Shall I return by the same path? I cannot; / The darkness of the night conceals it from me." [37] No doubt the vagrant movements and gestures expected from the actors at such points had their share in transforming the scenes into woods of terror, while the movements of fleeing and pursuing opened up a quasi-unlimited distance.

Sound effects are equally important. Gardens tend to be quiet—though often treacherously so. Wood scenes, however, are filled with various evocative noises. Shouts and excited calls are, in *A Midsummer Night's Dream* and elsewhere, exchanged between onstage and offstage.[38] And there are the noises of animals; in *The Two Noble Kinsmen* a soliloquy of the Jailer's Daughter, who is alone and astray in the forest at night, responds to the wolves' howling ("Harke, tis a woolfe"; "I have heard / Strange howles this live-long night"), with chirping crickets and screeching owls in the background.[39] The echo device, a heritage from pastoral literature [40] effectively dramatized in several Elizabethan wood scenes,[41] also suggests both wide range and deceptiveness. Special offstage sounds can identify a tree scene as a hunting grove; in *A Midsummer Night's Dream* the "musical confusion" of Theseus' hounds, along with the music of the hunters' horns, crystallizes the outcome of the night in

35. II.ii.36.

36. *The Birth of Merlin*, II.i.223 ff.

37. In *The Dramatic Works of Massinger and Ford*, ed. H. Coleridge (London, 1869), p. 399 (II.vi).

38. *A Midsummer Night's Dream*, III.ii.401 ff. Cf. *The Birth of Merlin*, II.i.61; Beaumont and Fletcher, *Beggars' Bush*, V.i.

39. *The Two Noble Kinsmen*, in *The Shakespeare Apocrypha*, III.ii.4, 11 ff., 35 ff. Cf. F. A. Shirley, *Shakespeare's Use of Off-Stage Sounds* (Lincoln, Nebr., 1963), pp. 11 f.

40. Cf. E. Colby, *The Echo Device in Literature* (New York, 1920).

41. For the echo in Dekker's *Old Fortunatus* see below, section IV. Cf. also *The Maid's Metamorphosis*, III.ii; Peele's *The Old Wives' Tale*, ll. 480 ff., etc.

the Athenian wood into an acoustic symbol. The short atmospheric scene that in *Titus Andronicus* (II.ii) introduces a forest sequence relies a great deal on hunting noise, which extends into the verbal imagery and strikes a keynote with which the varying situations in a highly ambiguous forest are as consistently connected as with the tree property; while Titus nobly hunts "the panther and the hart," Aaron tells Tamora's wanton sons how to rape "this dainty doe"; Tamora herself, when discovered in her embraces with Aaron (whom she has taken "for a stag"), is described as a false Dian.[42] The hunt as a whole, which had been arranged by Titus to celebrate a reconciliation, turns out to be his adversaries' opportunity for treason. Not only the noises, but also the actions connected with hunting, and not to forget the huntsmen's costumes, thus identify a tree scene as a grove and are at the same time linked up metaphorically with the deceptions and reversals of the plot. In Beaumont and Fletcher's *Philaster,* which contains a comparable example of this procedure, such a link is established at the very beginning of the forest sequence (IV.ii.1 ff.) in a dialogue between the woodsmen even before the verbal references to "these woods" and the tree set in.

III

The performance and the dialogue not only weave an appropriate but varying scenic atmosphere around the stage tree but also make both the property and the atmosphere release a complex of associations and meanings. To affirm that Shakespeare's woods, for instance, are reflections of the real Warwickshire forests would surely be a small part of the truth. The tree property, as well as the wood or garden it may stand for, can assume symbolic qualities and emblematic functions. By the way it is led up to, through the words and gestures delivered in it, and through the visual and verbal images it contains, a tree scene provides the audience's imagination with familiar motifs established by iconographic and literary traditions, the sheer multiplicity and disparity of which account for its ambiguous effects.

The forest image in particular offers a range of motifs, including com-

42. Cf. *Titus Andronicus,* II.ii. *passim;* I.i.493; II.i.117; II.iii.57 ff.

binations of motifs, most of which have their medieval, if not classical, literary precedents; [43] and these are concurrently played on in the dramatic tree scenes. Thus the medieval identification of wood and wilderness, of forest and desert, which can be traced from Old Saxon poetry to Sidney's *Arcadia,* is paradoxically unfolded in Shakespeare's *As You Like It,* and in tree scenes of many other Elizabethan plays, and parodied in *A Knight of the Burning Pestle* (II.175). This identification also implies that if tree properties marked forests they must also have marked deserts and wildernesses and that, for example, in the heath episodes of *King Lear,* although "for many miles about there's scarce a bush," there must have been a visual counterpart of Edgar's "happy hollow of a tree" and for "the shadow of this tree." [44] Equally traditional is the association of woods both with noble outlaws and with robbers; both use the stage tree for their respective activities (hiding and binding) in romance plays from *Common Conditions* to Beaumont and Fletcher's *The Pilgrim.* Robin Hood and his men, who are, indeed, a combination of the two, are represented or alluded to in tree scenes of several English plays ranging from Munday's *The Downfall of Robert Earl of Huntington* through Shakespeare's *The Two Gentlemen of Verona* and *As You Like It* down to Massinger's *The Guardian,* where the banditti are "imitating / The courteous English thieves" (V.iii). Even the hunts by which many tree scenes are brought to life may be assumed to have caused conflicting responses if one considers the humanists' depreciation of this sport as well as its aristocratic recommendation; this, too, is reflected in Shakespeare's treatment of the Forest of Arden. [45] The age-old *topos* of the dark forest, along with its symbolic associations with the concept of chaos, is also recreated on the stage; in *A Midsummer Night's Dream* the audience is made aware of it not only by the movements of the lovers in the Athenian wood, who, like the Red Cross Knight in Spenser's wood of Error, at once go astray, but also by the "drooping fog as black as Acheron" which Oberon orders to be spread

43. These are studied in detail by M. Stauffer, *Der Wald: Zur Darstellung der Natur im Mittelalter* (Berne, 1959).

44. *King Lear,* II.iv.300 ff.; II.iii.2; V.ii.1; cf. III.iv.46. See also Reynolds, " 'Trees'," pp. 155 ff.; and cf. Stauffer, *ibid.,* p. 98.

45. Cf. Claus Uhlig, " 'The Sobbing Deer': *As You Like It,* II.i.21–66, and the Historical Context," *RenD,* N.S. III (1970), 79–109.

over the scene; in an emblem of Henry Peacham's the dark forest ("Resembling Chaos, or the hideous night") is virtually located "by the banke of Acheron." [46] Yet another literary association of the wood motif is with madness, which is dramatically evoked when in *The Two Noble Kinsmen* Arcite asks Palamon "Is't not mad lodging here in the woods, cosen?," while in the following scene the Jailer's Daughter, unable to find Palamon in the same forest (by the same tree property), actually loses her wits (III.iii–iv); or when in Beaumont and Fletcher's *The Pilgrim* the plot leads the disguised heroine straight from the woods into a madhouse (III.v–vii). The pun of Shakespeare's Demetrius, who is "wood within this wood," [47] strikes a similar note. If Lear's madness on the heath was enacted in the presence of a tree property, it was by implication linked up with the wood image, which in turn seems to be related to Lear's nakedness, the nakedness of the mad hero in the woods having already been emphasized in Chrétien's *Ywain* or in Ariosto's *Orlando*.[48] Nor is it surprising that in *The Spanish Tragedy* Hieronimo in his madness should, as observed above, refer to his garden (marked by a bower) in terms that seem to suggest a forest. Moreover, the forest (and the desert) is a traditional place for penance, a fact of which we are reminded when in *The Two Gentlemen of Verona* news of Silvia's flight to the woods (where she is to meet both with the robbers and with her lover) is brought to the court by a friar who "in penance wander'd through the forest" (V.i.38). Lisander in Beaumont and Fletcher's *The Lover's Progress* is "in this thicket" when he resolves "To call my self unto a strict account / For my pass'd life, how vainly spent" (Act IV). Even the domestic drama of Thomas Heywood's *A Woman Killed with Kindness* culminates in a tree scene; the treacherous Wendoll, "with the sharp scourge of repentance lash'd" is left to "live in these shadowy woods / Afraid of every leaf or murmuring blast." [49] On the other hand,

46. *A Midsummer Night's Dream*, III.ii.357; cf. Henry Peacham, *Minerva Britanna or a Garden of Heroical Devices* (London, 1612), p. 182. For the "dark forest," cf. Rainer Lengeler, *Tragische Wirklichkeit als groteske Verfremdung bei Shakespeare* (Cologne, 1964), pp. 31 ff. See also E. Th. Sehrt, "Der Wald des Irrtums," *Anglia*, LXXXVI (1968), 463–491; J. M. Steadman, "Spenser's Errour and the Renaissance Allegorical Tradition," *NM*, LXII (1961), 22–38.

47. *A Midsummer Night's Dream*, II.i.191.

48. Cf. Stauffer, *Der Wald*, pp. 74–77.

49. Ed. R. W. van Fossen, The Revels Plays (London, 1961), xvi.33, 42 ff.

the forest has ever since the Greek romances been associated with love. In *Mucedorus* the forest in which the protagonist, banished for his love, lives like a hermit, is also inhabited by Bremo, the Wild Man, who describes it in idyllic colors in his *invitatio* with which he hopes to win Mucedorus' faithful princess.[50] The forest may be a *locus amoenus,* a refuge, a place where both lovers and pretending lovers are put to the test and made to discover their true selves. This association is, perhaps, the most frequent one to be dramatically signaled by the tree property, whether it is supposed to mark a forest or else (as in *Twelfth Night* or *Much Ado About Nothing*) a garden, or whether there simply is, as in Marston's *Parasitaster,* "a well-growne plain tree" via which the stubborn prince is lured into love.[51]

As for the eclectic landscape of the tradition of pastoral poetry, the realization in terms of stage setting of its pictoral patterns (as preserved, for example, in contemporary illustrations of Guarini's *Il Pastor Fido*) may be a special case where plays requiring a unified pastoral scene with its trees, bowers, banks, and cabins, such as Lyly's *Gallathea* or Beaumont and Fletcher's *The Faithful Shepherdess,* are concerned. For here the conventions of the masques may have to be taken into account. But even so a dominating tree is sometimes called for—as in *Gallathea*—[52] and seems to link up the pastoral setting with the tree scene of the public stage. That the tree property of the latter did in fact suggest pastoral themes is obvious enough in view of *As You Like It.* But there are numerous scenes in other plays as well in which the tree property is rhetorically pointed at in conventional idyllic complaints and comparisons between nature and court or city. In some cases the place of action is specified as a forest, as, for instance, in *The Two Gentlemen of Verona* ("This shadowy desert, unfrequented woods, / I better brook than flourishing peopled towns," V.iv.2 ff.); or as a garden like that of Iden in *2 Henry VI* ("Lord, who would live turmoiled in the court / and may enjoy such quiet walks as these"; IV.x.17); while the very indefiniteness of the visual tree property seems to be made use of when in Beau-

50. In *Shakespeare Apocrypha,* IV.ii–iii.
51. John Marston, *Plays,* ed. H. H. Wood (Edinburgh, 1938), II, 208.
52. Cf. Peter Saccio, *The Court Comedies of John Lyly* (Princeton, N.J., 1969), p. 19.

mont and Fletcher's *The Lover's Progress* Lydian declares: "these wild fields are my gardens . . ." (Act IV).

An enumeration of conventional motifs which performances of Elizabethan plays associate with the tree property could be carried on further; it would have to include, for example, the fairy lore which comes alive in the Athenian wood of *A Midsummer Night's Dream* and at Herne's oak in the Windsor Forest of *The Merry Wives of Windsor,* and also the ideas connected with the garden, some of which, like the enclosed garden image or the garden symbolizing paradise, have a biblical origin. The dramatic effects of a tree scene, however, depend on the artistry with which various and even conflicting associations are superimposed, combined, explored, or played off against one another. Thus in Shakespeare's *As You Like It* the whole range of wood motifs and motif clusters is made to converge in the green world. The Forest of Arden is described both as a paradise and as a wilderness; it is a refuge for distressed lovers as well as a place of danger; it is a giver and taker of life ("If this uncouth forest," Orlando reassures old Adam on entering it, "yield anything savage, I will either be food for it or bring it for food to thee" [II.vi.5]). It is the forest of noble outlaws (there are allusions to Robin Hood); it is a merry hunting grove (with Jaques criticizing the hunt); it is also a realm of melancholy and a place for penance, and it represents the mixed arcadian landscape which comprises both forest and pasture, and which is at the same time satirized by being confronted with divergent conceptions of the wood. Visually, the tree property itself is, indeed, dramaturgically functional and is used for its emblematic and evocative value. Under it Jaques listens to the "greenwood-tree" song and under it "the Duke will drink" (II.v). Here the tree seems to be related at one point to the description of a hoary oak offstage and at another point to a palm tree.[53] It may not be quite coincidental that in an emblem by Joachim Camerarius an oak interlinked with a palm tree signifies the impossibility of a Golden Age on earth;[54] for such a symbol seems to contain in a nutshell the meaning of what happens in Arden.

Indeed many Elizabethan tree scenes are highly disparate and para-

53. Cf. II.i.31; IV.iii.103; III.ii.163.
54. *Symbolarum et emblematum ex re herbaria desumtorum centuria una collecta* (Nuremberg, 1534); cf. A. Henkel and A. Schöne, *Emblemata* (Stuttgart, 1967), cols. 198 ff.

doxical worlds. In them illusions are fostered and shattered; in them many a romantic disguise plot reaches its climax; in them robbers may prove to be virtuous, protection may turn out to be dangerous, love may be converted into madness. The theatrical quality of a tree scene is fittingly exaggerated when in *A Midsummer Night's Dream* the mechanicals, who are meeting "at the Duke's oak" (which is at the same place as Titania's lavishly described resting place), convert "this green plot" into their stage, only to rehearse a play in which one scene takes place in a garden and the other in a wood.[55]

IV

The Elizabethan tree property, then, far from merely specifying a locality, is a symbolically charged focal point for the contrarious imaginative associations aroused by the dramatic tree scenes and their performance. The interaction of literary and theatrical factors which is at work in such scenes is to some extent mirrored in the texts of the plays; its mechanism can therefore be observed in detail. It must here suffice to look at two or three typical and structurally important examples of both "garden" and "forest" tree scenes.

A number of short "garden" scenes occur in Shakespeare's histories.[56] Most of them are independent of the plays' sources, and yet they are crucial to their thematic patterns; some of them have been classified as "mirror scenes." They are all the more striking for being inserted between scenes of council or warfare, the details of whose localities are usually left vague. A "garden," however, is almost invariably identified as the action reaches it, and the tree property is thus brought to the audience's attention. In the Temple Garden scene in *1 Henry VI* (II.iv) the rose bushes—also referred to as "trees" (l. 41)—which stem from the source and are required by the plot, help identify "the garden here," whose silence contrasts with the noisy quarrels in Temple Hall whence the lords emerge. But, ironically, the very rose "trees" that are marking a peaceful garden are also instrumental in rekindling the quarrel which

55. Cf. *A Midsummer Night's Dream*, III.i.3 ff.
56. M. H. Golden's "The Iconography of the English History Plays" (Ph.D. diss., Columbia University, 1964) contains useful material.

leads to civil war. Not only do the lords, by plucking and wearing red and white roses, form opposing factions; the dissension seems to grow out of the roses themselves. Warwick's pun equates the colors of the roses with rhetorical color and, by implication, with "base insinuating flattery" (l. 35). Epithets remind us of commonplace images associated with roses and their hues; "this maiden blossom in my hand" (l. 75) is opposed to "bleeding roses" (l. 72); but the opposition gets ironically inverted, and future events are symbolically foreshadowed by the reminder that white roses too extract blood from the fingers that pluck them "and thus paint the white rose red." Gesture also has its share in the rhetorical amplification. The color of either faction's roses is reflected in the faces of its opponents. Plantagenet, holding up his white rose, likens it to his adversaries' cheeks ("for pale they look with fear" [l. 63]), while Somerset sees the redness of his rose reflected in Plantagenet's shameful blushes (l. 66). This again proves to be ironically ambiguous; for paleness may also express anger, with "blood-drinking hate" behind it. In short, the tree property, by being extended into the dialogue, its rhetoric, imagery, and gestures, reveals the seeds of war that lie beneath an appearance of peace and is thus instrumental in providing a general exposition of the play. In the more famous garden scene in *Richard II* (III.iv), which need hardly be recalled, it is the tree-marked garden itself that reflects the theme; and its symbolism, based on traditional associations of the garden with the State and with paradise, radiates into the verbal garden imagery of the entire play.[57] Here, too, the tree both marks the locality and renders it ambiguous. The queen, after her unsuccessful attempts at playing various games have, among other things, served to create a garden atmosphere, withdraws with her lady-in-waiting "into the shadow of these trees" (l. 25). The gardener, whom she eavesdrops upon and who is the spokesman of truth, is in the light in front of the tree, pointing to the property (". . . bind up yon dangling apricocks . . . give some supportance to the bending twigs"). Again the tree property, with a significant configuration of characters (royalty hiding behind the tree, the gardener pointing to it), reflects an important point in the development of the play, inserted as this scene is between the scenes of Richard's surrender and his later deposition. The

57. Cf. Peter Ure's introduction to the [New] Arden edition (1956), pp. li ff.

tree property in these and many similar scenes (not necessarily "gardens") seems to suggest visually the ambiguousness of a state of apparent safety. The disguised King Henry VI, who after having safely crossed the Scottish border at "this thick-grown brake" is captured right there, is yet another example; and in *Julius Caesar* it is surely significant that an original stage direction should require Brutus to "enter . . . in his orchard" to meet the conspirators.[58]

Similar methods can be observed in "forests." Dekker's *Old Fortunatus*[59] offers a straightforward example; for here the ambiguity of the tree (and the forest) is palpably associated with the fickleness of Fortune. Moreover, this play shows that even in a court adaptation of a popular play (the only version extant) the tree symbolism may have been purposefully enhanced. Here it certainly has structural importance. The play is introduced by a wood scene; and though no tree is mentioned, as we shall see it may be argued that there in fact was one. The forest as such is established through Fortunatus' initial soliloquy. Its words suggest several of the devices already mentioned: the acoustic effect of the echo; the hero's vagrant and stumbling movements while he tries in vain to find "my best way out," cracks nuts, and names the animals he descries (and possibly hears), until in "this wildernesse without end" (l. 50) he finally falls asleep on the ground. The delusiveness of the wood is also reflected in Fortunatus' changeable behavior. It alternates between dejection and boisterousness (". . . and instead of sighing [I] will laugh and be lean"), echoes behavior typical of the morality Vice, and is also a common reflection of the fickleness of Fortune, whose "smiles and frowns" cause laughter and tears.[60] Appropriately, the goddess Fortune herself, praised by her jocund suitors and cursed by her distressed victims, then enters the scene and promises to "advance" him. Fortune's rule by smiles and frowns, which is to govern the action of the entire play, is progressively associated with the tree. In the second scene (not localized in the wood), the tree image emerges rhetorically in a debate about vice and virtue. Here Fortune is equated with the vices of the "World," and World / For-

58. *3 Henry VI*, III.i.1; *Julius Caesar*, II.i.1.

59. References are to Fredson Bowers' edition of *The Dramatic Works of Thomas Dekker*, Vol. I (Cambridge, Eng., 1953).

60. Cf. Werner Habicht, "With an Auspicious and a Dropping Eye," *Anglia*, LXXXVII (1969), pp. 147–166.

tune is associated with the crab tree: "Tis nor the crab-tree fac'd world neither that makes [my brows] sowre" (I.ii.62). Andelocia, one of Fortunatus' sons, retorts to this by associating virtue with the withering tree: ". . . wee florish like Apple trees in September, (which having the falling sickness) beare neither fruit nor leaves." This juxtaposition on the level of verbal imagery of the deceptively flourishing crab tree and the withering apple tree is then visualized. In the following scene (I.iii), in which Fortune reappears with the personifications of Vice and Virtue in her train (carrying a flourishing and a withering branch respectively), the goddess commands "these trees" to be planted in the ground. The juxtaposition of the dry and the flourishing trees, so common in Renaissance iconography and literature, is thus translated into visual terms.

In accordance with the play's plot the tree of vice then, indeed, flourishes—and also in a dramaturgic sense. In a later scene (IV.i) the action requires a solid tree; this is, of course, Fortune's crab tree, which may have been the "tre of gowlden apelles" mentioned by Henslowe. Arrogant Andelocia, who has eloped with Princess Agripyna by means of his wishing cap, lands in a wilderness (also referred to as "this wood"). Though the identification of a wood with a wilderness or desert is commonplace enough, it would still be surprising for such a place to be marked by an apple tree (or what appears to be one)—

> Heres neither spring nor ditch, nor raine, nor dew,
> Nor bread, nor drinke: my lovely Agripyne,
> Be comforted, see here are Apple trees.
>
> (IV.i.65–67)

—were it not for the overriding tree imagery already linked up with Fortune. Sure enough, the apples of the tree which Andelocia climbs are, like Fortune's rewards, outwardly sweet and inwardly bitter. The result of Andelocia's tasting them is his fall from prosperity into wretchedness, the loss of both princess and wishing cap, which leaves him destitute in the wilderness (the wood). He ends up in the same situation and posture in which we saw Fortunatus, his father, before Fortune had raised him from wretchedness to prosperity—falling asleep "under the tree." Fortune's wheel has, indeed, come full circle. The parallelism would have been pointless if it had not been emphasized by the tree property. Hence

it may be safe to assume that there actually was a tree to mark the opening scene of the play as described above, even if it is not explicitly referred to in the text. At that point the dramaturgic creation of a wild
wood atmosphere around it was more important. By the time we get to
the later tree scene (IV.i), however, the symbolical significance of the
tree has been fully established, though the physical property continues to
remind us of the atmosphere originally associated with it. Again, the
later scene, like the earlier one, is followed by an allegorical entry of the
goddess Fortune herself, who identifies the treacherously golden apple
tree (or crab tree) as the tree "planted here by Vice" (l. 160) and points
out its counterpart, the withering tree of Virtue. An apparent inconsistency in the extant text may, perhaps, be explained. Is the tree of
golden apples in Act IV, scene i, which must be strong enough to be
climbed, identical with one of the two branches planted in the ground at
Fortune's command in Act I, scene iii, which must be light enough to be
gracefully carried? If so, does the playwright after all fail to provide for
a tree in the opening scene? The inconsistency may, of course, be due to
the revision made for the performance before the court, which would
doubtless have affected the allegorical entries of Fortune. But even so
the scenic iconography remains a coherent one. There was one solid
tree in the first place; and there were the two small "trees" (perhaps
added to the court version) visualizing the image of the dry and flourishing tree, somewhat like the background trees common in illustrations of
emblems or in Ripa. The icon as a whole, as well as the wild and deceptive wood marked by it, are ultimately attributes of Fortune, whose
appearance on the stage visualizes, and whose speeches moralize, the
play's theme.

V

Most Elizabethan tree scenes are only sections within a play, and, except for a pastoral drama like *The Faithful Shepherdess,* the wood or
the garden is one of its several localities. One wonders, therefore, what
happened to the tree properties during the rest of the performance.
Theater historians who have been vexed by this problem usually remind us of the discovery space; besides, there is some evidence suggesting that the stage trap was employed to get trees on and off the

stage, as when in a dumb show of *A Warning for Fair Women* "suddenly riseth up a great tree."[61] Instances like these, however, look like special spectacular effects rather than the normal practice. In the plays discussed in the preceding section no such spectacularity is required. But their comparatively brief tree scenes occur at key points in the dramatic structure. The rose "trees" of the Temple Garden scene early in *1 Henry VI* constitute an emblematic nucleus out of which the political action is made to develop. The garden image visualized at the center of *Richard II* symbolically reflects the pivotal situation of the plot. In the two wood scenes in *Old Fortunatus* the decisive manifestations of Fortune's control over the action take place. Considering this structural importance of the tree scenes, it is perhaps not altogether unjustified to suggest that the tree properties which evoked a garden, a wood, or a wilderness remained on the stage throughout the performance as a contrapuntal visual token of what was being unfolded. If this is correct, then the tree scenes must not be thought of as isolated units, as would appear from a modern printed text. The visual impression of the tree property would have radiated through the play in its entirety.

The dramaturgy of the tree property implied in many Elizabethan and notably in Shakespeare's plays seems to confirm that effects of this sort were intended. Even the "great tree" raised for the dumb show of *A Warning for Fair Women,* the felling of which symbolizes a murder, may have remained on the stage to mark the forest (and "the bushes") where the actual murder takes place and where subsequently the murderers repent. In Kyd's *The Spanish Tragedy* the bower is first used by Horatio as a shelter for his love; then Horatio is hanged on it; and next it is connected with Hieronimo's madness, which was caused by Horatio's death. Similarly, in *Titus Andronicus* the tree (which marks the hunting forest in Act II) is first referred to by Aaron when he prepares his villainy ("He that had wit would think that I had none, / To bury so much gold under a tree"): in Act V the same property is still present, for ironically it is needed then as gallows for Aaron ("A halter, soldiers! Hang him on this tree"). Earlier in the play it was identified as a "dismal yew" and an "elder-tree"—both associated with death—and it also served as a visual correlative of the verbal image which described

61. In *The School of Shakespeare,* ed. R. Simpson (New York, 1878), II,284. Cf. also Chambers, *Elizabethan Stage,* III, 89 ff.

ravished Lavinia as a mutilated tree.[62] A comparable irony can be observed in *Macbeth*. Doubtless there was, at the very beginning of the
play, a tree "upon the heath" (I.i.7), where the hero is accosted by the
witches, just as there was one on the heath of *King Lear*. It is not unusual that a stage tree should be associated with magic and that magic
action should externalize a hero's moral delusion. And it can hardly be
a coincidence that at the end of the tragedy the tree element reappears
as the moving Birnam wood—as the delusion by which Macbeth is de-
feated. Interestingly enough, the messenger's announcement that "the
wood began to move" calls forth Macbeth's threatening but vain reference
to a more solid tree: "Upon the next tree shalt thou hang alive." [63] Moreover, the cauldron scene in the middle of the play, whether or not it is
Shakespeare's, clearly contains a visual and verbal link between the
witches' tree and Birnam wood: the Third Apparition (conjured up by
the witches) has "a tree in his hand," which is, of course, a genealogical
tree, but which also forebodes Birnam.[64] In *A Midsummer Night's
Dream* and in *As You Like It* it seems even more important that the
tree or trees that marked the Athenian wood and the Forest of Arden
should have remained permanently visible. Are not these extended
sequences of wood scenes fantastical explorations of the conflicts and
paradoxes hidden beneath the surface of the courtly world whence the
characters come and into which they are finally again dismissed? The
actual incursion of the wood into the court which takes place at the end
of *A Midsummer Night's Dream* would be aptly underlined by the continued visual presence of the tree.

Far from being merely an incidental stage image, the tree may be said
to have been one of the essential properties on the Elizabethan public
stage. Precisely because it was an "emblematic" rather than a realistically
localizing item, it could be variously supplemented for the realization of
the "tree scenes" mapped out in dramatic literature. And yet at the same
time it was a unifying element—a focal point of the heterogeneous associations evoked in the "tree scenes," and a permanent visual reminder
of a play's central themes.

---

62. Cf. *Titus Andronicus*, II.iii.1 f.; V.i.41; II.iii.107, 277; II.iv.17.
63. Cf. *Macbeth*, V.v.34 ff.
64. *Ibid.*, IV.i.86 ff.

Elizabethan Stage Practice
and Marlowe's The Jew of Malta

J. L. SIMMONS

IT IS A TRUISM that Renaissance drama needs to be interpreted by what
dim light our knowledge affords of Elizabethan stage practices. Although much of this knowledge is speculative, piece by piece speculation
begins to substantiate or to refute itself. Certainly our deductions of
Elizabethan staging cannot be drawn only from the evidence of literal
stage directions. Such evidence, after all, tends to be neither hard nor
fast. Moreover, it is not very plentiful. We must follow, in our theatrical
imaginations, Hamlet's advice to suit the action to the word, the word to
the action; for this advice applies not only to the actor and his gestures
but to the actor and his movement on a particular stage with particular
facilities. With discretion as our tutor, deictic words and passages, requiring dramatic reference to properties or to parts of the stage, help to
flesh out what Rudolf Stamm has called "the theatrical physiognomy"
of the play.[1]

In this essay I will speculate, for a complex of important and related
reasons, on a problematical moment in the staging of Marlowe's *The*

1. "Elizabethan Stage-Practice and the Transmutation of Source Material by
the Dramatists," *ShS*, XII (1959), 64–70.

93

Jew of Malta. I believe that this crux in the staging can generally bear witness to the basic structure, the facilities, and the use of the Elizabethan stage. Specifically, we can test the conviction of a growing number of stage historians that the Yard was occasionally used for dramatic action, particularly involving exits and entrances.[2] The crux in the staging can also be related, with mutual illumination, to a textual crux, offering one more bit of evidence that the Quarto of 1633, as J. C. Maxwell has argued, is not so corrupt as is usually assumed.[3] Finally, the stage action which I believe is pointedly begged in the text is a symptomatic indication of Marlowe's symbolic and dramaturgical strategy. Contemplation of a few minutes of this play-in-performance helps to clarify what kind of play Marlowe created. Although my argument contains much that is conjectural, the speculation falls piece by piece into a coherent picture which I hope encourages approval. At the very least, the possibilities deserve consideration.

Early in Act V, the Governor of Malta has ordered Barabas, Ithamore, the courtesan, and Pilia-Borza away to prison. Unknown to all but

2. See especially J. W. Saunders, "Vaulting the Rails," *ShS*, VII (1954), 69–81; and Allardyce Nicoll, " 'Passing Over the Stage,' " *ShS*, XII (1959), 47–55.

3. "How Bad Is the Text of *The Jew of Malta?*," *MLR*, XLVIII (1953), 435–438. On bibliographical evidence one can argue only that the text is carelessly printed. But "an overwhelming proportion [of these errors] are identifiable and (within limits) curable." The problem posed by the Quarto's late date per se is largely imaginary: "Manuscripts, unlike apples, do not become corrupt simply by lying in a drawer" (p. 438). The argument for *Jew* as an unreliable text reflecting corruption and revision depends upon critically distinguishing Acts I–II from Acts III–V on the basis of the "deterioration" in the characterization of Barabas. On this matter Maxwell cites P. H. Kocher: "The play begins with too lofty a treatment, one that could not be maintained when the plot really began to move. Marlowe recognized that in the second act, and threw the character away" (*Christopher Marlowe* [Chapel Hill, N.C., 1946], p. 286). I would argue on the basis of the play as "transitional": the Barabas of the first two acts is dynamic and "realistic"; daringly, but not without resulting awkwardness, Marlowe sufficiently establishes the character's virtue to let Barabas function positively, in relation to the Christians, as a Vice—a static and "allegorical" type. The same incoherent "deterioration" of character from dynamic and complex realism to static and simplistic moral type is seen in Mortimer and Queen Isabella in *Edward II*. In the case of *Jew,* the evidence for revision (other than Thomas Heywood's acknowledged Prologues and Epilogues for the Court and the Cockpit) has only a mistakened admiration for a hypothetical Marlowe to recommend it.

Barabas and the audience, the latter three villains are about to die, the three minor vices having been poisoned by the Vice himself. The death report follows six lines after their exit:

> My Lord, the Curtezane and her man are dead;
> So is the Turke, and *Barabas* the Jew.[4]

Bosco, like the audience, is surprised only by the totally unexpected news regarding the hero: "This sudden death of his is very strange." The dialogue indicates that the feigning Barabas is brought back on stage while the Governor reminds his fellow Christians that "the heavens are juste." His lines and those following then indicate a puzzling action not elucidated by any literal stage direction:

> For the Jewes body, throw that o'er the wals,
> To be a prey for Vultures and wild beasts.
> So, now away and fortifie the Towne.   [*Exeunt.*]
>
>   BARABAS
>
> What, all alone? well fare sleepy drink
> I'le be reveng'd on this accursed Towne;
> For by my meanes *Calymath* shall enter in.

With his fakery thus revealed, the scene continues, but now clearly representing a different location, one outside the walls from which Barabas has evidently been thrown. For revenge, he betrays the city to the invading Turks.

T. W. Craik's note sums up editorial comment on this staging crux and offers the best solution to date:

At this point the body of Barabas is supposed thrown over the walls. This cannot have been performed with any realism. Dyce's stage-direction reads "Exeunt all, leaving Barabas on the floor." Bennett suggests that the body was carried off-stage, and subsequently revealed by opening the inner-stage curtains. But more probably the body was simply tossed forward and allowed to roll towards the front of the platform. (The Governor's "So" certainly suggests that his command has just been executed to his satisfaction.) It would then lie for a moment in full view, an object of anticipatory interest, until Barabas's rising.[5]

---

4. I have cited the text of the Quarto (1633) from the three copies in the Folger Shakespeare Library. The Quarto text is divided into acts but not scenes.

5. *The Jew of Malta,* New Mermaids Series (London, 1966), p. 93.

I would object, however, that the structure of the stage did allow for a realistic representation of the act ordered by the Governor. In fact, the scene demands, when taken with what follows, an attempted realism. One might accept a pantomimed action such as Craik suggests for Barabas' ejection over the walls. But unless some properties or constructions are available, one must surely question Marlowe's theatrical flair a few lines later when Barabas specifies the employment of troops for the capture of the city with elaborate details, details which the following "alarums" must somehow reflect:

> . . . here against the Truce,
> The rocke is hollow, and of purpose digg'd,
> To make a passage for the running streames
> And common channels of the City.
> Now whilst you give assault unto the wals,
> I'le lead 500 souldiers through the Vault,
> And rise with them i' th middle of the Towne,
> Open the gates for you to enter in,
> And by this meanes the City is your owne.

I am convinced that these deictic lines are clear instructions for staging and that the instructions are contingent upon the earlier action of tossing Barabas over the wall. If the facilities of the stage and the conventions of the playing area are fully considered, this theatrical crux illuminates, almost photographs, the structure and the excitement of Marlowe's playhouse.[6]

The difficulty posed by the staging vanishes when one considers that the Yard could be occasionally employed as playing area and as an additional resource for spectacular effects involving entrances and exits. The Governor's satisfied "So" follows an easily achieved and theatrically effective representation of his command, the bodily ejection of Barabas from the platform stage into the Yard below. When the Turks join him there, having entered in procession into the Yard, Barabas points

6. By the early nineties, *The Jew of Malta* would no doubt be performed exclusively at the Rose. In the late eighties, however, when the play is usually dated (ca. 1589), the stage history is more complicated and uncertain, the theatrical companies less distinct and exclusive. Marlowe's play might well have been launched at the Theater or the Curtain. Needless to say, I am concerned with Marlowe's intentions in relation to the original playhouse, not with later revivals, specified on the title page of the Quarto, at Whitehall and the Cockpit.

to one of the pillars supporting the stage—the textually crucial "Truce"—
and lifts the drapery hiding the supports to allow for the exit of all except
Calymath. Calymath assaults the stage, while Barabas and the other actors
disappear beneath the platform. The following stage direction, then, is
quite exact:

> [Alarums. *Enter Turkes, Barabas,
> Governour and Knights prisoners.*]

No entrance is required for Calymath, who has catapulted onto the stage
and is the first to speak to those who emerge from the tiring house:
"Now vaile your pride you captive Christians." The realism is sufficient;
so sufficient, in fact, that one can take Marlowe's lines as an indication of
what we cannot see: Barabas enters the tiring house through a trap door,
perhaps one within some "place of discovery." When he opens the door—
the gates of the city—the illusion of Barabas' martial strategy is complete.

The Quarto reading "Truce" does not have to be emended to "sluice"
or glossed, unconvincingly, as "either (1) contrary to the treaty or (2) in
anticipation of the cessation of hostilities." [7] The spelling is approximately
phonetic; the careless printing of the Quarto can account for the somewhat unusual form (the *OED* cites "truse" and "trus" among the
variants), if such accounting is necessary. Modern editions should read
"truss," a deictic word which fuses a part of the actual structure of the
playhouse with the imagined wall surrounding Malta. Barabas points to
"a projection from the face of a wall, often serving to support a cornice,
etc.; a kind of large corbel or modillion" (*OED,* 6b). That image blends
with the kind of supporting structure which Burbage, with his knowledge as a joiner, had supplied for the permanent trestles of the Theater
(1576)—"a framework of timber or iron, or both, so constructed as to
form a firm support for a superincumbent weight, as that of a roof or
bridge" (*OED,* 6). The first usage cited by the *OED* of the latter definition of "truss" is in an unpublished report of 1654 to London's Court
of Aldermen from the Company of Carpenters regarding safety regu-
lations for the construction of chimneys:

7. *The Jew of Malta,* ed. Richard W. Van Fossen, Regents Renaissance Drama
Series (Lincoln, Nebr., 1964), p. 99.

When any Chimney for any buildings shalbe sett upon a trusse of timber
That it be sett two foote 6 inches from the upside of the trusse to the upside
of the floore.[8]

In such a context, however, the Company would not adventure linguisti-
cally but would use the most common term for what is architecturally
the same construction as the timbered support under the stage. At any
rate, the use of "truss" as a projecting support, as a part of either a wall
or a trestle, was definitely established by 1589.

The stage action as I have constructed it requires, in addition to the
entrances from the tiring house, means of access directly onto the Yard,
something precisely like the large "Ingressus" on each side of the acting
area as designated in the DeWitt sketch of the Swan.[9] Two plays contemporary with *The Jew of Malta* offer evidence to support my image
of Calymath and his Turks proceeding from such an entrance into the
Yard and around to the front of the stage. The first example is from
Robert Wilson's *The Cobler's Prophecy,* published in 1594 but clearly to
be dated in the immediate post-Armada days. The opening stage direction all but inescapably implies the use of an entrance, an exit, and a
processional area quite distinct from the platform stage:

> [*Enter* Jupiter *and* Juno, Mars *and*
> Venus, Apollo, *after him,* Bacchus,
> Vulcan *limping, and after all* Diana
> *wringing her hands: they passe by,*
> *while on the stage* Mercurie *from one*
> *end* Ceres *from another meete.*][10]

The second example, from Thomas Kyd's *The Spanish Tragedy* (ca.
1587), likewise argues more playing area than the platform stage and two
tiring-house doors; but the evidence in this case depends more upon
deictic words than literal stage directions. In the second scene, *"A tucket
a farre off"* heralds to the Spanish court the victorious return of the
army:

8. First printed in E. B. Jupp, *An Historical Account of the Worshipful Company of Carpenters* (London, 1848), p. 316.

9. Nicoll, " 'Passing Over the Stage,' " p. 53; Saunders, "Vaulting the Rails," p.
75.

10. Malone Society Reprints (Oxford, 1914).

> [*The Armie enters;* Balthazar *be-*
> *tweene* Lorenzo *and* Horatio *captive.*]

The King responds to the processional: "A gladsome sight: I long to
see them *heere*" (italics added). After *"They enter and passe by,"* the
King takes up a few moments to establish the identity of the significant
trio in the procession and to allow the actors time to get in place before
he orders a second processional:

> Goe, let them march *once more about these walles,*
> That, staying them, we may conferre and talke
> With our brave prisoner, and his double guard [italics added].[11]

The army then enters again and exits, all except the three important
characters, who join the royal group. The demonstrative words, which I
have italicized, have dramatic implications regarding gesture and staging.
Such words are, as Stamm insists, "of considerable importance . . .
They usually point to parts of the stage, to figures or properties on the
stage, or to objects, places or events to be imagined beyond its limits."[12]
In this case, however, the limits beyond the stage do not have to be
imagined. The processional moves in the Yard about the edge of the
stage. The height of the platform satisfyingly represents, as in *The Jew
of Malta,* the walls of the city. The separation of stage and Yard affords
the spatial distinction necessary not only for the theatrical illusion but
for the practical accommodation of the designated action.

The second requirement for my suggested staging of Marlowe's scene
is an access from beneath the stage to the tiring house. For evidence of
this access we need look no farther than Old Hamlet's Ghost when he
exits and then *"cries under the stage."* Stage directions in the later drama
indicate entrances from under the stage onto the platform—entrances not
to be accounted for by trap doors on the main stage. Nicoll cites an
instance from Thomas Heywood's *The Silver Age* (1613) which introduces an action to represent Hades:

> [Hercules *sinkes himselfe: Flashes of*
> *fire; the Divels appeare at every cor-*
> *ner of the stage with severall fire-*
> *workes. The Judges of hell, and the*

11. *The Works of Thomas Kyd,* ed. Frederick S. Boas (Oxford, 1901), p. 10.
12. Stamm, "Elizabethan Stage-Practice," p. 66.

> *three sisters run over the stage,* Hercu-
> les *after them: fire-workes all over
> the house.*][13]

In the concluding scene of Thomas Dekker's *If This Be Not a Good
Play, the Devil Is in It* (1612), there is a similar *jeu d'esprit:*

> [*The play ending, as they goe off,
> from under the ground in severall
> places, rise up spirits, to them enter,
> leaping in great joy,* Rufman, Shackle-
> soule, *and* Lurchall, *discovering be-
> hind a curten,* Ravillac, Guy Faulx,
> Bartervile, *a Prodigall, standing in
> their torments.*][14]

What the plays by Heywood and Dekker have in common with *The
Jew of Malta* is at once apparent. The two plays represent a survival of
the naïve morality elements long after the mainstream of the drama had
absorbed the allegorical world into the realistic world of history. In
Hamlet, the magnificent achievement of Shakespearean realism still
maintained, as evidenced by the Ghost and his passage beneath the stage,
a philosophical and theatrical recognition of the outer mystery. But at
the Red Bull, Dekker and Heywood revealed to their rather unsophisti-
cated audiences an access to a literal and uncomplicated Hell.[15] Dekker's
play, incidentally, requires for one of the discovered "torments" the
hellish emblem which concludes Marlowe's play, the stage property noted
in Philip Henslowe's possession, "i cauderm for the Jewe":[16]

13. Nicoll, " 'Passing Over the Stage,' " pp. 50–51.

14. *The Dramatic Works of Thomas Dekker,* ed. Fredson Bowers, (Cambridge,
Eng., 1953–1961), III, 201.

15. Granting the unusual requirements such stage directions entail, George F.
Reynolds suggests that "perhaps the actors scrambled up over the edge of the
stage" (*The Staging of Elizabethan Plays at the Red Bull Theater* [New York,
1940], p. 91).

16. For the emblematic properties of the cauldron, see G. K. Hunter, "The The-
ology of Marlowe's *The Jew of Malta," JWCI,* XXVII (1964), 211–240. The staging of the cauldron scene presents difficulties unrelated to my discussion, but I
believe that those difficulties can easily be obviated. When the Governor cuts the
rope, Barabas disappears from the upper stage, the "gallery," and is "discovered"

I am perboild, I am stewd, I am sod in a kettle of brimstone pottage.—it scaldes,—it scaldes,—it scaldes,—it scaldes—whooh.

As a transition play in which a historic, realistic world holds fairly intact a morality figure, *The Jew of Malta* appropriately associates the Vice-like Barabas with the secularized infernal regions of the playhouse, and this association symbolically reveals as much about Barabas and his play as does the emblematic and fantastic cauldron.

One theatrical exigency remains to be considered. Although the hearty Elizabethans would not likely be timorous, what of the safety hazard to the groundlings around the open stage? (The actor would, of course, know how to take the fall.) A playwright whose previous production had exacted the death of a child and a pregnant woman might hesitate to call for the exuberant stage business I have suggested.[17] Perhaps there was a practice of roping off a section of the Yard, if the play required its use. I have even suspected that the specification in the contract for the Fortune—that the stage should be "paled in belowe with good, stronge and sufficyent newe oken bourdes"[18]—refers not to an innovation to board up the space under the stage, as the instructions are usually interpreted, but to the kind of palings which lined the Elizabethan tiltyard and protected both performer and spectator. Certainly the most evident meaning of "pale in" indicates that the stage was to be "fenced" as a means of exclusion. It would not take the acting companies long to recognize the need and the means to prevent the audience from pressing too close. Of course the pales would be irresistible to the groundlings either as a perch or as a boundary to cross; and therefore when the Porter in *Henry VIII* prepares for the processional following Elizabeth's christening, he and his man have to berate what Saunders suspects are two members of the actual audience in order to clear the processional area:

---

after a dramatic pause in a cauldron on the main stage. A trap door here would be unnecessary; moreover, for this "fall," it would be quite dangerous. One may clearly infer from the stage direction that the audience is not to see Barabas literally fall through a trap door.

17. I refer to the accident of 16 November 1587, during Act V of *2 Tamburlaine*. A man also received a serious head injury from the actor's wild shot. See E. K. Chambers, *The Elizabethan Stage* (Oxford, 1923), II, 135.

18. The contract is printed in Chambers, *ibid.*, II, 436-439.

MAN

You great fellow,
Stand close up, or I'll make your head ache.

PORTER

You i' th' camlet, get up o' th' rail;
I'll peck you o'er the pales else.[19]

But this is much later. For an earlier drama, when the interaction between audience and actor was freer, surely the ample warning of several "heave-hoes" ad libitum could prepare the groundlings for Barabas' ejection and make the danger negligible. And in a subliminal way, the groundlings should be able to anticipate the action as not only surprising and delightful but as inevitable. In terms of the morality tradition, a tradition which Marlowe ingeniously manipulates, the Vice's relationship is more with the audience than with the dramatis personae. Marlowe's *coup de théâtre* climaxes a communion between the audience and Barabas which is characteristic of the Vice's homiletic derivations. The Vice, as Bernard Spivack points out, stands "outside the play." And Barabas is all the more separable because his dramatic lineage, even more than his moral and ethnic background, is so distinct from the realistic, literal world of Malta.[20]

The communion between the Vice and the spectators was mainly achieved by the dissembler's honest direct address and asides to the audience, but it was enhanced by physical contact and perhaps even by the use of the character as a kind of stage manager.[21] Whatever the "place" on which the earlier sixteenth-century moralities were performed, it was clearly an area used by both players and audience; and the Vice frequently served to admonish the spectators from pressing forward. In John Heywood's *Love* (ca. 1525), for example, there is the important stage direction regarding the Vice, *"ronnynge sodenly aboute the place*

19. V.iv.84–87. See Saunders, "Vaulting the Rails," pp. 70–71. Saunders' suggested staging does not account for "the pales."

20. *Shakespeare and the Allegory of Evil* (New York, 1958), pp. 31 ff., 111–120, and *passim*. On the "dual aspect in the play's exposition," see David M. Bevington, *From "Mankind" to Marlowe* (Cambridge, Mass., 1962), pp. 218–233.

21. Spivack, *Shakespeare and the Allegory of Evil*, p. 464, n. 17. See also Leslie Hotson, "False Faces on Shakespeare's Stage," *TLS,* 16 May 1952, p. 336.

among the audyens." [22] In *Clyomon and Clamydes,* a play bearing marks
to distinguish it as one of the earliest texts for a fixed stage, Subtle Shift
prepares for a processional which will apparently engage the Yard;
for as in the scene from *Henry VIII,* no pressing crowd is on stage.
Subtle Shift enters, appropriately, "like a Wiffler":

Rowme there for a reckning, see I beseech you if thale stand out of the way,
Jesu, Jesu, why do you not know that this is the day
That the combat must passe for *Mustantius* and the Queene?

.   .   .   .

Well here they come, roome there for the King, heres such thrusting of women
  as it grieveth mee.[23]

Nathaniel Woodes's *The Conflict of Conscience* (1581), although not
written for the popular playhouses, indicates that the Vice must shake
hands with random spectators at his final exit, homiletically confirming
with the audience an immoral alliance:

But needes I must be packing hence, my fellowes stay for me,
Shake handes before we do depart, you shall see mee no more:
And though *Hypocrisie* goe away, of hypocrits heere is good store.[24]

When the Christians toss Barabas into the Yard, Marlowe confirms
with a startling twist the special alliance between his hero and that hero's
only confidant. Throughout the play Marlowe's use of the traditional
interaction between the Vice and the audience grows out of a totally new
dramatic strategy. With the fantastic Barabas, Marlowe is stalking secular
and realistic prey—those agents of justice who triumph with the policy
of genuine Machiavels while they self-righteously appeal to heaven.[25] As a
descendant of the Vice, Barabas is still a homiletic agent. But Marlowe
is concerned with exposing an evil more insidious than any in the world
of the morality. Real hypocrites and dissemblers bear no identifying names

22. See Richard Southern, "The Contribution of the Interlude to Elizabethan
Staging," in *Essays on Shakespeare and Elizabethan Drama in Honor of Hardin
Craig,* ed. Richard Hosley (Columbia, Mo., 1962); and Robert Carl Johnson, "Au-
dience Involvement in the Tudor Interlude," *TN,* XXIV (1970), 101–111.

23. Malone Society Reprints (Oxford, 1913), ll. 1677 ff. The play was not printed
until 1599, but it dates from the late seventies or early eighties.

24. Malone Society Reprints (Oxford, 1952), ll. 1930–1932.

25. See Howard S. Babb, "Policy in Marlowe's *The Jew of Malta,*" *ELH,* XXIV
(1957), 85–94.

and wear no revealing costumes; they cannot declare themselves to the audience, even if they would, because they do not know themselves. Barabas therefore insists upon his own moral superiority:

> . . . as good dissemble that thou never mean'st
> As first meane truth, and then dissemble it,
> A counterfet profession is better
> Then unseene hypocrisie.

In the stage action, symbolizing his moral function, Barabas exuberantly leads all the Elizabethan young Turks in undermining the moral pretences of the Establishment and in opening the gates to expose "unseene hypocrisie." [26]

26. I am grateful to the authorities of the Folger Shakespeare Library for the summer fellowship which enabled me to prepare this essay.

Tamburlaine *in the* Theater: *Tartar, Grand Guignol, or Janus ?*

NANCY T. LESLIE

O F ALL MARLOWE'S PLAYS, literary critics are least familiar with modern stage performances of *Tamburlaine the Great*. While the efforts early in this century of William Poel, Sir Frank Benson, the Phoenix Society, and the universities have led to many later revivals of *Doctor Faustus, Edward II,* and *The Jew of Malta,* there has been only one well-known mounting of *Tamburlaine,* Sir Tyrone Guthrie's confla- tion of Parts I and II in 1951 and in 1956. In spite of several university and repertory company revivals that attest to *Tamburlaine's* theatrical via- bility, the fact remains that for theater and literary critics alike the play still arouses the antithetical responses the Guthrie production elicited from T. C. Worsley, J. C. Trewin, and Sir Donald Wolfit, respectively:

> Only the inflated hyperboles of the film handouts can do justice to this vast, sprawling, truly horrible and, in the last analysis, worthless play.

> *Tamburlaine* is an extraordinary relic—cloth-of-gold or fustian, according to your viewpoint.

> Clearly, Marlowe was an expert dramatist.[1]

1. T. C. Worsley, "Tamburlaine the Great," *New Statesman and Nation,* XLII (1951), 336; J. C. Trewin, "Catching a Tartar," *John O'London's Weekly,* 12

Given opinion so polarized, a study of *Tamburlaine* in its modern theatrical element may enlighten us not only about Marlowe's directors, but, more importantly, about Marlowe's play. Acting versions, directors' notes, and reviews of the productions raise provocative questions about abridgments of Parts I and II, about major and minor characters, and about audience reaction to Tamburlaine's megalomaniacal thirst for power. I shall attempt therefore to combine theater history and literary criticism in a discussion of numerous production variables and a study of the relationship between what is omitted in three of the staged versions and the possible reasons for these excisions.

Tamburlaine's popularity in its own day is well documented,[2] yet there is no evidence of a single performance between the reopening of the theaters in 1660 and the twentieth century. Tragedies of the same name by Charles Saunders (1681) and Nicholas Rowe (1701) were performed, but they are completely independent of Marlowe's work. A single performance of an abridged *Tamburlaine* at Yale in 1919, of *Tamburlaine, Part II*, at Oxford in 1933, and of another conflation of Parts I and II at Yale in 1946 take us up to the Guthrie production of *Tamburlaine* that ran for five weeks at the Old Vic in 1951, and for two subsequent weeks at Stratford, with Donald Wolfit in the title role. *Tamburlaine* next appeared when Guthrie essentially reproduced this version five years later for Canadian and American audiences, with Anthony Quayle as Tamburlaine, supported by ninety-two members of the Stratford (Ontario) Shakespearean Festival Company. Guthrie's *Tamburlaine* was virtually a box-office bonanza during the fortnight's tryout in Toronto,[3] but in the

---

October 1951, p. 596; and Donald Wolfit and Tyrone Guthrie, "Introduction," *Tamburlaine the Great: An Acting Version* (London, 1951), p. xiii (cited hereafter as W-G). See also Tyrone Guthrie, "*Tamburlaine* and What It Takes," *Theatre Arts*, XL, no. 2 (February 1956), 21–23, 84–86, and Erwin Beck, "*Tamburlaine* for the Modern Stage," *ETJ*, XXIII (March 1971), 62–74, for a careful analysis of the Guthrie abridgment and a plea for its reprinting.

2. *Henslowe's Diary*, ed. R. A. Foakes and R. T. Rickert (Cambridge, Eng., 1961), pp. 23–33; *Tamburlaine the Great*, ed. Una Mary Ellis-Fermor (London, 1930; repr., New York, 1966), p. 16; and C. F. Tucker Brooke, "The Reputation of Christopher Marlowe," *Transactions of the Connecticut Academy of Arts and Sciences*, XXV (June 1922), 365 ff.

3. The $75,000 production grossed $54,700 for thirteen performances in the Royal Alexandria, a 1,525 seat theater. See Herbert Whitaker, "Show Business,"

face of mixed reviews and poor attendance the play was withdrawn from New York after less than four weeks of a projected eight weeks' run. Since then, there have been at least three separate revivals of Tamburlaine in England: [4] an outdoor production at Oxford, 14 June 1960, a mounting by the Tavistock Repertory Company, London, 4–19 December 1964, and a revival by the Marlowe Theater, Canterbury, in October 1966. Such a recent interest in *Tamburlaine* calls into question both Wilbur Sanders' dismissal of the play as "the indulgence *ad absurdum* of the 'humour of monarchising'"[5] and Ivor Brown's judgment that after Guthrie "nobody wanted to give that monster another outing. . . ."[6]

All of the directors who have chosen to take *Tamburlaine* out of the closet have had to contend with what W. A. Armstrong aptly pointed out: "Three of the greatest playwright-producers in the history of the English theatre—Ben Jonson, Bernard Shaw, and Harley Granville-Barker—have made adverse pronouncements on the stageworthiness of *Tamburlaine*."[7] Jonson thought the diction unnatural, having "run away from nature" and "flown from all humanity," and the acting "scenical strutting" and "furious vociferation," such as would appeal to

the (Toronto) *Globe and Mail,* 20 December 1955 and 6 January 1956, for further statistics. I am grateful to Mr. Irwin Simpkins, Reference Librarian, Emory University, and to Mr. Paul Myers, Curator of the New York Public Library's Theater Collection at Lincoln Center, and his staff for much of the factual material in this essay.

4. See also the (London) *Times,* 21 March 1964, p. 6, and the *Listener,* 26 March 1964, p. 532, for reviews of the B.B.C. broadcast of *Tamburlaine* (the third during this century), 19 and 20 March 1964. An Audience Reaction Report was prepared 27 April 1964 by B.B.C.'s Audience Research Department. In America, *Tamburlaine* was revived by the Peninsula Little Theater, College of San Mateo, California, in 1958 and was given a concert reading by the Harvard Theater Club, 26 and 28 February 1964.

5. *The Dramatist and the Received Idea* (Cambridge, Eng., 1968), p. 222.

6. "How Bright a Boy?," *Drama,* Journal of the British Drama League, LXXV (1964), 27.

7. *Tamburlaine: The Image and the Stage* (Hull, Eng., 1966), p. 3. This essay is virtually a definitive restatement of the modern "romantic" readings of *Tamburlaine* that have come from Harry Levin's seminal work, *The Overreacher* (Cambridge, Mass., 1952). The counterview is expressed by Roy W. Battenhouse, *Marlowe's "Tamburlaine": A Study in Renaissance Moral Philosophy* (Nashville, Tenn., 1941).

"ignorant gapers." [8] Ironically, Jonson had celebrated the skill of Edward Alleyn, the first Tamburlaine, in a well-known epigram (lxxxix) one year before this allusion to the play was made, and, of course, it is he who coined the phrase about "Marlowe's mighty line." Shaw, however, considered the tradition that Marlowe was a great dramatic poet to be "infernal," and one that threw "all the blame for his wretched half-achievement on the actor," as he wrote Granville-Barker in 1903; he concluded, "Marlowe had words and a turn for their music, but nothing to say—a barren amateur with a great air." [9] Nonetheless, Shaw's own plays are closer to Marlowe's, *mutatis mutandis,* than he ever would have admitted. Granville-Barker, on the other hand, was blind to Marlowe's dramaturgy simply because he could not resist faulting Marlowe for not being Shakespeare, regrettably a common myopia. Had he tried to mount *Tamburlaine,* he might have been less apt to chide what he called Marlowe's "orgy of declamation," first for failing to individualize the characters so that their speech would distinguish them, and secondly for elevating the poetry *qua* poetry above "the demands of the play." [10]

In view of Jonson's, Shaw's, and Granville-Barker's strictures, it is significant that producers of *Tamburlaine* have felt compelled to fuse Parts I and II. Stephen Vincent Benét and the actor-director Edgar "Monty" Woolley were the first modern adapters of *Tamburlaine.* They were complimented by Professor C. F. Tucker Brooke in his review of their 1919 production: "The decision . . . to present a condensed version of the two parts . . . involved a difficult choice, which, on the whole, the results justified. . . . So judiciously have the cuts been managed that little indeed of Marlowe's grandiose rhetoric failed to get a hearing. . . . The result of this amalgamation of the two parts was to accentuate the preponderance of stage action over plot interest and to increase the pageant effect." [11] Similarly, Tyrone Guthrie and his collaborator, Donald

8. *Timber, or Discoveries,* ed. C. H. Herford and Percy and Evelyn Simpson (Oxford, 1947), VIII, 587.

9. *Bernard Shaw's Letters to Granville Barker,* ed. C. B. Purdom (London, 1956), p. 18.

10. *On Dramatic Method* (London, 1931), pp. 54–57.

11. *Yale Daily News,* 17 June 1919, p. 3 (cited hereafter as *YDN*). Information supplied by Judith A. Schiff, Chief Research Archivist, Yale University Library. The manuscript acting version with annotations can be found here (Yale MS W) and the edition printed by Yale University Press, 1919.

Wolfit, sought a pageant effect—a "ritual dance" mated with a "savage oratorio" that could be performed in three hours' running time, even though this meant "cutting nearly half the text" (W-G, pp. x–xi). They argued that such excision did not pervert the original, and Ivor Brown (*Observer,* 30 September 1951, p. 6) allowed that in their version "the two plays have been wisely contracted into one. " Of course, if one believes, as Brown does, that *Tamburlaine* is a vehicle for a solo instrument, then it is necessary to remove the counterpoint. Conversely, a more recent director of *Tamburlaine,* Robert Pennant Jones, argues persuasively in the unpublished notes to his production, to which I shall turn later, that conflation of Parts I and II need not result in a monochromatic scale. Nonetheless, in his review of the Jones production (*Spectator,* 11 December 1964, p. 813) Malcolm Rutherford speaks for those who consider the entire text sacrosanct: "The trouble with cutting is that the work becomes more not less repetitive, and any development of character tends to disappear altogether. For, inevitably, whatever variety Marlowe himself provided is the first to go."

An examination of the staged versions of *Tamburlaine* in only three productions—Benét and Woolley's, Guthrie and Wolfit's, and Jones's—substantiates Rutherford's contention in some measure, but not totally. Let us begin with the 1919 performance at Yale. As an undergraduate, Benét was an accomplished and published poet, as precocious in his own way as Marlowe. After the open-air performance 14 June, the distinguished teacher and editor H. S. Canby asked Benét and Woolley to publish their version. Even though they were scrupulously faithful to Marlowe's text—there is no rewriting[12]—Benét and Woolley imposed quite a rein on the epic sweep of Parts I and II by scene compression and scene omission. They chose to dispense with the horrors both of slaughtering the Virgins of Damascus and of shooting the Governor of Babylon. By omitting from Part II the episode of Sigismund and the perjured Christians, as well as the Theridamas-Olympia subplot, they pared the plot to skeletal proportions, five scenes in the first act, seven in the second.

12. Such restraint is in marked contrast to the Basil Ashmore acting version of *Tamburlaine* (London, 1948); this is interlarded with pirated lines and "miniscenes" inserted to heighten the love interest, on the order of Tate's *King Lear,* and Bajazeth and Zabina are removed altogether.

The first five scenes at Yale marked successive horizontal stages in Tamburlaine's conquest both of the Eastern kingdoms and of the captive princess Zenocrate. There was no real vertical thrust to the plot line because Tamburlaine's opponents were not represented as increasingly difficult. Marlowe's embellishment of Cosroe by his minions was cut, while the farcical stage business between Tamburlaine and the fatuous Mycetes was retained. Cosroe's lengthy speeches on Tamburlaine's bad faith were omitted, as was his death on stage and his curse on "devilish presumption." [13] The entrance of Bajazeth in great pomp (Part I, III.i), with its latent parody of Tamburlaine's own rhetoric, was excised. Bajazeth did not enter until III.iii, and after his downfall the textual surgery worked against any sense of his majesty in misery. However, the student reviewer, Thornton Wilder, did commend "the scenes about the cage . . . as the most dramatic in the play" (*YDN*, p. 12). Bajazeth and his queen Zabina presumably were on stage after their suicides, since there is no stage direction to the contrary, but Tamburlaine's speech as he points to their bodies and to that of Zenocrate's first love, Arabia— "And such are objects fit for Tamburlaine / Wherein, as in a mirror may be seen / His honor, that consists in shedding blood / When men presume to manage arms with him" (Part I, V.i.475–477)—was cut, I suspect, lest there be any dramatic irony evoked.

In short, the structure of the first five scenes in the Yale version reinforced a sympathetic portrait of a conqueror whose abilities are rewarded and whose questionable ethics are rarely, if ever, subjected to irony. Tamburlaine's base birth was not stressed; during the first scene he did not cast off his "shepherd's weeds" to assume complete armor and cutlass. He appeared from the outset to be a Mongolian Robin Hood, ridding Persia of its lamentable cankers. Professor Brooke contended that there was nothing in the costuming to suggest either Tamburlaine's base origins or his supernatural martial prowess: "The white décolleté of the first scenes made him look like Mercutio; in the last scenes he looked a darker and drearier Macbeth" (*YDN*, p. 5). But Louis Loeb's portrayal of Tamburlaine was acclaimed by William Lyon Phelps as

13. *Tamburlaine the Great, Parts I and II*, ed. John D. Jump, Regents Renaissance Drama Series (Lincoln, Nebr., 1967), pp. 39–42. All subsequent references to the play are from this edition.

"thoroughly intelligent . . . never dull . . . never grotesque" (*YDN*, p. 8).

Loeb's performance thus kept the tedious and the ludicrous at bay, the danger of anticlimax that must harry every producer of *Tamburlaine,* particularly in the scenes from Part II. The second act at Yale opened with the tableau of Tamburlaine, Zenocrate, and their three sons on "fair Larissa plains," and it set a different mood from that of the entire first act. (Guthrie and Wolfit also chose to open the final act of their conflation with this tableau.) Tamburlaine's lecture on bearing a "mind courageous and invincible" (Part II, I.iii.69–84) was then combined with his self-inflicted wounding as he attempts to shame his cowardly son Calyphas (III.ii.95–129). The comedy of the escape of Callapine, Bajazeth's vengeance-ridden son, with his opportunist jailer, Almeda, intervened before the protracted death of Zenocrate. But Tamburlaine was not so maddened by his wife's death that he conflagrated Larissa, erected the pillar forbidding its rebuilding, or carried Zenocrate's coffin from camp to camp thereafter. He recovered from his grief to taunt the defiant Callapine, to tease the erstwhile jailer, and to murder his recalcitrant son, Calyphas.

Significantly, Benét and Woolley retained Calyphas' Falstaffian lines about honor, since A. J. Fox, the Yale Calyphas, provided the most striking challenge to Tamburlaine's *virtù* in the play. Tamburlaine's famous entrance drawing the captive kings—"Holla, ye pampered jades of Asia!" (IV.iii.1)—was delayed until *after* his very sudden illness (V.i.216–222). But since Tamburlaine did not burn Mohammed's holy books, there was no chance for the audience to draw any causal moral between sacrilege and illness. Death, Tamburlaine's only conqueror, simply came, after the triumphal "To Babylon, my lords, to Babylon!" (IV.iii.98–133). The chariot was not brought back on in the death scene for Tamburlaine's final herculean gesture—scattering Callapine's legions with a glance. The map of the world was called for, but Tamburlaine did not drag himself across it like a wounded beast (as he was to do for Guthrie); he merely pointed to the west as he repeated, "And shall I die and this unconquered?" (V.iii.150). Finally, in this version few of Marlowe's hyperboles were omitted, but the short eulogy with its apotheosis of Tamburlaine was cut at the end. The audience heard as the final line, "For Tamburlaine, the scourge of God, must die."

In effect, Benét and Woolley, from start to finish, produced a Tartarian Robin Hood-turned-Napoleon who dies a natural death, an untimely one to be sure, but one hardly called down by Jove, Mohammed, or conventional morality. Significantly, Benét removed practically all of Marlowe's references to Jove, except for Tamburlaine's threat to make Jove stoop in the refusal of Zenocrate's plea for mercy on Damascus (Part I, IV.iv.71–72). What iconoclasm there is in Marlowe's *Tamburlaine,* e.g., that the oaths of Christians are no better than those of infidels, that the Koran makes a lovely fire (not necessarily impious, however, from a Christian standpoint, as Harry Levin points out),[14] that there may not be a God in heaven—"The God that sits in heaven, if any god" (Part II, V.i.199)—Benét and Woolley skirted by excisions. Tamburlaine's barbarous cruelty was mitigated not only by omitting the deaths of the Virgins and of the Governor of Babylon, but also by severely cutting the taunting of Bajazeth. Tamburlaine's rhapsody on beauty (Part I, V.i.135–173) was not followed by the jolt of "Hath Bajazeth been fed today?" (V.i.192), since that line was cut.

Ultimately, the dramatic structure of this *Tamburlaine* resulted by default in an almost exclusively "romantic" reading of the play. Tamburlaine "became a most puissant and mighty monarch," as the Yale title page asserts, copying the 1590 octavo, and he did *not* go mad at the end. While Benét and Woolley steered clear of endorsing Tamburlaine's methods or of pointing his heterodoxy, as a substratum it is unmistakable. This is not surprising in view of the literary consensus on Marlowe in 1919. For Thornton Wilder, it was a "world of superlatives that the performance . . . understood and dwelt upon" (*YDN,* p. 12). As Brooke had pronounced in 1910, "The dominant trait of Marlowe's genius is its youthfulness; and we approach nowhere else so near to the essential character of the poet as in these two early plays. . . . It remains a very open question whether the gain in form and objectivity in the later dramas brings with it an altogether sufficient compensation for the decrease in boyish ideality."[15] Benét and Woolley chose to dramatize just this boyish ideality.

To turn from the Yale post-World War I production to Guthrie's is to

---

14. "Marlowe Today," *TDR,* VIII, no. 3 (Summer 1964), 28.
15. *The Works of Christopher Marlowe* (Oxford, 1910), p. 3.

see Tamburlaine almost transformed from heroic Tartar to Grand Guignol. T. S. Eliot is reported to have remarked after the opening night, "This . . . makes *King Lear* look as if it might have been written by Sir James Barrie." [16] Guthrie argued that the horrors of World War II prepared the audience for seeing Tamburlaine's incredible metaphors made literal on stage; he therefore conceived the entire play as an "orgy of sadism by the light of meteors . . . the inflamed power-dream of a genius that never reached maturity" (W-G, p. x), a dream, moreover, with no subtlety in rhetoric whatsoever. The savage carnage of the original was thus retained and exaggerated, with as much of the play's epic proportions as Guthrie and Wolfit could encompass in one evening by trimming the classical allusions and by doing away with the Sigismund and Olympia sequences from Part II. Wolfit believed that many of the printed versions of Elizabethan plays were fuller than the actual playhouse versions; he excised where he thought a line or passage was for the study only. Against all derogators, Wolfit strongly defended Marlowe's dramaturgy by arguing that "interplay of character, which had seemed hidden in the printed page, leapt up before us as we spoke it aloud . . . characters became clear and distinct, and humour shone here and there" (W-G, p. xiii).

Wolfit's flamboyant performance, as he moved from initial jocularity to psychosis, from rampant ambition to prostration, was universally acclaimed, as was Anthony Quayle's strikingly similar portrayal five years later.[17] But Guthrie's singular talents for stage spectacle did not always delight. Many critics felt that the demonic zest and pace of both the Old Vic and the Stratford Festival Company productions led Guthrie to neglect the spoken word. Richard Findlater, who very much admired Guthrie's genius, chided him for not believing in "the primal function of the word in the theatre." [18] While magnificent in its own right, the lavishness of Leslie Hurry's lurid scenery—an immense tented background in 1951, which became an actual three-hundred-pound gold lamé tent in 1956—and the props, among them a lion-headed chariot and imposing cage, gave some credence to this charge. On the other hand, there was

16. Peter Fleming, *Spectator,* CLXXXVII (1951), 392.

17. See the *Times,* 25 September 1951, p. 8, and 11 January 1956, p. 12.

18. "The Producer," *Theatre Programme,* ed. J. C. Trewin (London, 1954), p. 171.

PLATE 3. From the 1956 production of *Tamburlaine* given by the Stratford (Ontario) Shakespeare Festival Company. Anthony Quayle as the young Tamburlaine surrounded by enemies. Set by Leslie Hurry. Reproduced by permission of Mr. Herb Nott, the photographer, and Mr. Paul Myers, Curator or the New York Public Library's Theater Collection at Lincoln Center.

PLATE 4. From the 1956 production of *Tamburlaine* given by the Stratford (Ontario) Shakespeare Festival Company. Bajazeth (Douglas Rain) in his cage, with Zabina (Coral Browne). Set by Leslie Hurry. Reproduced by permission of Mr. Herb Nott, the photographer, and Mr. Paul Myers, Curator of the New York Public Library's Theater Collection at Lincoln Center.

much critical carping about the costuming in 1951;[19] not only had Wolfit nothing to compare with Edward Alleyn's red velvet breeches, but his entourage was said by the *Spectator*'s critic to end as they began, "looking like members of an impecunious water-polo team." As a result, Guthrie was led to extremes in 1956, one hundred and twenty-five costumes in all. The emphasis on the visual that was Guthrie's genius and nemesis is best exemplified, however, by the costume that evoked the loudest outcry, Tamburlaine's final one: "If only he would abandon that last unfortunate fur coat!" J. C. Trewin cried in the *Illustrated London News* (13 October 1951, p. 594). Under this weight, Tamburlaine dragged himself across the face of an immense map that had been pulled on by six slaves. The dramatic effect, and its length, was doubtful. The animality of Tamburlaine, a wolf come down on the fold of the East, had been stressed from the outset; here at the end, like a fever-ravaged grizzly, he stumbled lamely and then prowled on all fours, unable to evoke pathos or pity but rather, it seemed, anxious to capitalize on the monstrosity of his being.[20]

Because Guthrie chose not to play any variations on the theme of ingratiating shepherd become despot, it fell to the supporting cast to add dissonance or complexity. Cosroe had little chance, however, since his supporters' speeches were omitted, and to add insult to injury Guthrie had Tamburlaine declaim the famous "thirst of reign" speech (Part I, II.vii.12–29) to a dying Cosroe propped up before him. Guthrie's Bajazeths, Leo McKern and Douglas Rain, tried valiantly to play the eagle or lion to Tamburlaine's Machiavellian fox. Tamburlaine's conquering Bajazeth is pointless if there is no majesty to conquer, and both actors created a believable growth in character from bravado to wisdom. Both Zabinas, Margaret Rawlings and Coral Browne, clattered about the stage under the weight of huge balls and chains, but they managed

---

19. See Eric Keown, *Punch,* CCXXI (1951), 416. In contrast, the costumes, based on Oriental illuminated manuscripts in the Bodleian, for Nevill Coghill's production of *Tamburlaine,* Part II, at Oxford in 1933, were applauded by the *Times* (13 June 1933, p. 12); Tamburlaine's was copied from an Indian miniature that once belonged to Alexander Pope.

20. Norman Marshall, *The Producer and the Playwright* (London, 1957), p. 255; see also Audrey Williamson, *Old Vic Drama 2: 1947–1957* (London, 1957), pp. 77–83.

to impart enough pathos to transform Zabina's last dying frenzy from the ludicrous to the sublime, in a superb revelation of the peculiar sanity that is inherent in madness.

Additionally, the stage Zenocrates did play a constant countertheme to Tamburlaine's increasingly diabolical bloodletting. In 1951 Jill Balcon chose to stress Zenocrate's strange mental unbalance, while in 1956 Barbara Chilcott applied the sensuality and inscrutability of Shakespeare's version of the more famous Egyptian to Zenocrate. But Zenocrate's death was marred by having her corpse, a ghoulish puppet, bandied about at the end of the scene, thus upstaging any Marlovian pity. Finally, among the supporting cast, neither Theridamas nor Calyphas in the Guthrie productions—in spite of very creditable performances was directed to reveal the ironic counterthrusts of the original. The audience was so distracted by the convulsive twitching of Calyphas' body, in a macabre imitation of a slaughtered animal's death throes,[21] that what the murder reveals about Tamburlaine, that lust for power brooks no dissent, even filial, was buried in the theatrical effect. Furthermore, the Callapine-Almeda scenes were played so broadly that whatever serious point might have been furnished by this comedy from Part II was obviated by the stage business; the rotund Almeda appeared to have just stepped out of a seraglio. The minor character, however, about whom all critics remarked was the Governor of Babylon, precisely because of Guthrie and Hurry's tour de force in designing the arrow-riddled costume.

For Eric Bentley (the *New Republic,* 13 February 1956, p. 20), the "cries of Bravo when the Governor was hoisted in the air and transfixed by arrows were a true index to Mr. Guthrie's interpretation," and that Bentley viewed very critically: "Where Marlowe was defiant, Mr. Guthrie is only amused; where Marlowe, in his colossal error, was at least spunky, Mr. Guthrie, behind all the external false energy, is tired and perhaps even bored. . . . Marlowe and Guthrie are both as sophisticated as you

---

21. Harold Clurman, *Nation,* CLXXXII (1956), 99–100. Erwin Beck, cited above, admits, "All evidence considered, Guthrie apparently went too far with his scenes of staged violence. . . . what *Tamburlaine* demands in order to be fully appreciated today is a production which carefully modulates the violence by not adding more than Marlowe's text requires and by relegating to offstage action those deeds that the 1590 text so specifies" (*"Tamburlaine for the Modern Stage,"* pp. 73–74).

can get, but while Marlowe's sophistication is youthful, nihilistic, and
intellectual, Mr. Guthrie's is blasé, apolitical, and trivial." Such comment
is harsh indeed, but Guthrie was so zealous about transfusing the
theatrically moribund *Tamburlaine* that, for many, he created simply a
showpiece for a sadistic villain. For proof, we need only glance at the
headlines of the 1956 coverage of the play: "A Tale of Sound and Fury,
Illustrated," "Two Butcheries," "The Terrible Tempered Tamburlaine
Storms In," "Classical Thunder," and "Overflowing Bucket of Blood." [22]
Guthrie chose to stress neither Tamburlaine's lucid recognition of
mortality nor his awareness of an irrational universe. Furthermore, in the
scenes taken from Part II, Guthrie resorted to madness as a motive for
Tamburlaine's behavior, rather than frustration, resentment, outrage,
or shock. Guthrie thus avoided the monotony that Malcolm Rutherford contends plagues all conflations of the original, but he did not entirely avoid the grotesque or the melodramatic. [23] The post-Guthrie
revivals have managed not to exploit the horrific aspects of *Tamburlaine*, [24]
and I should like to consider briefly one of these—Robert Pennant
Jones's adaptation at the Tower Theatre, London, in 1964—before concluding.

22. Respectively, Henry Hewes, *Saturday Review*, 4 February 1956, p. 20; Wol-
cott Gibbs, *The New Yorker*, 28 January 1956, p. 58; *Cue*, 28 January 1956; Brooks
Atkinson, *New York Times*, 29 January 1956, sec. 2, p. 1; George Jean Nathan,
New York Journal-American, 28 January 1956, p. 16; see also "Savage Drama of
Elemental Passions," *Theatre Arts*, XL, no. 3 (March 1956), 18–19.

23. See Phillip Hope-Wallace, *Manchester Guardian*, 26 September 1951, p. 3,
on this aspect of the Old Vic production. I cannot agree with Robert B. Heilman,
Tragedy and Melodrama (Seattle, Wash., 1968), pp. 167–168, who contends that
Tamburlaine is "high-level" melodrama: for him, the audience shifts "from one
unambiguous emotional posture to another," and "neither in the relationships nor
in the scope of individual personalities is there the subtlety or depth that would
force us into an exacting, troubling experience where incompatible claims are both
urgently present." Such generic placing denies all irony in *Tamburlaine*.

24. See *Sunday Times* (London), 19 June 1960, p. 35; *The Stage* (London), 23
June 1960, p. 17; and Kenneth Tynan, *Tynan Right and Left* (New York, 1967),
pp. 25–26, for reviews commending the highly stylized Oxford University Dramatic Society's production. The *Times* (15 June 1960, p. 4) mixed praise with
blame. For a review of the "notably robust, straightforward, and well-spoken account of the play" that the Marlowe Theatre mounted, with Wolfe Morris in the
title role, see the *Times*, 19 October 1966, p. 17.

The Jones production was an extremely sensitive attempt to present *Tamburlaine* to a modern audience, and it played to virtually full houses during December, one of the heaviest theater months in London. Quite naturally, it is unfair to compare either the resources or the actors of a repertory company with those of the Old Vic or the Stratford Shakespearean Festival Company, but there are several aspects of this production worthy of comment. Contrary to Mr. Rutherford's opinion that all conflations simply remove verbal and non-verbal complexity to rush through the plot, the excisions in the Jones acting version of *Tamburlaine* intensify the Janus-like nature of the original. Unlike either the Benét or the Guthrie version, here each of Tamburlaine's opponents was given his unexcised measure of stature, which is necessary to depict the power of Marlowe's currency of kingship, namely, "working words," as the director states.[25] Making a strong case for common sense in the play, Theridamas was permitted all of the lines [26] in which he reacts to Tamburlaine's rhetoric much as Shakespeare's Dolabella does to Cleopatra's. Mr. Jones omitted none of Marlowe's own oscillations between comedy and violence; he did eliminate what he considered to be "wooden" or "contrived," notably the Olympia and Theridamas sequence, and the "routine bombast" of many of Marlowe's classical allusions. Finally, since the relative merits of Christian versus pagan morality are no longer a meaningful subject of debate for modern audiences, one can hardly fault Mr. Jones for cutting from Part II the Sigismund sequence, clearly the most topical aspect of the original, in spite of its historical ironies.

In the production itself, Mr. Jones's ingenious doubling of parts did more than imitate a custom common in Marlowe's day or get maximum utility out of thirty-six actors; it demonstrated quite an original insight into the play. Bajazeth, significantly, became his own son Callapine, thus underlining the constancy of resistance to tyranny, while with symbolic intent the same actor played the roles of Agydas, Arabia, and Calyphas.

25. I am grateful to Mr. Jones for supplying me with his acting version and production notes and to Mr. Dorsett for photographs of his set. Mr. Jones also directed me to a limited and little-known edition of *Tamburlaine* (London, 1930) ingeniously illustrated after Aubrey Beardsley by R. S. Sherriffs.

26. From Part I: I.ii.106; II.v.66; II.v.91–92; III.iii.224. From Part II: III.iii.11–12; III.iv.78–79; IV.i.96; V.iii.54–55.

For Mr. Jones, "This character-composite represents the threat to Tamburlaine's personal, i.e., non-military, authority, as guardian, as husband, and as father. All die, but not without having made an important point about Tamburlaine's character." Their deaths, indeed all the killings on stage, were executed with merciless speed, in marked contrast to the Guthrie production; Jones argues, "Death itself is its own moralist." The spirit of this 1964 production thus closely followed the contention in Harry Levin's essay ("Marlowe Today," p. 30) of that same year that "Tamburlaine's chariot fascinates us less than Bajazeth's cage."

To emphasize the Icarian nature of *Tamburlaine,* symbolized by the chariot and the cage, John Dorsett designed a powerfully emblematic set. The audience faced a "mountain" constructed of large slabbed steps, painted deep bronze, and arranged in ascending layers that reached a flat apex area on which the Persian throne was set in the beginning. This "mountain" defined one focus of the production. To point the other emphasis, two actual drawbridges were placed on either side of the stage, initially to hold the thrones for the queens' flyting and later to hold Bajazeth's cage. Additionally, the splendid use of color that Marlowe devised, the white, red, and black motif to underscore Tamburlaine's conquests, was retained, heightened, and set off by costuming the three different factions—Persian, Egyptian, and Turkish—in identifiably contrasting colors. In short, Jones and Dorsett did prove that an abridged *Tamburlaine* is playable today. But ultimately the question must be asked: is either a cut or an uncut Tamburlaine worth mounting in our time? Is the play mimetic only of Marlowe's era, or is it a universal "image of man's interaction in time" [27] that speaks—because of its universality—to whatever is problematical for its auditors in their time?

One can hardly prove hypotheses about audience reaction to any play, but the fact that there have been audiences for *Tamburlaine* in this century provokes speculation. Since none of the recent revivals attempted a full-scale reproduction of the original, or gave impetus to the afternoon and evening sequence at Chichester of which Mr. Rutherford dreamed in 1964, it is unlikely that entirely antiquarian motives prompted

27. Jackson Barry, *Dramatic Structure: The Shaping of Experience* (Berkeley, Calif., 1970), p. 10.

serious interest in the play. *Tamburlaine* is an extraordinary relic, but it also seems to be something more. When he reviewed the Guthrie revival in 1951, Ivor Brown argued, "Tamburlaine is not just an animated waxwork from the Chamber of Horrors. He is relevant to modern savagery" (*Observer,* 30 September 1951, p. 6). Yet in 1956 opinion split over the contemporaneity of *Tamburlaine:* many felt that Tamburlaine's resemblance to Hitler, Mussolini, and Stalin was so glaring that revulsion negated both profit and pleasure; others argued that the *exemplum* of absolute power was an unpleasant lesson worth heeding.[28] At issue, of course, is whether *Tamburlaine* glorifies Machiavellian *virtù,* denigrates it, or asks us to suspend moral judgment; is the play immoral, moral, or amoral? No two *Tamburlaine* productions have pointed this question in the same way. The unbridled ambition that leads to an insatiable lust for power is subject to as many responses as there are directors to prompt them—and one man's bias is another's insight. For different reasons, neither Benét and Woolley nor Guthrie and Wolfit asked for or expected a complex intellectual response to *Tamburlaine;* Mr. Jones did— and with good cause.

Contemporary audiences have witnessed the virtual establishment of what was known in the sixteenth century as "the doctrine of natural law as the normative basis of moral ideas" to appropriate D. J. Palmer's phrase.[29] If man's state in nature is swayed by wild and anarchic forces, if there are no permanent allegiances, only ceaseless selfishness, then the conflict of individual wills is inevitable: the strong man will surface always to subjugate the weaker. Even as we may denounce it, for audiences familiar with the plays of Sartre, Camus, Artaud, and Genet, Marlowe's "naturalism" is an accurate and pragmatic definition of the human condition, upon which one is quite free to impose irony in the interests of his sanity. Recent literary criticism of Marlowe recognizes the irony in *Tamburlaine,* regardless of disagreements about the uses and

28. See John Beaufort, *Christian Science Monitor,* 28 January 1956, p. 6, as an example of the first point of view; and George Boolos and Michael Freedman's letter to the Drama Editor, *New York Times,* 12 February 1956, sec. 2, p. 3— "Tamburlaine has turned out to be scathingly prophetic"—as an illustration of the second.

29. "Marlowe's Naturalism," *Christopher Marlowe,* ed. Brian Morris (London, 1968), p. 154.

intent of that irony.[30] Many critics speak of *Tamburlaine*'s consummate lack of resolution, its amorality, and its almost quintessential paradoxes— ideas quite foreign to the play's earlier modern admirers.

Tamburlaine is a paradigm of self-contradiction on stage or off: the audience is presented at the beginning with a protagonist who is determined to prove quite literally that a man's reach need not exceed his grasp. But as he keeps turning metaphor into fact his actions become increasingly monstrous or simply incredible. His word is his deed; Bajazeth *is* his footstool. He rides in triumph through Persepolis, but the progress of pomp is at once glorious, ridiculous, and abhorrent, since that triumph is juxtaposed with the thousands of human carcasses in Asphaltis' lake and with the Governor's riddled body hanging on the walls of Babylon. For J. R. Mulryne and Stephen Fender, "Our judgement of Tamburlaine, though it may on occasion appeal to basic humanitarian instincts, normally acts through a sense of proportion, a recognition of extravagance and triviality which is morally neutral. The only lesson that the death of Tamburlaine teaches is the existential one of man's common mortality."[31] The only question—and that is enough— that the life of Tamburlaine poses is the essential one of man's common violence. Whether a given production, such as the Guthrie that employed a professional whipcracker, revels in *Tamburlaine*'s violence or chooses with Mr. Jones to let that violence speak for itself, it is no longer possible to deny the violence of the original as Benét and Woolley did. *Tamburlaine* is unquestionably controversial for armchair critics; the staged versions would indicate that it is controversial for all of us.

30. See Katherine Lever, "The Image of Man in *Tamburlaine, Part I*," *PQ*, XXXV (1956), 427; David Bevington, *From "Mankind" to Marlowe* (Cambridge, Mass., 1962), pp. 199–217; Douglas Cole, *Suffering and Evil in the Plays of Christopher Marlowe* (Princeton, N.J., 1962), pp. 86–103; Robert Kimbrough, "*1 Tamburlaine*: A Speaking Picture in a Tragic Glass," *RenD*, VII (1964), 20–34; Donald Cary Freeman, " 'Brave to Be a King': A Stylistic Analysis of Christopher Marlowe's Dramatic Poetry" (Ph.D. diss., University of Connecticut, 1965), pp. 79–88; David H. Zucker, "Stage and Image in the Plays of Christopher Marlowe" (Ph.D. diss., Syracuse University, 1968), chaps. 1–2; and Barry Phillips, "Marlowe: A Revaluation" (Ph.D. diss., University of Connecticut, 1969), pp. 154–161.

31. "Marlowe and the 'Comic Distance,'" *Christopher Marlowe,* ed. Morris, p. 56.

Armor and Motive in Troilus and Cressida

DAVID J. HOUSER

Recent critics have expressed an increasing interest in the contribution of staging to the over-all effect of Shakespeare's plays. R. A. Foakes calls for study of "dramatic imagery," something "different from poetic imagery," study which would take into account "stage effects, properties and other direct 'images' [which] all help to make a play," while Maynard Mack warns that critics "have been too much concerned in this century with the verbal, which is only part of the picture." By providing a visual context, the way a play is staged can supplement, reinforce, or qualify the effect of verbal imagery. Taking this fact into account, studies of emblematic tableaux, the effects of possible blocking or gesture, repeated visual motifs, and the significant use of costuming have revealed a type of artistic achievement that previously had been largely unattended to.[1]

1. Foakes, "Suggestions for a New Approach to Shakespeare's Imagery," *ShS,* V (1952), 82; Mack, "The Jacobean Shakespeare: Some Observations on the Construction of the Tragedies," *Jacobean Theatre,* ed. John Russell Brown and Bernard Harris, *Stratford-upon-Avon Studies* (London, 1960), I, 32. For examples of such studies, see Maurice Charney, *Shakespeare's Roman Plays: The Function of*

Shakespeare's use of such visual techniques in *Troilus and Cressida,* however, has not been studied in detail. Instead, most of the critical examinations of the play, primarily investigations of genre, characterization, and theme, have taken the text out of the theater in an attempt to deal with the basic questions which W. W. Lawrence explicitly poses after contrasting Shakespeare's *Troilus and Cressida* to earlier tellings of the tale: "His version is like no other; what effect did he aim to produce? How did he mean his play to be understood?"[2] In their efforts to answer those questions, critics have failed to reach agreement, though clearly the play and its characters cannot be all things. If, for example, the play is seen as essentially tragic it can hardly be essentially comic and satiric as well. Troilus cannot be both noble as an aspirer to the ideal in love and base as a self-limited "sexual gourmet," or Hector both admirable in his pursuit of chivalric honor yet also the most culpable among the Trojans in the consciousness of his rejection of morality and reason in order to press that pursuit.[3] Frequently in such questions of character (and underlying them, in questions of tone, of effect, of how Shakespeare meant his play to be understood) the key consideration is

---

Imagery in the Drama (Cambridge, Mass., 1961); Alan C. Dessen, "Hamlet's Poisoned Sword: A Study in Dramatic Imagery," *ShakS,* V (1969), 53–69; John Shaw, "The Staging of Parody and Parallels in '1 Henry IV,' " *ShS,* XX (1967), 61–73; and Leo Kirschbaum, "Shakespeare's Stage-Blood," *PMLA,* LXIV (1949), 517–529.

2. *Shakespeare's Problem Comedies,* 2d ed. (New York, 1960; 1st ed., 1931), p. 124.

3. The quoted term is Oscar J. Campbell's, from *Comical Satyre and Shakespeare's Troilus and Cressida* (San Marino, Calif., 1938), p. 212. His low opinion of both the Greeks and Trojans has been supported with qualifications by a number of later critics. Among the better recent treatments are those of David Kaula, "Will and Reason in *Troilus and Cressida,*" *SQ,* XII (1961), 271–283; and Alice Shalvi, " 'Honor' in *Troilus and Cressida,*" *SEL,* V (1965), 283–302. G. Wilson Knight, *The Wheel of Fire,* 4th ed. (London, 1949; 1st ed., 1930), and some later critics such as Willard Farnham, "Troilus in Shapes of Infinite Desire," *SQ,* XV (1964), 257–264, have attempted to argue the supreme admirability of the Trojans. Conflicting assignations of genre can be seen in Lawrence and in Thomas Marc Parrott, *Shakespearean Comedy* (New York, 1949), both of whom consider the play to be in some sense comic; see also Theodore Spencer, *Shakespeare and the Nature of Man* (New York, 1942), and Brian Morris, "The Tragic Structure of *Troilus and Cressida,*" *SQ,* X (1959), 481–491, who argue for tragedy; and Campbell, who stresses a specific satiric technique.

one of motive, and it is in revealing motive that attention to nonverbal effects is especially valuable in this play. In *Troilus and Cressida,* Shakespeare uses both emblematic tableaux and a related, recurring visual motif—armor and the act of arming or disarming, fighting or refusing to fight—with the effect of emphasizing, comparing, and defining motive.

Customarily, critics have separated two lines of activity in *Troilus and Cressida,* the events predominately concerned with love and lovers and those concerned with the war,[4] and the principals of each part of the plot speak much and loftily about their motives for acting. Troilus, Paris, and even Achilles claim at appropriate times to be guided by their love and elsewhere join with such as Hector, Ajax, Aeneas, and Diomed in jealously maintaining their honor. Within the action framed by the judgment and pressures of Priam, Ulysses, and Agamemnon at one extreme of surface respectability, and the comment and perspective provided by Pandarus and Thersites at the other, desires for honor and the fruits of love would seem to be the two primary motives of the men in this play. But "honor" and "love" can be, of course, elevating euphemisms for various degrees of pride and sensual besottedness or lust. From the first scene Shakespeare invites us to test the exact flavor of what is meant each time these words are used, and from that first scene he uses armor and the issue of fighting or refusing to fight, arming or disarming, to guide our evaluation.

After the Prologue, the first words of the play are Troilus': "Call here my varlet; I'll unarm again" (I.i.1). Although we can only speculate about his exact appearance and action, it is clear that he is armed for battle. The natural gesture here would be to set aside a shield, perhaps, or to remove a helmet and sword while pacing in frustration. For an Elizabethan, both the terms in which he describes his state and his subsequent interview with Pandarus would make iconographic sense of such action. He says he cannot fight because he is "mad / In Cressid's

4. Indeed, Norman Rabkin, *"Troilus and Cressida:* The Uses of the Double Plot," *ShakS,* I (1965), 265–282, studies the communication of theme through Shakespeare's manipulation of the "two distinct plots, as independent of one another as any in Shakespeare: the affair between Troilus and Cressida on the one hand, and the Greek ruse to bring Achilles back into the war and thus end it on the other" (p. 266).

love" (ll. 50–51), a love which not only drives him to unarm but which also has made him "weaker than a woman's tear" (l. 9), unmanned,

> Less valiant than the virgin in the night,
> And skilless as unpractis'd infancy.
>
> (ll. 11–12)

Troilus' situation echoes a classical myth which Shakespeare clearly uses in *Venus and Adonis* and *Antony and Cleopatra,* the disarming of Mars by Venus. The work of both Raymond B. Waddington and Robert P. Miller indicates that the Mars and Venus story was interpreted to exemplify either besotting love or the tempering of extremes to provide new and gentle harmony. Miller shows that the former is operative in *Venus and Adonis,* in which the lover if controlled is weakened by his lust and is deprived of his armor or weapons as well as his desire to use them. Waddington sees as finally dominant in *Antony and Cleopatra* the other view of the union of the gods of war and love, emphasizing a sense of the fruitful reconciliation of extremes, especially in the two death scenes.[5] But consistently, the marks which distinguish the besotted Mars, besides the removal of weapons and armor, are an associated loss of manly dignity and the will to warlike action. In this first scene Troilus calls for his man and perhaps literally casts aside part of his armor, declares his state and its cause, and demonstrates his weakness and lack of control by virtually wooing Pandarus, subjecting his will and dignity to the whim of a soft man who is not a fighter but who is instead the means to pursue the delights of Venus. Troilus' motive is marked by what he says, and it is recognizable as besottedness. With the reinforcement of staged disarming, the significance of his lines is more likely to be noticed and understood.

The parallel to the Venus-Mars seduction is not the scene's only comment on Troilus' motives and love. Other critics have discussed the revealing terms of his complaint about his lover's pains, "the open ulcer of my heart" (l. 52), the gash that love has given him into which

---

5. Miller, "The Myth of Mars's Hot Minion in 'Venus and Adonis,' " *ELH,* XXVI (1959), 470–481; Waddington, "Antony and Cleopatra: 'What Venus Did with Mars,' " *ShakS,* II (1966), 210–227. Miller's treatment of the myth presses on to a consideration of Christian exegesis which is perhaps more appropriate to a study of the poem he is examining than it would be here.

Pandarus' talk of Cressida lays "The knife that made it" (l. 62).[6] Such language and his final decision to go to the battle after all, to attend the "sport abroad" (l. 114) because the sexual sport at home is unavailable, serve to confirm the effect of what has come before. While Troilus is to be imagined off fighting Greeks, we watch as his lady and his procurer exchange bawdry, so that when Troilus' boy requests Pandarus to attend his master we are conscious of the significance both of their meeting place and Troilus' activity there: "At your own house; there he unarms him" (I.ii.266).

The use of staged action to help an audience become aware of a correspondence between Troilus and the besotted Mars does more than direct attention to the words and motives of a single character, however. Troilus is only the first of several men in the play who do not merely disarm or appear unarmed but who abandon weapons and armor specifically for lust. For example, in Act III, scene i we see Paris no longer armed, as he had been when crossing the stage in Act I, scene ii, but in softer clothes appropriate to lovemaking. While others fight outside the walls, he is luxuriating with Helen in what they at least call love. This is the only appearance of Helen, one that assumes special importance since the Prologue, an armed man himself, has reminded us that the glorious "princes orgulous" (Prologue, l. 2) have vowed

> To ransack Troy, within whose strong immures
> The ravish'd Helen, Menelaus' queen,
> With wanton Paris sleeps—and that's the quarrel.
>
> (ll. 8–10)

The flat deflation that has been noted in that last line[7] is continued here as Helen, "the mortal Venus, the heart-blood of beauty, love's invisible soul" (III.i.31–32), jokes as bawdily as a Doll Tearsheet. The presence of Pandarus again serves to underline the quality of "love" in the scene, not simply by carrying his staining name with him but also by evoking Paris' definition of love as lust: "He eats nothing but doves, love;

6. See as representative Spencer, *Shakespeare and the Nature of Man*, pp. 115–116; Rabkin, "The Uses of the Double Plot," p. 273; and Derick R. C. Marsh, "Interpretation and Misinterpretation: the Problem of *Troilus and Cressida*," *ShakS*, I (1965), 185.

7. See Shalvi, "'Honor' in *Troilus and Cressida*," p. 285, and Marsh, "Interpretation and Misinterpretation," p. 186.

and that breeds hot blood, and hot blood begets hot thoughts, and hot thoughts beget hot deeds, and hot deeds is love" (ll. 122–124). When Paris announces that he "would fain have armed to-day, but my Nell would not have it so," and asks, "How chance my brother Troilus went not?" (ll. 130–131), he does more than simply mark himself as besotted in his lust and remind us that Troilus shares his state. He proves what other characters have asserted, the shallowness of the "argument" for the war itself, a point insisted on here as Helen is asked to greet the Trojan champion at his return from battle:

> You shall do more
> Than all the island kings—disarm great Hector.
>
> (ll. 146–147)

The effect of the lust that dominates certain of the play's young men extends to Hector and through him to all Troy; repeatedly Shakespeare uses scenes which recall the disarming of Mars by Venus in order to make us aware that it is indeed besottedness and not healthy love we are witnessing.

But the play involves more than tainted love attachments. Various characters on both sides of the conflict claim a quite different motive for action in the war: the pursuit and maintenance of honor. Two prime examples in the Greek camp are Achilles and Ajax. Musing in Act III, scene iii, about the strange behavior toward him exhibited by Agamemnon and the Greek lords, Achilles talks of the loss of honor that man is subject to, and Ulysses tailors his vocabulary to fit Achilles' vision of himself when he warns that "Perseverance, dear my lord, / Keeps honour bright" (ll. 150–151). When not engaged in flattery, however, Ulysses and the rest of the Greeks cite pride as the true motivation for the actions of Ajax and Achilles, and again it is in deciding whether to arm and fight that the motive is made clear. The force which Ulysses says has disrupted the maintenance of degree is "an envious fever / Of pale and bloodless emulation" (I.iii.133–134), and his chief example is Achilles who refuses to do battle, "Having his ear full of his airy fame" and growing "dainty of his worth" (ll. 144–145). Agamemnon calls him "over-proud / And under-honest" (II.iii.119–120), and Ulysses declares, "He is so plaguy proud that the death-tokens of it / Cry 'No recovery'" (ll. 172–173). When Ulysses finally goads Achilles temporarily into action, he does so by playing on that same trait. That which duty, his generals' entreaties, and his faction's good cannot make him do, Achilles' hurt pride can. Ajax is presented as a less intelligent version of the same man.

The refusal to arm is not always and simply a sign of wrong motive. Instead, moments in which the decision must be made provide situations in which a variety of reasons for acting can be aired and tested. For example, in the Trojan camp the question of "honor" is also crucial in getting men to arm, but by means of the debate in Act II, scene ii—over returning Helen, over whether or not to continue to fight —Shakespeare clearly delineates exactly what "honor" means in this play. Hector, Helenus, Priam, and Cassandra speak in turn against keeping Helen, offering arguments which Troilus and Paris reject generally by means of appeals to honor. Hector's immediate response to Priam's request for judgment expresses a caution that an audience, aware of the outcome of the Trojan War, can only view as great good sense: "Who knows what follows?"—the expense which already has been too much can only increase (ll. 13 ff.). Troilus denies that such considerations can outweigh "the worth and honour of a king / So great as our dread father's" (ll. 26–27), and answers Helenus' rebuke with a scornful railing against reason.

> Nay, if we talk of reason,
> Let's shut our gates and sleep. Manhood and honour
> Should have hare hearts, would they but fat their thoughts
> With this cramm'd reason.
>
> (ll. 46–49)

Honor is again the basis of his response when Hector labels as "mad idolatry" (l. 56) Troilus' attempt to create worth in Helen by simply declaring her worthy. If a man take a wife he cannot reject her although his "will distaste what it elected. . . . There can be no evasion / To blench from this and to stand firm by honour" (ll. 66–68). One can neither change one's mind nor fail in the assertion of will and still maintain honor. As Paris shortly says, it would mean disgrace

> Now to deliver her possession up
> On terms of base compulsion!
>
> (ll. 152–153)

Cassandra's "high strains / Of divination" and Priam's rebukes both fail
to

> distaste the goodness of a quarrel
> Which hath our several honours all engag'd
> To make it gracious.
>
> (ll. 123–125)

Once again the issue of whether or not to fight has been used to examine
reasons for acting. The exchange has clearly revealed that in Troilus'
mouth, at least, his motive of "honor" means disregarding reason and
submitting to rashness, disregarding cost, ignoring divination, and maintaining the reputation of being able both to kill well and to take Helen,
Greeks or no, and keep her.[8]

The total effect is devastating visually as well as logically. On one side
of the debate are an older warrior who, as the Trojan champion, must
be of necessity the most physically impressive man on stage, a priest
most naturally dressed in such a way that his occupation is clear, a
king, and a prophetess who enters raving in a manner which marks her
function. Against these opponents stand two young and passionately
irrational men, Troilus too young even for much beard, a subject for
laughter earlier in the play. The scene invites reinforcing blocking that
places the participants in the debate in two roughly grouped factions
facing each other across the stage, perhaps before a throned Priam. Hector would most naturally deliver his final comments from a dominant
position in front of his faction, accomplishing a final deflation of Paris
and Troilus as "young men, whom Aristotle thought / Unfit to hear
moral philosophy" (ll. 166–167), whose "reasons" are appeals to passion,
whose arguments violate the "moral laws / Of nature and of nations"

8. In Farnham's reading of the scene, truth in honor indeed has been defined,
but differently: "It is loyalty, fidelity, constancy, steadfastness. It means keeping
one's word to the death when one has solemnly promised adherence to a person
or a cause. It means a reality that lies in the word one has given and not in the
changing array of 'facts' in one's surrounding world, which may appear, but according to Troilus can do no more than deceitfully appear, to make the given
word of no validity" ("Troilus in Shapes of Infinite Desire," p. 261). This is an
eloquent summary of Troilus' arguments which assumes that against them the
anwers of Hector, Helenus, and Cassandra carry no weight. But not even a viewer
sympathetic to Troilus will trust his judgment here, having just seen its faultiness
in evaluating Cressida.

(ll. 184–185) alike, and whose resolve "extenuates not wrong, / But makes it much more heavy" (ll. 187–188). A Hector so placed would almost automatically leave his original faction and shake the hands, clap the shoulders of the two reasonless young men as he declares that he will abandon his opinion "in way of truth" (l. 189) to embrace the cause upon which their "joint and several dignities" (l. 193) depend. So staged, Hector's abandonment of a reasoned opinion in favor of an emotion-based one is paralleled by a physical movement away from those characters who embody insight, stability, and mature consideration to another group displaying a vigorous but immature passion. Troilus' words provide a final indirect interpretation of his brother's action: Hector will fight to keep Helen who is

> a theme of honour and renown,
> A spur to valiant and magnanimous deeds,
> Whose present courage may beat down our foes,
> And fame in time to come canonize us;
>
>   (ll. 199–202)

Hector puts aside his opinion "in way of truth" to assert his will and establish his reputation, and this is called honor.

Diomed sums it up well in a "despiteful'st gentle greeting" (IV.i.34), part of an exchange with Aeneas which again turns on the difference between being armed or not. Aeneas has wished him health in truce,

> But when I meet you arm'd, as black defiance
> As heart can think or courage execute.
>
>   (ll. 14–15)

In terms which reveal motive, Diomed responds with a prayer for Aeneas' long life if they do not meet on the field,

> But in mine emulous honour, let him die
> With every joint a wound, and that to-morrow!
>
>   (ll. 30–31)

His response to a question from Paris soon labels the cause as a quarrel between a cuckold and a lecher over a whore, significant only as an excuse to exercise "mine emulous honor."

Essentially the same values underlie Pandarus' praise of Hector and Troilus as they pass in Act I, scene ii, for there too action is judged literally by its surface appearance and not by its innate worth. What we see emphasizes the substance and significance of what is said as the focus is again on armor now marked by their fighting: "There be hacks." (l. 200), with Troilus seen to be especially praiseworthy because of his bloody sword and "his helm more hack'd than Hector's" (ll. 223–224). But the fight of Ajax and Hector provides an especially clear-cut example of the disregard of underlying worth in the service of "mine emulous honor." Hector's challenge is ridiculous but in a way so romantic that its shallowness can be missed. He shall

> make it good or do his best to do it:
> He hath a lady wiser, fairer, truer,
> Than ever Greek did couple in his arms.
>
> (I.iii.274–276)

But the romanticism is stripped away when the challenge is filtered through the old, musty, but experienced Nestor who will meet Hector, if need be, and

> will tell him that my lady
> Was fairer than his grandame, and as chaste
> As may be in the world.
>
> (ll. 298–300)

As Achilles says, Hector will meet "such a one that dare / Maintain I know not what; 'tis trash" (II.i.121–122). Since the argument is indeed trash, the only motive for fighting is the potential gain in the reputation of being able to kill well, and Ajax is very frank in admitting this: though Hector declines to kill his kin, Ajax declares he "came to kill thee, cousin, and bear hence / A great addition earned in thy death" (IV.v.140–141). Hector has displayed a subtle qualification of his pursuit of reputation, an insistence on acting within the rules of chivalry —a handsome enough code elsewhere, but in this play little other than a way to make fighting without worthy purpose seem to be almost a dance, a ritual, and a thing of honor.

The staged action again underlines the judgment of motive and event which has been both implicit and explicit in the dialogue. The fierce encounter of two armed men ends in a discarding of weapons, helmets, and shields as Hector first lets Ajax feel the weight of his arm in an embrace rather than a blow and then, with shows of cordial warmth, goes to Agamemnon's tent and later to Achilles' feast. The effect is to stress the hollowness of the motives which led to deadly fight between men who can find no reason not to be friends except the competition for reputation.

All these strands are woven together in the final battle and the preparations for it, as men again decide or decline to arm in scenes that both balance each other and refer back to what has been presented earlier in the play. First Achilles, the greatest of the Greek warriors, puts aside his vow to meet Hector on the field (V.i). Polyxena, his Venus, would not have it so, and Achilles obeys. He breaks his vow for an inadequate reason, an unadmirable motive.

Two scenes later the greatest of the Trojans, Hector, is seen in a corresponding situation. The arguments presented to dissuade Hector from his intent to arm and fight are the same as those used against Troilus and Paris in the council scene, and as he rejects each of them, Hector again chooses to assume the position which he himself earlier proved to be folly. Andromache calls him "ungently temper'd" (V.iii.1) as she urges, "Unarm, unarm, and do not fight to-day" (l. 3). She has dreamed and Cassandra seconds her admonitions. But Hector has vowed and will not turn back, even as Paris and Troilus insisted on unswerving consistency: "Be gone, I say. The gods have heard me swear" (l. 15). Cassandra and Andromache rationally puncture that argument ("The gods are deaf to hot and peevish vows. . . . Do not count it holy / To hurt by being just. . . . It is the purpose that makes strong the vow;/ But vows to every purpose must not hold" [ll. 16, 19–20, 23–24]), but Hector values "Mine honour" (l. 26) above such considerations. A different issue, the cost of what is risked by Hector's resolve, is the point of Cassandra's warning to Priam,

> now if thou lose thy stay,
> Thou on him leaning, and all Troy on thee,
> Fall all together.
>
> (ll. 60–62)

Priam himself joins Cassandra in foreboding divination. But Hector wills; he will "forth, and fight, / Do deeds worth praise and tell you them at night" (ll. 92–93). That desire to win praise, fulfill his vow, and maintain his faith engaged to the Greeks leads him to reject good sense and reason, ignore excessive cost, dismiss divination, and go against the will of Priam; and all this is done to satisfy passion and "mine emulous honor." Unlike Achilles, against whom he is balanced, Hector keeps his vow in spite of many adequate reasons not to.

The issues underlying this debate are those of the Trojan council, and the particular way Shakespeare has chosen to review those issues invites blocking parallels with the earlier scene. Priam enters and performs again the function that was his the only other time he appears; he presides as an ineffectual judge between opposed factions. Priam most naturally would stand or be seated at the same place on stage that he occupied before as once more two passionate warriors assert their honor from one side of the stage and figures urging the sway of tempering reason speak from the other. Hector has adopted Troilus' ideas here; the suggested staging reinforces the dialogue by placing him visually in the position that had been Troilus'.

In contrast to Act I, scene i, Troilus is now ready to buckle on his armor and fight, and shrugs off the fact that Hector is urging him not to, but again the motive is wrong. In Act V, scene ii, the observation of Diomed and Cressida, we watch the passion build that lies behind his resolution. A sort of externalized reason in the form of the coldly rational Ulysses governs Troilus there,[9] but in his argument with Hector he exhibits only the thinnest veneer of self-control:

> For th' love of all the gods,
> Let's leave the hermit pity with our mother,
> And when we have our armours buckled on,
> The venom'd vengeance ride upon our swords,
> Spur them to ruthful work, rein them from ruth!
>
> (V.iii.44–48)

Whatever one may think of the devotion to chivalry that lies behind Hector's response to this speech, a subject yet to be explored, the judgment of Troilus' lines is accurate. They are "savage" (l. 49), indeed. But they also assume more dignity than is justified by the actual battle with Diomed which follows. Granted that Thersites is an uncertain touchstone, "in everything illegitimate" (V.vii.19), it nevertheless is through the frame of comment which he furnishes that we watch them

9. Including Thersites, Spencer comments that "Passion, reason and cynicism form the discordant chorus to action" (*Shakespeare and the Nature of Man,* p. 118).

struggle: "Hold thy whore, Grecian; now for thy whore, Troyan—now the sleeve, now the sleeve!" (V.iv.23–24). When Troilus suffers partial defeat and calls for the "traitor Diomed" to turn "And pay thy life thou owest me for my horse" (V.vi.6–7), there is a laughable pun on "whore." Troilus has lost to Diomed two beasts he was wont to ride.

The climactic meeting, however, is that between Achilles and Hector. When Ajax and Achilles arm, Nestor exults, "So, so, we draw together" (V.v.44), but in fact they only incidentally work to the same end. The Greek draught-oxen have come to plough up the wars, but for personal revenge and stung pride not for cause or duty. "Ajax hath lost a friend" (l. 35), as has Achilles. The death of Patroclus, Achilles' masculine whore, provides a direct parallel to Troilus' reason for such great anger.

In the first encounter with Achilles, Hector displays that "vice of mercy" (V.iii.37), that chivalry, which was first seen in the match with Ajax. The courtesy which Achilles disdains leads directly to Hector's death but not till a final and especially effective use of the armor motif stands as an emblem of the cause of his defeat. When Hector pursues a Greek for his "goodly armour" (V.viii.2) and gets it only to find the man contained in its beauty to be a "Most putrified core" (l. 1), S. L. Bethell sees in the event a vivid expression of the "fair without, foul within" theme that pervades the play.[10] This is certainly true, but I agree with Alice Shalvi that the particular fair without that Hector pursues is identifiable.[11] In Act V, scene iii Troilus rebukes his brother for sparing Greeks made helpless before him. What Hector defends as chivalrous "fair play" Troilus calls "Fool's play, by heaven, Hector" (l. 43). Troilus' wish to abandon pity when in armor may be savage, but it is also based in a clear-sighted evaluation of battle: "Hector, then 'tis wars" (l. 49). In his pursuit of reputation through chivalry, through an artificial construct of values that attempts to deny the harsh nature of war and make it fair, Hector may be accused in Cassandra's last words, "Thou dost thyself and all our Troy deceive" (l. 90). On the battlefield he pursues an emblem of his chivalry, the goodly armor, and achieving it, both metaphorically and literally, disarms himself (V.viii.4 s.d.).

Achilles enters, and once again we see an encounter of the Greek

10. *Shakespeare and the Popular Dramatic Tradition* (Durham, N.C., 1944), pp. 125–127.

11. " 'Honor' in *Troilus and Cressida*," pp. 292–293.

and Trojan champions, though now with a difference. Before, two armed
men faced each other on equal terms till Hector's prowess asserted itself. To make sensible Hector's invitation to "Pause, if thou wilt"
(V.vi.14), Achilles must show his weariness, perhaps by being forced
to his knee or by having his sword or shield beaten from him. Hector's
physical superiority is clear simply from what we see. But now Hector
blindly has deprived himself of shield and weapon, and he faces not a
single champion but a cluster of baser henchmen who hack him without
suffering so much as a returning blow. Achilles is left alive and in the
posture that connotes strength, standing over the corpse, as he sheathes a
sword which has remained bloodless and gives orders that the body
of the man who granted him mercy be desecrated. Achilles does not
"forgo this vantage" (V.viii.9). He is Troilus' kind of man—"Hector,
then 'tis wars."

Thersites sings but one song, "Lechery, lechery! Still wars and lechery!
Nothing else holds fashion. A burning devil take them!" (V.ii.194–196).
Through reinforcing blocking, emblematic tableaux, and the repeated
visual motif of armor and arming or disarming. Shakespeare has insisted
that we see the motives for the actions of his characters to be indeed
self-feeding pride in war and self-deluding, besotted lust. The result is
dishonorable action, death, a Troilus raging for his lost horse, whore, and
brother, and a Pandarus inviting you to see the play as part of your
own world by smilingly bequeathing you his diseases.

Florimène *and the Ante-Masques*

STEPHEN ORGEL

O F THE MANY INNOVATIONS introduced into the life of the Caroline court by Queen Henrietta Maria, few were more shocking to British public opinion than the staging of plays in which the queen and her ladies took speaking roles. In the year after King Charles's accession, 1626, she appeared in Sieur de Racan's *Les Bergeries, or L'Artenice,* a popular pastoral that had been presented at the Hôtel de Bourgogne seven years earlier.[1] The queen's participation was considered sufficiently scandalous to cause severe embarrassment to the king, and such a produc-

---

1. The play, referred to in English sources merely as a French pastoral of the queen's, was identified by Louis Arnould in the standard modern critical edition, *Les Bergeries* (Paris, 1937), pp. v–vii. In 1960, W. A. Jackson and Jean Parrish published an account of a copy of the play in the Houghton Library, with contemporary annotations that further confirm Arnould's identification ("Racan's *L'Artenice,*" *HLB,* XIV, no. 2 (1960), 183–190). Astonishingly, however, Jackson and Parrish did not consult the only modern edition of the work, and therefore claimed that they had made a new addition to the English dramatic canon. The scholarly injustice is further compounded by G. E. Bentley, in *The Jacobean and Caroline Stage* (Oxford, 1941–1956), VII, 60, where the *Harvard Library Bulletin* article is routinely cited as the source for the discovery.

tion was not attempted again until 1633. This time the queen played the lead in Walter Montagu's *Shepheard's Paradise,* a drama of Neo-Platonic love that took almost eight hours to perform and evidently both baffled its audience and bored them to tears. A few weeks later William Prynne's *Histrio-Mastix* was published, with the famous index entry, "Women-Actors, notorious whores." Though Prynne claimed this was not intended as a slur on the queen, a reader aware of the royal theatricals could hardly have drawn polite conclusions. Prynne was tried in the Star Chamber on a charge not of libel but of high treason; he was convicted and fined £5,000, sentenced to life imprisonment, disbarred and expelled from Lincoln's Inn, pilloried, deprived of his academic degree; and his ears were cut off by the public executioner. *Histrio-Mastix* is an exercise in sheer lunacy, and the fact that both courtly and Puritan readers took it seriously is a measure of the importance of theater to the life of the time. Charles and Henrietta Maria set as great store by their plays as Prynne did by his principles; the loss of Prynne's ears and livelihood did not seem to the court too severe a penalty for attacking the royal charades, nor did it seem to the Puritans a punishment suffered in a trifling cause. In a very profound way the theatrical medium was the king's and queen's truest realm. Charles fashioned a heroic world for himself in the increasingly ambitious masques that Inigo Jones annually created, while Henrietta Maria presented, through Jones, complementary pastoral retreats where love and chastity gained their divine rewards in the harmony of marriage and peace.

The third and last of the queen's pastoral dramas was presented in 1635, the year following the crown's victory over Prynne. It was an anonymous French play called *Florimène;* the performers were the queen's French ladies, and the production was by Inigo Jones. There is some evidence that it was originally planned for the king's birthday, 19 November,[2] but it was in fact not given until 21 December. Henrietta Maria, who was within a week of the birth of her daughter Elizabeth, was present with the king, but did not take a part; nevertheless, the Caroline monarchs were at the center of the entertainment. The queen's pastorals, like her interest in Neo-Platonism, have regularly been dismissed by modern critics as flippant and irrelevant, mere courtly games. But if we consider them in their historical context, we shall see them as

2. See Bentley, *Jacobean and Caroline Stage,* VII, 99.

important indices to the royal will. These are the years of prerogative rule, and the queen's philosophy is a political assertion exactly consonant with, and indeed implied by, the king's absolute monarchy. About the queen revolved all passion, controlled and idealized by her Platonic beauty and virtue, as about the king revolved all intellect and will. This may be poetry, but in the world of Caroline England it was also politics.

The text of *Florimène* has not survived, but an English summary of the play was licensed by Sir Henry Herbert on 14 December, 1635, and published before the end of the year. In addition, a curious addendum to the play has been preserved. The Huntington Library owns an apparently unique copy of a pamphlet entitled *The Ante-Masques,* by Aurelian Townshend.[3] Hitherto unidentified, it is the text of a tiny comic epilogue to *Florimène,* which served to conclude the queen's elegant French pastoral with a courtly version of an English jig. The identification of the piece rests on clear internal evidence. Both line 46 and the conclusion suggest that the work was performed in the presence of the king and queen; it followed a production given by French ladies who played shepherdesses (ll. 51–54), the plot of which involved four couples (l. 62), disguises including changes of sex (ll. 15–18, 71–72), marriages arranged by a deity (ll. 81–82), and information imparted by Fame (l. 65). This does not fit the plots of either *L'Artenice* or *The Shepheard's Paradise,* and the latter, moreover, did not have a French cast. But the 1635 pastoral fills the bill precisely, even to the appearance of Fame, who speaks the prologue.

Both the Argument of *Florimène* and Townshend's *Ante-Masques* are here reprinted for the first time. They are discussed in fuller detail in the forthcoming *Inigo Jones,* by Stephen Orgel and Roy Strong, which includes reproductions of all the designs for the staging of the entertainment.

I

THE ARGUMENT / Of the PASTORALL of *Florimene* / with the Discription of the / Scoenes and Intermedii. //

3. The text consists of five printed pages without title page or colophon, but with a decorative border at the beginning. It is described by Bentley, *ibid.,* V. 1231.

PRESENTED BY THE / Queenes MAJESTIES Command- / ment, before the Kings Majesty in the / Hall at White-hall, on s. THOMAS / day the 21. of *December*. / *M.DC.XXXV.* // LONDON : / Printed for *Thomas Walkley*, neere / White-hall. 1635

The names of the Persons in this Pastorall.
Florimene a shepheardesse.
Filene, a shepheard of *Arcadia,* disguised in the habite of a Woman, cals himselfe *Dorine,* in Love with *Florimene.*
Anfrize, a shepheard in love with *Florimene.*
Lucinde, a shepheardesse in Love with *Aristee.*
Aristee, a shepheard, brother to *Florimene,* in Love with the faigned *Dorine.*
Lycoris a shepheardesse of *Arcadia,* disguised in the habite of a Man, in Love with *Filene.*
Florelle a shepheardesse, friend to *Florimene.*
Damon a shepheard, Friend to *Filene.*
Filandre a shepheard, Friend to *Anfrize.*
Diana, a Goddesse.
Clarice, Diana's Nymph.

THE DESCRIPTION OF the Scœne.
The Ornament inclosing the Scœne, was made of a Pastorall invention, proper to the subject, with a figure sitting on each side, representing a noble shepheard and shepheardesse, playing on Rurall instruments, over them Garlands held up by naked Boyes, as the prize of their Victory.

Above all, ranne a large Freese, and in it children in severall postures, imitating the Pastorall Rights and sacrifices, in the midst was placed a rich compartment, in which was written *FLORIMENE.*

The curtaine being drawne up, the *Scœne* was discovered, consisting of Groves, Hills, Plaines, and here and there scattering, some shepheards cottages, and a far off, to terminate the sight, was the mayne *Sea,* expressing this place to be the Isle of *Delos.*

Fame enters and speaks the Prologue to his MAJESTY.

Should I appeare holding, etc.

Exit *Fame.*

The Introduction.

The Scœne changeth into a stately Temple, with a Portico of two rowes of Collumnes, and in the midst on a Pedestall was raised the Statue of *Diana,* unto whom this Temple was dedicated.

The Musicke enters, representing the Priests of *Diana,* with the Arch Flamine and Sacrificers, who sing this Song.

Solue du Solier[4] *Honneur, etc.*

The while the Priests sings, the high Priest passeth betweene them, and goeth into the Temple, all the Shepheards and Shepheardesses present their offrings to *Diana,* after which is sung this song.

Fny devant nostre solicl,[5] *ctc.*

The Scœne returnes to the Isle of *Delos.*

Actus I. Scœna prima.

Damon a Shepheard, dwelling in the Isle of *Delos,* having visited *Filene* a young shepheard, one of his intimate Friends, living in *Arcadia,* perswadeth *Filene* to go with him into his Countrey of *Delos,* to see the solemnity which by the shepheards and shepheardesses, were to be celebrated in honour of *Diana;* and beeing there arrived, *Damon* conducted him to the Temple, where after *Filene* had wel considered the beauty of all the shepheardesses, fell deepely in Love with *Florimene:* Hee findes his Friend *Damon,* and tels him of his new flame, which having never felt before, desires his helpe to ease his passion. *Damon* promiseth him all favourable assistance: hee knowing best the humor of *Florimene,* beeing his Kinswoman, and his sister *Florelle* her daily Companion, hee perswades *Filene* to disguise himselfe in the habit of a woman, and call his name *Dorine,* and promiseth him that his sister *Florelle* shall bring him to see *Florimene,* to which *Filene* consenting, they go to finde out *Florelle.*

4. ? Salut au soleil
5. ? Icy devant nostre soleil

Scœna 2.

Anfrize comes foorth with his Friend *Filandre,* to whom he recounteth how much the beauty of *Florimene* had ravished his senses, and that hee can no longer live without expressing his affection to her: *Filandre* who beeing free from the passions of Love, counsels him to leave that fond inclination; but seeing hee could not divert him, promiseth to treat with *Florimene's* friends to that purpose: *Anfrize* satisfied with that promise, gives him thanks, and then goes forth.

Scœna 3.

Florimene being yet free from any touch of Love, comes to seeke some sollitary place, where she might entertaine her selfe with the pleasure of her free thoughts: thither *Damon* and his sister *Florelle* immediately come, and espying *Florimene, Damon* sends his sister to her to speake in favour of *Filene,* who at that time was at her house, disguising himselfe in the habite of a woman: *Florelle* comes to *Florimene,* and tels her there was a young Shepheardesse, lately come from an neighbouring Iland, to see the celebration of the great feast which was prepared in honour of *Diana,* and that if shee pleased to see her, she should finde her a Shepheardesse accomplished in all perfections: *Florimene* desirous to see her; *Florelle* willed her to stay at that Fountaine, whilst she fetcheth the strange Shepheardesse.

Scœna 4.

Aristee a shepheard of the Ile of *Delos,* is followed by *Lucinde* a young shepheardesse, passionately in love with him, she tels him the paine she suffers by his unkindnesse, but hee contemnes her, and leaves her to her plaints. *Lucinde* seeing her selfe dispised, yet takes courage, and resolves the more *Aristee* disdaines her, the more she wil follow him, hoping in the end he will love her, for her constancy.

The first Intermedium.

The *Scœne* is changed into a snowy Land-schipe with leave-lesse trees, and a dusky skie, and here and there some houses for shelter, expressing the Winter.

Winter *Enters.*

An old Man, and sings some French Verses in prayse of the King: after him followes foure old Men leaning upon their staves; in habits of the old fashion. They dance, and so goe off.

Actus 2. *Scœna* 1.
The Scœne, the Isle *of* Delos.
Diana *discends in her Chariot.*

Diana out of her affection to the Inhabitants of *Delos,* having left the Heaven, and discended unto the Earth, to take the pleasures of hunting, to which effect she called one of her Nymphs to follow her in that exercise.

Scœna 2.

Florimene sitting at the Fountaine, thinkes that *Florelle* stayes too long; but seeing her comming with the young shepheardesse (which was the disguised *Filene*) hindred her further reprehension: *Florimene* seemeth well pleased with the acquaintance of *Dorine,* and *Dorine* much joyed to bee in the presence of *Florimene.* Their salutations being past, *Dorine* speaketh with *Florelle,* imbracing her with great joy; *Florelle* desires her not to shewe her selfe to be transported, least *Florimene* might suspect some thing: after many complements passed on both sides, *Florimene* desires *Dorine* not to take it unkindly, If she leave her company so soone, and prayes her to be excused because it is late, and desires her to continue the affection professed to her, and promises to meet her in the same place the next day, to have the honour of her conversation; and so goes out: *Dorine* sayes to *Florelle,* they must goe seeke *Damon,* to tell him of their successe.

Scœna 3.

Aristee brother to *Florimene,* beeing hidden behind a Bush, the whilst his sister and *Dorine* speake together, and taking *Dorine* for a woman, fals in Love with her; and to the end hee may discover his passion to her, hee resolves to be there the next day in the same place, and goes his way.

Scœna 4.

Anfrize meeting with his friend *Filandre,* demaunds of him what hee hath done, who answeres him, that it is not in his power to perswade *Florimene* from her cruelty, but seeing how much paynes *Anfrize* suffred; he tels him of a young shepheardesse which lodges at *Damons* house, who is so much in the good opinion of *Florimene,* as he beleeves shee can perswade her to bee more gracious unto him, if he doe entreate her, to speake for him. *Anfrize* assuring himselfe of the curtesie of that shepheardesse,[6] goes to attempt that way.

Scœna 5.

Licoris a shepheardesse in love, and disdained of *Filene* puts her selfe into mans apparrell, and resolves never to leave him, untill she perswades him to love her.

The second Intermedium.

The Scœne is varied, and there appeares a spacious Garden, with walkes, perterraes, close Arbours, and Cypresse trees, and in the farthest part stands a delicious Villa, all which figureth the spring.

The Spring enters.

And sings, after which enters three young couple of men and maids, they dance and so retyre.

Actus 3. Scœna 1.
The Sceane; the Isle of Delos.

Damon having met with the fained *Dorine,* doth congratulate with him of the good successe which his disguise had procured him with his Mistresse, and Councels him to loose no time, but discover unto *Florimene* the affection he beares her: *Filene* having dissigned to follow his Councell, tels him that a young shepheard, called *Anfrize,* taking him for a woman, hath intreated him to speake to *Florimene* in his behalfe, and under the pretext of speaking for another, hee hopes to dispose the thoughts of *Florimene,* so well as to bring her to taste the power of

6. shephearnesse Q

love; he entreateth *Damon* not to leave him, for his presence would imbolden him to entertaine *Florimene* with that subject, who presently comes in.

Scœna 2.

Florimene seeing *Dorine* and *Damon* together, said to *Damon,* that without doubt, he was in love with *Dorine,* and that she judged so by his melancholy countenance: *Damon* marvailes to here her speake of love, which had alway so much disdayned it: *Florimene* answered, that love being a trouble to the thoughts, and a depriving of liberty, shee hated the very name of love: *Dorine* taking her at that word, answered, that all things created had their being, and their contentments from love, and then tels her of the great affection which *Anfrize* had borne her, and seeing her well disposed to here her discourse of him, she continues to speak further in his favour, until she was interrupted by *Anfrize,* who comes in.

Scœna 3.

Anfrize seeing *Florimene,* kneeles downe, and desires her to heare him, he tels her of the great paines, hee hath long suffered for her, which he never durst presume to tell her, untill now: *Florimene* having heard him speake, shewed her selfe to bee very sencible of his paines, and tels him hee may hope to be rewarded for his long sufferance, and the more to assure him of her inclination to love, she invites him to sit downe by her under those Elmes, and *Dorine* to come with her, who stayes behinde a while, exclaiming against fortune, and blaming her owne tongue, for having so well spoken for her rivall: But resolves to be revenged on *Anfrize* if he leaves not the love of *Florimene.*

Scœna 4.

Aristee comes to finde *Dorine,* whom hee verily beleeves to be a woman, and speakes to her of the love he bares her, and as shee refuseth him, *Lucinde* who is in love, but scorned by *Aristee,* comes in; who seeing him thus rejected by *Dorine* rejoyceth to see him punished in the same kinde as he disdained her: *Dorine* being troubled with *Aristees* importunity, goes her way: And *Lucinde* not able to perswade *Aristee* to love her, leaves the place: *Aristee* resolves to gaine the love of *Dorine,* and purposes to put on his sister *Florimenes* clothes, unto whom he is very like, and being dressed like a woman, may be taken for her, hoping by that meanes to sound the thoughts of *Dorine.*

Scœna 5.

Clarice a young Nymph comes to seeke *Diana,* whom she thinkes to be in the woods, she discourses of the pleasure of hunting, and the discontentments suffered by lovers.

The third Intermedium.

The Scœne is turned into fields of Corne, meddowes with Hay-cocks, and shady woods, shewing a prospect of Summer.

Ceres enters

Representing Summer, and sings, after her enters five reapers, having sickles in the one hand, and ripe corne in the other: they dance and then go forth.

Actus 4. Scœna 1.
The Scœne the Isle of Delos.

Dorine comes to look for *Florimene,* to the end she may tell her who she is, and discover her passions unto her; but shee is met by

Scœna 2.

Aristee, apparrelled in his sister *Florimenes* clothes, and he is so like her, as *Dorine* takes him for *Florimene,* and in that beleefe, discovers unto him that she loves *Florimene,* which hath beene the cause of her disguise: *Aristee* astonished to heere that *Dorine* is a man, goes his way without more speech, *Dorine* seeing himselfe unkindely used: goes forth.

Scœna 3.

Aristee coms in againe, much confused in knowing *Dorine* to be a man, and now repents him of his disdaine to *Lucinde,* and goes away with a resolution to seeke her out, and to tell all the world of the Imposture of *Filene.*

Scœna 4.

Licoris a shepheardesse of *Arcadia* who loved *Filene* having taken the habit of a shepheard persevering in her love to him, and perceiving *Lucinde* to complaine of the ingratitude of her lover *Aristee,* she coms neere her; and asks her if she knows Filene, and tels her he is his elder brother; *Lucinde* saies if he be in that Countrey, he wil not faile to come to that Fountaine, where all the shepheards do use to meete, and having well beheld *Lycoris* taking her for a man, fals in love with him, and presently began to discover her affection, but *Lycoris* not willing to abuse her, tels her the cause of her disguise, *Lucinde* hearing that *Lycoris* was a maide, is ashamed, and went her waies, and *Lycoris* goes forth to looke for *Filene.*

Scœna 5.

Anfrize and *Filandre* speake together of the disguise of *Filene: Anfrize* feares that when *Filene* shall discover himselfe, and askes pardon of *Florimene,* she will forgive *Filene,* and disgrace him; and therfore to hinder that misfortune, he desires *Filandre,* as his friend, to doe his best to keepe him in his mistresse grace.

Scœna 6.

Florimene comes and knowing the desccit of *Filene,* complains of *Florelle* that she did unkindly in not discovering unto her his disguise, being as shee conceives impossible, but she should know it, and forbids *Florelle* ever to speake any more of him to her. The meane while *Lycoris* who heard all that was said of *Filene,* was ravished with joy, and comes neere to *Florimene,* and tels her what she is, and that her love to *Filene,* caused her to leave her owne Countrey of *Arcadia,* and desires *Florimene* to speake to *Filene* in favour of her who so much loves him, the which *Florimene* promises, and *Filene* comes in.

Scœna 7.

Filene tels *Damon,* that he is much griev'd that his disguise is discovered to *Florimene,* not knowing how to remedy what is passed: hee desires *Damon* to councel him; *Damon* adviseth him to speak to *Florimene* himselfe, and humbly aske her pardon, which he doubts not but he may obtaine; in the meane time *Lycoris* drawes neere, and makes knowne to him the great paines which she hath long endured for him, and desires him to have pitty on her. *Filene* saies the same to *Florimene,* and kneeling downe, desires her pardon for his fault, and to have pitty of his long sufferance. But *Florimene* will by no meanes heare him speake, but goes away with *Florelle;* that suddaine departure, put *Filene* into despairation; *Damon* seeks by perswasions to appease him; and *Lycoris* speaks to him againe of her love; but *Filene* wil not give her any hope of his affection, untill she can obtaine his pardon of *Florimene:* *Lycoris* promises him to doe what she can possible, and goes her way: *Damon* still comforts *Filene* with fresh hope: they goe forth.

Scœna 8.

Florelle shews unto *Florimene* the misery of *Filene,* whom she hath put unto despairation, *Florimene* beginning to relent; confesses she never hated *Filene,* but hath alwaies affected him; wherefore she desires *Florelle* to goe with her to *Dianes* Temple, to pray the goddesse that she may enjoy his love.

Scœna 9.

Aristee meeting with *Lucinde* desires him to forgive him his neglect of her love; praying her now to accept him as her servant: But *Lucinde* rejects him, and saith that she cannot now love him, and so goes away; but hee stil followes her, desiring her to have pitty on him.

The fourth Intermedium.

This Scœne becomes Hills of easie ascent, set all with Vines, the trees and verdures, seeming somewhat faded, and in some parts are placed those vessels fit for vintage, to expresse the propriety of *Autumne.*

Bacchus Enters.

Representing *Autumne,* supported by two *Satyres* and followed by two *Sileni,* they sing; after them enter three boone Companions; the first attir'd like a *Dutch-man,* having a bottle in his hand; the second like a *Souldier,* with a Tobacco pipe and *Bolonia* Sausages; the third drest in a Fantasticall habite, with a Gammon of Bacon, and other provision tyed in a Napkin; they dance, and then sit downe to their

Colation: When on the suddain, foure *Satyres* come leaping in, at which affrighted, they runne away, leaving their Victuals behinde them; the *Satyres* strive for the Bottle, and then drinke one to the other, till being heate with Wine, they dance with wanton Action, and so fal downe a sleep: whilst they sleep, the *Dutch-man* and the rest come softly in, and steale away the Bottle of Wine, and their Meate.

Pan enters and dances, then awake the *Satyres;* they kneele to *Pan,* as craving pardon; they dance about him, and carry him out.

Actus 3. *Scœna* 1.

The Temple of Diana appeares varied from the first; for no Scœne but that of the Pastoral was twice seene.

Florimene being now enamour'd of *Filene,* confesses her errour in refusing the love of such an accomplished shepheard, resolving that when she sees him, she will make knowne unto him how much she loves him, whereupon *Lycoris* enters.

Scœna 2.

Lycoris comes forth to *Florimene,* and as much as shee may with modesty, desires her to admit *Filene* to see her, and speake with her, at first *Florimene* seemes to refuse her, but in the end she consents, and at that instant *Filene* comes in: *Lycoris* goes to him, and tels him that she had obtained of *Florimene* to heare him speake: so *Lycoris* goes her way, fearing to heare him protest more love to *Florimene* then she desires to know.

Scœna 3.

Filene approaching neere to *Florimene,* prostrates himselfe at her feete, desiring her pardon, which *Florimene* willingly grants him, and moreover promises him ever hereafter to love him; and that the jealousie of *Anfrize,* had beene the cause of her discourtesie towards him: *Filene* ravish'd with joy, to finde himselfe beloved of his Mistresse, gives thankes to the Gods, that his disguise had brought his dessignes to so good effect. During this discourse, *Filandre* being hidden, heares all their talke, and goes to tell his friend *Anfrize,* who presently comes in, in great fury, to reproach *Florimene* of her inconstancy, just as *Florimene* and *Filene* were giving assurance to one another of their mutuall affections.

Scœna 4.

Anfrize seeing *Filene* so neere to *Florimene,* begins to quarrell with him, but *Filene* answered him so, that *Anfrize* became extreame furious, and passing the bonds of civell respect, would have killed him with his dart, if *Florimene* had not hindered him with her sheepe-hooke, telling him that for this indiscretion, he must never pretend any part in her affection. *Anfrize* kneeles downe before her, and desires her to excuse him, and that she would be pleased to remember that he was the first that had the honor to love her, *Filene* kneeling downe, sayes as much for himselfe: But *Florimene* tels them both, they must goe to the Temple of *Diana,* and there pray *Diana* to declare which of them her deity would appoint to be her husband, which she promises not to refuse after sentence given by the goddesse: when they are gone she prayes her selfe to *Diana,* that shee may enjoy *Filene.*

Scœna 5.

Aristee continueth his pursuite of *Lucinde,* who still contemnes him: *Lycoris* comes in to looke for *Filene: Aristee* comes to her, and prayes her to speak to *Lucinde* in his favour; but *Lycoris* could obtaine nothing of her more then himselfe. The meane while they are interrupted by the comming of the goddesse *Diana,* who enters, and they all kneele downe.

Scœna 6.

Diana commands *Lucinde* to love *Aristee,* and to take him for her husband, and then tels *Lycoris,* that *Filene* is her owne brother, and that *Montan* is not her father, as shee hath ever beleeved, but that he tooke her from *Orcan,* which had saved her from the cruelty of a Satyre, which stole her from her Father *Tytire* in *Arcadia: Diana* having ended her discourse, sees *Filene* and *Anfrize,*

Scœna 7.

Who came to make their request to *Diana,* as *Florimene* commanded them, *Diana* bid *Anfrize* speake first, who having recounted al his wealth and riches, which he more presumed on then all other reasons, that he could alledge for his marrying of *Florimene:* then *Diana* commands *Filene* to speake, who could not vaunt of his riches, but saith, hee had onely his vertue to deserve her: *Diana* pronounceth her sentence in favour of *Filene,* and gives *Lycoris* to *Anfrize* for his wife, *Florelle* who hath heard all this, wisheth that her couzen *Florimene* knew the newes, At which

Scæna 8.

Florimene appeares; *Florelle* goes to her, and tels her the sentence of *Diana,* concerning her marriage, with which *Florimene* was much joyed, she presently perceiveth *Filene* with all the other shepheards and shepheardesses standing before the Temple. *Diana* seeing *Florimene,* to confirme her joy, tels her she must have *Filene* for her husband, and commands them both to continue their affections, and bids *Anfrize* to content himselfe with that beauty which she hath appoynted for him. They all give *Diana* thanks.

Here the Heavens open, and there appeare many deities, who in their songs expresse their agreements to these marriages.

At which time the lovers and their mistresses doe protest one to another their mutual affections, and ful contentments: After which *Diana* dismisseth them.

FINIS.

II

[Decorative Border]

The Ante-Masques.

The first that enters is A Man of Canada.

From Canada, both rough, and rude,
Come I; with bare and nimble feet;
Those Amazonian Maides to greet,

Which Conquer'd them that us subdu'd: 5
        Love is so Just,
        Our Victors must
Were Chaines, as heavy as ours bee:
Fetters of Gold, make no Man free.

The second are 2. Ægyptians.

From Memphis, with Prophetick soule,
Come wee, these wonders of the West,
Within her Temple, ever Blest,
To reverence; and not controule:
        Thrice happy then,   15
        Those worthy Men,
Whom love transformes to such as They;
Tooke they their Shapes, but for a Day.

The third are 3. Pantaloones.

From Bergamo, the Antient Seat,   20
Of Zanies, and of Pantaloones,
Come we, with very little meat,
A-foot, to save a few Doubloones;
        And see those eyes,
        That did surpryse,   25
All People wheresoere they came;
For we would burne in such a flame.

The fourth are 4. Spaniards.

The Spanish Pace is ever slow;
Our looke and language alwayes Grave;   30
So when wee come, we grace a shew,
The Men we praise, are counted Brave.
        The women Chaste,
        And Angell fac't:
Light Nations value little things: 35
Our Approbation honors Kings.

A Song.

Draw neere! And let not your Condition,
Meane though it be, dismey your Harts,
Vales, have sometimes as full fruition,   40
Of the bright sunne, as higher Parts:
    And should as oft, if some proud Hill
    Cast not his shadow, on them still.

So Mountaines of the Moone deprive us,
Yet Her sweet Influence wee feele;   45
And these Great Planets both revive us,
To whom as Houshold-Gods we kneele,
    And what our poore Soyle yeelds professe,
    To pay ye backe, in Thankefulnesse.

[Decorative border]

The Subject of the Masque.   50

Not in Arcadia, but the fertile fields,
And Plains of Beauce, that such plenty yeelds,
Of fleecie Sheep, and swelling Eares of Corne,
Were these sweet flowres, of Sheperdesses borne;
As if the Soyle, which was so rich before,   55
By this addition, labor'd to bee more,
And grow an Indies; Nor doe Lovers pryse,
Dymonds so much, as their Loves sparkling Eyes:
Vertues beside, to many a Pretious Stone,
Authors ascribe, when they inherit none: 60
But these are full, by Purchase, and Descent
Finish't all fower, to the least Complement:
What Education, can to native Grace,
Any way adde, is full in every Face;
Which Fame divulging, drew these Shepherds streight,   65
Like fishes tempted by a dainty Beight,
To leape at that; And over and above,

Swallow the hooke; which hooke they say is Love;
Whose Operation, in a noble brest,
Is violent; and gives the limbes small rest.   70
So like their shadowes, they these Nymphes pursue,
Changing their Country Habits into new;
And for their sakes, could they the secret finde,
Would gladly weare the Habit of their Minde,
Tred in their steps; And in their Cabbins rest: 75
For what is neerest unto them, is best;
But ere Man may such happinesse attaine
He must drinke Lethe; And no signe remaine
Of folly in him; Or of former flame,
But in white paper write his Virgins name: 80
That done; the Deity that doth reside,
In yonder Grove, shall point One out a Bride,
So well indow'd: her Attributes will strive,
To make him thought, the happiest man alive:
The rest may pause; And without Envie stay;   85
T'is Joy enough, to Hope for such a Day.

A Pigmees Speech.

If I should tell yee whence I come,
Some I should please, and anger some,
But by my Stature, yee may see,   90
Not much above a Ladies knee;
Sometimes, they lay me in their lappes,
And give me kisses, sometimes Clappes;
And then I talke, and so doe They:
But there's an end, and come away;   95
Lords take your Ladies by the hands,
Let yours be Questions, Theirs Commands,
Bee not so nice! you'l meet anon!
When Lights are out, and people gone:
The Night is shorter now than I;   100
Loose it not all, too mannerly;
Rest would doe well, If ye can get it;

Beshrew their fingers would permit it,
Untill the Morning Clocke strike Ten;
Speake out like Clerks, and cry Amen.　　　105

My owne Excuse

To the most Magnanimous and Unanimous
KING and QUEENE.

So many are the faults I make,
In this loose Paper; that I feare,
Onely for this poore Poëms sake,
I may hereafter loose your eare:
　I would, by your Two bounties live,
　But now; If yee forgive, yee give.

AURELIAN TOUNSHEND.

The Traffic of the Stage
in Calderón's
La vida es sueño

ALAN K. G. PATERSON

C ALDERÓN'S FIRST VOLUME of printed plays, the *Primera parte* of 1636, opens with *La vida es sueño*. Surely a craftsman's pride placed it there as a brilliant herald, the risen sun of his perfected art. Yet the play embodies the accumulated experience of much past theater, his own and others', and of much past literature. Revolutionary in its boldness of emotion and significance, the play gains ascent from inherited elements recast. The following study is an attempt to uncover some of the submerged traditions upon which new art was laid. Some of these belong to a literary background of a humanistic nature, others to a more specifically dramatic one, to patterns of action and image incorporated from the repertory of Calderón's own day, and above all to the craft of acting itself. While literary models and the poetic texture of the play have received frequent attention, I hope to show that the dramatist's process of creation involved a sensitive response to the spectacular elements of theater; the vision of *La vida es sueño* is a rich one because Calderón drew the resources of its own medium into cooperation with imaginative activities which we can recognize in isolation as intellectual and poetic.

155

Calderón's use of older dramatic material has been documented and discussed by A. E. Sloman; his study suggests a dramatist whose response to tradition was of paramount importance in the creation of new theater.[1] N. D. Shergold has brought light to bear on this feature of Calderón's work from quite another angle: in all probability, he argues, *La vida es sueño* was written for a particular company of actors, that of Antonio de Prado.[2] This being so, we may then imagine how the dramatist acknowledged very practical demands of performance; the particular aptitudes and styles of a group of players were absorbed into the writing of a play. Living theater, embodied not only in the skills but in the personalities which these actors had created before their audience, provided fresh energy for a new play; between dramatist and performers there was an exchange of talents. Prado's players seem to have acquired a high level of professional identity. There is the evidence of the *loa* written for the company's 1635 season of plays, a light-hearted advertisement for themselves and also a subtle exploitation of the relationship which their professionalism had set up with audiences in the *corral*. Prado, appearing reluctant to shoulder the troubles of a new season, is shown a triumphal tree whose branches hold the members of his troupe, reunited after the Lenten break. The trunk is rooted in Prado's pockets. A second vision shows another tree, hung this time with empty moneybags; the musicians sing a popular refrain of disillusionment:

mas a la fe, compañía,
que los sueños, sueños son.[3]

The troupe's sense of professional unity comes over clearly: they are a composite family, united by complementary skills, flowers in the

1. *The Dramatic Craftsmanship of Calderón: His Use of Earlier Plays* (Oxford, 1958). All quotations from the play in this article come from Sloman's edition (Manchester, 1961).

2. "*La vida es sueño:* ses acteurs, son théâtre et son publique," in *Dramaturgie et société,* Editions du centre national de la recherche scientifique (Paris, 1968), pp. 93-109.

3. Luis Quiñones de Benavente, *Loa que representó Antonio de Prado,* in E. Cotarelo y Mori, *Colección de entremeses,* Nueva biblioteca de autores españoles, eighteen (Madrid, 1911), Tomo I, Vol. 2, pp. 515-517. For details of dating, see Shergold, *Dramaturgie et société,* p. 104, and H. E. Bergman, *Luis Quiñones de Benavente y sus entremeses* (Madrid, 1965), pp. 332-341.

Prado meadow. They act together to make their living, as any group
of craftsmen in the audience.[4] But the *loa* is more than an appeal for
their practical workaday identity to be recognized. The actors are
craftsmen of make-believe, whose workshop, the stage, is a world of
poetry and illusion. Prado's wife may have to sell a dress in order to
satisfy the rising wage demands of the employees, but she reacts by
burlesquing Góngora's sweet lament on passing time:

> Hoy sin un vestido estoy,
> y ayer con muchos me vi:
> aprended, damas, de mi
> lo que va de ayer a hoy.[5]

The dialogue is a brisk to-and-fro of literary allusion and pun; the
reluctant Prado drowses like the "convidado de piedra," observes the
gracioso Frutos Bravo; Isabel is a Góngora by name and by virtue of
her solitude; the *mosqueteros* are addressed as a collective Don Gaiferos
by a supplicant actress in distress. So the players at once introduce
themselves as part of our prosaic world, asserting their professional
cares and identities, and also shift themselves away from it, revealing
their mastery of fantasy, of a magic game in which all the cast, musicians
too, offer sparkling variety grounded in each actor's conscious knowledge
of his part within the acting craft.

There is one part in *La vida es sueño* in which the contrast and
exchange between the role and the actor, between the stage and life,
acquire a deep significance. It is the part of Clarín, played, according
to Professor Shergold, by the *gracioso* Frutos Bravo. From the *loa*,
Bravo appears to have been a clown with a speciality for theatrical
jesting. He arrives on stage out of an impressive contraption—the
bofetón—and apes an apocalyptic angel, armed with a sword and breath-
ing cosmic reproach over the sleeping Prado:

4. Prado's own sense of belonging to an established craft is attested by his role
as a signatory founder of the actors' guild formed in 1631, the *Cofradía de repre-*
sentantes. See J. Subirá, *El gremio de representantes españoles y la cofradía de*
Nuestra Señora de la Novena (Madrid, 1960), p. 42.

5. Luis Quiñones de Benavente, *Loa*, p. 516b. Compare with Góngora's *letrilla*,
"Aprended, Flores, de mí," ed. R. Jammes in *Don Luis de Góngora: Letrillas*
(Paris, 1963), p. 18, and also with Góngora's other delicate poem on loss, "La más
bella niña," in Millé's *Obras completas* (Madrid, 1961), p. 43.

O eres racional camello,
o eres tizón de la esfera,
o eres epacta de jaspe,
o el convidado de piedra.
Sacude dormitaciones
y con lo que representas
crujan los ejes coluros,
gima esa máquina arteria.

PRADO

No lo entiendo.

FRUTOS

Yo tampoco.

Frutos Bravo presents the two fantastic visions and departs at the end to tidy up his appearance, as he tells us, presumably for the next performance. Frutos' humor is consciously histrionic; his exaggerations are born of the boards, exaggerations which he confronts and exposes with a nod and a wink toward the tiring room. Clarín's role offers a parallel. The character's discourse is fashioned from his actor's profession; he copes with complexity by reducing it to an entertainer's terms. His reaction to the clank of Segismundo's chains ("Cadenita hay que suena") suggests a knowing glance toward the off-stage box of effects. Threatened by Clotaldo, he reduces himself to something in between Humility and Pride, a role which is a non-role and whose genesis he explains:

Y si humildad y soberbia
no te obligan, personajes
que han movido y removido
mil autos sacramentales, . . .

(I, ll. 347–350)

The Tower jailers, their faces covered, erupt on stage and Clarín greets the masquers' arrival ("¿Enmascaraditos hay?"). The endearing diminutive, as before, is the clown's comfort in the face of peril; these hooded fellows are only part of theatrical business. When he presents himself at Court, here was a spectacle, Clarín declares, that had no need of an admission ticket; his own eyes are better boxes from which to view. Mistaken for Segismundo in Act III, he assumes the role with a shrug:

fuerza es hacer mi papel.

A novel twist is given to this type of jesting when the banter turns
clearly toward Calderón himself, as Clarín outrageously parodies, by
dint of exaggeration and a note of apology ("perdóname"), his author's
elemental horse, a verbal icon which by 1635 must have been established
as one of the dramatist's favorites.[6] Clarín is an actor of many parts,
taking his cue from circumstances; or he assumes no part at all, as
when he opts out of battle and hides behind a rock, pulling faces at
Death:

> que yo, apartado este día,
> haré el papel de Nerón
> que de nada se dolía.
> Si bien me quiero doler
> de algo, y ha de ser de mí;
> escondido, desde aquí
> toda la fiesta he de ver.

(ll. 3047–3053)

Such humor, which reaches far into the play's meaning, called upon
a clown who was alert to the relevance of his fooling and conscious
of his role as a serious trifler. As he dissociates within himself the
actor from his role, or as he annotates the action as if he were a mere
bystander at another's play, he presents an ironic, diminishing analogy
to the greater drama of Basilio, the king whose kingly role led him
to deny a father's love, and of Segismundo, the prince who has been
stripped of his part and relegated to playing a non-role in the Tower.
As we shall see, Clarín's sustained awareness that life is acting links
up with the master phrase of the play, "la vida es sueño."

Besides this, Clarín is haunted by Fortune. In his nightmare in the
Tower, flagellants rise and fall, like kings on Fortune's wheel, (ll. 2204–
2212); there, too, he shuffles the cards with Death,

si me da, o no me da.

We are reminded of Garzoni's well-known register of folly, *The Hospital
of Incurable Fools,* in which Dame Folly is introduced as the beneficiary
of Madam Fortune.[7] As he commutes part for part, Clarín bears out

---

6. Ll. 2672–2687. Sloman suggests a parodic element.

7. The preface reads: "To the good old Gentlewoman, and her special Benefac-

this traditional relationship between the fool and Fortune, which is consummated by the chance bullet that prizes him from his hiding place on the battlefield; whereupon the world of the fallen fool, governed by chance, confronts that of the falling king, who as he tried to govern the unpredictable came himself under the unstable sway of an illusion.

Here, there is complete unity between the fool and the play. Clarín's style of wit is close to the humor of the 1635 *loa,* which depends on the players' artful exploitation of their own professional ambiguity between reality and illusion. Calderón has grasped that mode of humorous discourse and threaded it into the weave of *La vida es sueño.*

The opening scenes of the play have an imaginative thrust from which familiarity hardly detracts. The play bursts into sudden life, magical in its tone and setting. The spell has been borrowed from high romance, quickened by an exuberant theatrical fantasy. Rosaura descends from the upper stage, dressed as a man. She curses her untrustworthy horse, a violent hippogriff. Her allusion to the fickle flying horse of Ariosto's *Orlando furioso* not only evokes a mood but imparts Rosaura's identity: the glamorous heroine engaged on an amorous quest in foreign parts, loyal yet shrouded in confusion.[8] The atmosphere

---

tresse, Madam Fortune, Dame Folly (Matron of the Hospitall) makes curtesie, and speaks as followeth." Of the thirty kinds of fools noted by Garzoni, Clarín possibly fits into the twenty-first category, "scoffing fooles" who make merry the world and play the sedulous ape: "These be they that sweepe the courts of Princes and great men." I have quoted from the English version, *The Hospitall of Incurable Fooles* (London, 1600).

8. The obvious evocation of the romantic epic has been glossed over in the effort to invest the animal with moral-symbolic meaning. Valbuena Briones initiated the fashion: "El caballo representa los instintos pasionales que agitan el pensamiento, primordialmente el apetito carnal y el orgullo. El jinete es la facultad razonadora que puede dirigir y frenar esas tendencias. La caída o la estampida significan la pérdida del gobierno de la pasión" ("El simbolismo en el teatro de Calderón," *RF,* LXXIV [1962], 61). Margarit S. Maurin followed this theme through, seeing "no mere horse" but a symbol of Segismundo himself ("The Monster, the Sepulchre and the Dark: Related Patterns of Imagery in *La vida es sueño,*" *HR,* XXXV [1967], 164). Cesáreo Bandera settles for the horse's symbolic status as "la pasión sexual" in "El itinerario de Segismundo en *La vida es sueño,*" *HR,* XXXV (1967), 71. Wild horses (without wings, I suspect) had of course emblematic associations with unreason; see E. Panofsky's discussion of Dürer's *Large Horse*

of romance intensifies; in the twilight, a dark tower appears at the foot of crags. In spirit, the travelers are moving through the deadly labyrinth that guards the Fata Morgana's keep with its imprisoned paladins, or is it the fortress garden of Falerina? It is of no matter; atmosphere and expectations count. Rhetoric, setting, and Rosaura's transvestite appearance work like a catalyst on the audience's memories of glittering romance and mystery. Chevalier describes the residual material of the *Orlando* as being, by Calderón's time, "un très vague canevas," neither too much nor too little.[9] At the same time, within this fantasy, a different reference can be detected, one that is owing to the old tradition of the multiple stage with its symbolic levels of heaven, earth, and hell. Rosaura's descent from above is an emblematic journey to Hell; she falls from the mountaintop whose forehead burns in the sun to a pitiless desert down to the very mouth of Hell ("la funesta boca") within which night is engendered. The stage movement recalls a traditional moral architecture whose Fall significance is caught and pointed in poetry. Whereupon romantic fantasy and Christian association are shifted aside; fanciful mystery gives way to moving human agony and the traditional sinners' Inferno becomes the inner hell of Segismundo's torment. Old literature has been transformed into something new and poignant.

Segismundo, chained and dressed in skins, emerges from the inner stage, where the guttering light which had first announced his presence images reason entrenched within dark confusion. The progress of his monologue through the three elements of air, earth, and water, the scheme closing with the fire of Segismundo's passion for freedom, leads through order to a misery that contradicts order:

---

and *Small Horse* in *The Life and Art of Albrecht Dürer* (Princeton, N.J., 1955), p. 88. But let us not forget that the flying horse's home stable is the *Orlando*, an allusion carried forward, at the level of names to begin with, by the introduction of Clotaldo (a later addition to the Ariostan paladins, appearing in Nicolás Espinosa's *La segunda parte de Orlando* [Zaragoza, 1555]), and by, of course, Astolfo. In the *comedia*, the persistent tone of many reworkings of the *Orlando furioso* was one of light mockery, not absent in Calderón's treatment of the underplot characters; see M. Chevalier, *L'Arioste en Espagne* (Bordeaux, 1966), Part II, chap. III, *passim*.

9. Chevalier, *L'Arioste en Espagne*, p. 426.

¿Qué ley, justicia o razón
negar a los hombres sabe
privilegio tan süave,
excepción tan principal,
que Dios le ha dado a un cristal,
a un pez, a un bruto y a un ave?

(ll. 167–172)

The notion of cosmic order and the degree to which each verbal icon
contributes enlarges the scope of Segismundo's alienation; he is estranged
not from freedom alone but also from love. In his view from the
Tower of the unrestrained world beyond, the Prince has learned of
Nature's *piedad* and felt the lure of freedom. Denied of both, he
would willingly turn against himself and ravage his own heart. It is
strange to consider that this intense expression of anguish is built
largely out of borrowed material; the image of the chain, of the self-
pitying man, together with the progress of his reasoning are formed
from Pliny's sober discourse on man as the disinherited creature within
nature (quoted here in the robust translation by Jerónimo de Huerta
of 1624):

Sólo al hombre ha hecho [la naturaleza] desnudo, y en tierra desnuda, y
el día que nace comiença a habitarla con quexido y llanto. En ningún otro
animal ay lágrimas, sino en el hombre, y estas luego en el principio de su
vida. Las fieras y animales que nacen entre nosotros quedan libres en naciendo,
y sueltos todos los miembros; pero el hombre infelizmente nacido llorando
está caydo, ligado de pies y manos, siendo animal que ha de mandar a los
demás; y como por mal agüero comiença su vida por prisiones y castigos, y no
por otra culpa, sino por auer nacido . . . Los otros animales conocen su
naturaleza: y assi unos exercitan el correr, otros volar en alto, otros usar de
sus fuerças, otros nadar: pero el hombre ninguna cosa sabe sin ser ense-
ñado . . .[10]

This borrowing is only an opening phase to the appropriation and
adaptation of antique material; by a dazzling stroke of imagination,
Calderón saw, I believe, the possibility of merging Pliny's bleak assertion
with an even more ancient tale, of theatrical stock, the myth of the
Titan Prometheus. From the conflation and reformation of these two
elements, the core of *La vida es sueño* was formed.

10. *Historia natural de Cayo Plinio segundo traducida por el licenciado Ge-
ronimo de Huerta* (Madrid, 1624), Book VII, Prelude.

I am not saying that Calderón necessarily knew the *Prometheus Bound* of Aeschylus, though there are echoes between the two plays. Prometheus, chained at the command of Zeus to a crag in the wild Caucasus, laments before the winged daughters of Oceanus over his exclusion from the pity of men and of the father of the gods. Suffering makes him eat his heart out. Segismundo, chained within the Tower in Poland's wilderness, yearns for pity before the listening Rosaura (borne before him on the wings of the hippogriff). He would as lief tear his heart from his chest. A line can be drawn plausibly between these two great peaks of European theater. But to trace it aright, we must follow the course of Prometheus down into the tangles of humanist exegesis.

Having fashioned the statue of man from mud, Prometheus was carried to heaven by Minerva, where he stole a brand from the wheel of the chariot of the sun. Zeus had the Titan chained to a mountain as a punishment; there, his heart was to be devoured eternally by an eagle. The exegetical views of the mythographers are diverse. There is Boccaccio's euhemeristic interpretation, whereby Prometheus, Japhet's heir, was

absorbed as a youth by the sweetness of learning, and abandoned his children to the care of his brother Epimetheus. He went away to Assyria. After listening to famous Chaldeans, he ascended to the summit of Caucasus where he meditated long over and acquired insight into the course of the stars, the nature of the thunderbolts, the causes of many things. He returned to the Assyrians, and taught them astrology, and the meaning of lightning, and the customs of civilized men, of which they were utterly ignorant; for until then men had been rude and savage, living like wild beasts. Prometheus left them civilized, as though formed anew.[11]

Prometheus was the sage (the *homo doctus*) who changed natural man (*homo naturalis*) into civilized man (*homo civilis*). Natalis Conti put the latter idea more colorfully: "Prometheus called men from the forest to a life in the city, built houses for them, formed their language, and taught them the science of the stars . . ." Prometheus, Conti adds, signifies Forethought.[12] According to both mythographers, the imprison-

11. *Genealogiae deorum gentilium libri quindecim* (Venice, 1472), Book 4, chap. xliv, fols. 66ᵛ–67ᵛ (my translation).

12. *Natalis Comitis mythologiae sive explicationum fabularum libri decem* (Ven-

ment in the Caucasus stands for the sage's solitude, and his torture by the eagle signifies his arduous labor for truth. It was Ficino who synthesized such fragments into an influential psychology of thought in the *Quaestiones quinque de mente,* a Neo-Platonic meditation communicated to his pupils from Mount Cellano, Promethean-wise. As reason seeks its right end, which is the true and the good, Ficino states, it is deterred by the senses; either it finds what it would rather not, or does not find what it would. Man is the most perfect of animals, for he can aspire to perfect knowledge; for that reason he is the most imperfect, unable to reach the ultimate perfection toward which he is privileged to aspire:

Nothing indeed can be imagined more unreasonable than that man, who through reason is the most perfect of all animals, nay, of all things under heaven, most perfect, I say, with regard to that formal perfection for the sake of which the first perfection is given. This seems to be that most unfortunate Prometheus. Instructed by the divine wisdom of Pallas, he gained possession of the heavenly fire, that is, reason. Because of this very possession, on the highest peak of the mountain, that is, at the very height of contemplation, he is rightly judged the most miserable of all, for he is made wretched by the continual gnawing of the most ravenous of vultures, that is, by the torment of enquiry. This will be the case, until the time comes when he is carried back to that same place from which he received the fire, so that, just as now he is urged on to seek the whole by that one beam of celestial light, he will then be entirely filled with the whole light.[13]

Here the Promethean myth has entered the Renaissance as its flattering symbol of philosophical inquiry and the willing act of self-sacrifice in exchange for knowledge. Whatever its ancient significance, the classical myth gives shape to a thoroughly Renaissance concept of mind and civilization.

Brilliantly, Calderón freed the imaginative hoard shut up within the mythographers' handbooks. Their motley Prometheus simply divides

---

ice, 1568), Book 4, chap. vi. "Est autem Prometheus . . . mens quae res futuras multo ante praevidet," fol. 100ᵛ. Olga Raggio's survey, "The Myth of Prometheus: Its Survival and Metamorphosis up to the Eighteenth Century," *JWCI,* XXI (1958), pp. 44–62, is very useful.

13. "Five Questions Concerning Mind," trans. J. L. Burroughs, in *The Renaissance Philosophy of Man,* ed. E. Cassirer, P. O. Kristeller, and J. H. Randall, Jr. (Chicago, 1969), p. 208.

into two, a Basilio and a Segismundo. Within Basilio (*el docto*) are the configurations of the Assyrian astrologer-king, of Prometheus whose name signified Forethought, the founder of cities and statecraft. Within Segismundo appear those of the suffering Prometheus, bound as a consequence of knowledge. If Ficino saw himself as Prometheus the sage, standing severe and proud at the very frontiers of thought, imparting the good and the true to men, Calderón has seen beyond such a stance into a world where knowledge generates action, action doubt, doubt alienation. Basilio, acting in the City in the name of science and civilized order, recreates the Wilderness with its dark Tower of confusion and its victim, gnawed by a man made absurdity. The contrast of the City and the Wilderness, so central to the play, expresses basic antimonies in the nature of knowledge so familiar to our own culture yet derivative from what must be the most ancient source material in the play. As the Renaissance myth of intellectual optimism was absorbed into Calderón's play, it yielded a voice of despair, appropriated in part from Pliny.

Past erudition has been recovered and regenerated; it develops before us in a manner free from the narrow didactic attitudes of the mythographers. To explain this, we must recognize that the Promethean material is carried into the theater in the company of dramatic images of a well-established order and power. Behind Segismundo there is the Wild Man of the Woods, guardian of the cave, the rock, or the castle, whose theatrical origins go back to festive pageants in which the Wild Man seems to have supplied an element of contrast in the ritual celebration of power; he stood as a rival whose might at once challenged and yet subsisted with royal authority.[14] The figure of the Wild Man had been renewed in court drama. In Act I of Lope's *El premio de la hermosura* (performed in 1614),[15] Wild Men armed with clubs guard the cave where the lovelorn prince Cardiloro is put gently to sleep by the magician Ardano; they reappear in Act III as representatives of a crazy paganism, half-humorous, half-fearsome captains with thun-

---

14. Ample documentation concerning the woodwose in "processions, tournaments and festivities" can be found in N. D. Shergold, *A History of the Spanish Stage From Medieval Times Until the End of the Seventeenth Century* (Oxford, 1967); see index, s. v. "salvaje."

15. *Ibid.*, pp. 252–255.

derous names, enlightened anthropophagi who legislate against cannibalism in their realm (with the exception that foreigners may be eaten) and who proceed solemnly to sacrifice an alien in order to appease the chaste Diana. A similar mixture of clownish roguery and awe lends a protean identity to Segismundo; his monologue over, he throws a *salvaje*'s tantrum and in lines comically sibilant and jingling threatens to squeeze Rosaura to bits in his brawny arms:

> Pues la muerte te daré,
> porque no sepas que sé
> que sabes flaquezas mías.
> Sólo porque me has oido,
> entre mis membrudos brazos
> te tengo de hacer pedazos.
>
> (ll. 180–185)

Locked up once more, his muffled voice threatens the heavens from behind the door with a titanic rebellion. The part of Segismundo must have been an exacting, if rewarding, one for its actor; he had to master swift transitions from deliberated pain to snarling fury, from love to petulant rage; if he made good the acting variety called for by the part in its opening stages, then he had established the twisting profile of a character which could later undergo yet stranger mutations. Basilio, too, suggests a character modeled on a pageant king. He *is* the King, at least by antonomasia. The rapid obsequies of Astolfo and Estrella, the formal advance of a noble retinue to the sound of "tanto sonoro instrumento," the chorus of the courtiers who applaud his resolve and magnify his name with one voice, all these theatrical touches define and isolate the royal image with a force and economy that are in contrast to the crowded metaphors of kingship found in the earlier plays. In new guise, the Wild Man and the King face each other throughout the play, heroic figures of might and power whose old magic is revived for a new end.

Before *La vida es sueño,* Calderón had exploited audience recall of the pageant king and hairy savage. In *La gran Cenobia,* Aureliano appears "vestido de pieles" in the wilderness, a figure exiled with his pride, who courts a *hubris* which will lead to his humiliation. The royal image, too, is present in the golden scepter and laurel crown that hang from a branch on the cliff face, tempting Aureliano to translate himself from being the self-crowned king of beasts to being king over men; scepter and crown signify a divine order that is threatened by a wild ambition:

> Salid, fieras,   salid de las oscuras
> cárceles que os labraron peñas duras;
> venid, venid corriendo,
> y a mi coronación asistid, viendo
> cómo mi honor pregono,
> cuando rey de estos montes me corono.
> *Toma la corona y pónesela, y el cetro.*
> Pequeño mundo soy, y en esto fundo
> que en ser señor de mí, lo soy del mundo.[16]

Here the ruling intention is simple and exemplary. In *La vida es sueño*, the area of mystery encircled by Act I is deeper than moral catechizing; its vision of conflict is to be wondered at, not resolved. With Basilio's address to the court, that opening cycle of conflict is near completion. Prompted by a desire for knowledge, Basilio had scrutinized the heavens; a subtle mathematician, he sought certainty of knowledge from the uncertain events that marked his son's birth. He predicted from his son's horoscope his own and his kingdom's disaster. To forestall disaster, the Tower was built and his son encarcerated; duty overcame love, *por ver*. From within that Tower, Segismundo, too, scrutinized Nature, not to perceive a predestined order but to enter into communion with its freedom from order. Enshrined in two characters are two concepts of Nature, each underpinned by her enigma; for the convulsive disorder that challenged Basilio at Segismundo's birth parallels the mindless movement observed by the Prince from the Tower. Here is the play's problem of knowledge, which overlaps one of identity: in order to test his science (contingent in his mind with civilized order), the philosopher-king denies his private self, the father he is, and abandons his son to being a man of no destiny. Having chosen his part, Basilio plays it out in action. In his deliberation before the court, he stresses his loyalty to the state; out of that loyalty, Segismundo will be freed. One final detail completes this phase of Basilio's quest for certainty and turns us again toward the inner man, to the motive concealed in the public action: in Act II the King tells Clotaldo alone of his private

16. *Obras completas* (Madrid, 1966), I, 72a.

motive for Segismundo's release; the burden of this speech is "quiero examinar":

> Quiero examinar si el cielo
> (que no es posible que mienta,
> y más habiéndonos dado
> de su rigor tantas muestras
> en su cruel condición)
> o se mitiga o se templa . . .
>
> (ll. 1102–1107)

Once again, *por ver*. Basilio is forever driven by the need to know; upon this need, his loyalty and his cruelty are built. His tragic purifying will mean first the renunciation of knowledge and then the abdication of kingship.

So we come to the experiment; it is prefaced by a scene between Basilio and Clotaldo that has the flavor of the laboratory, with intimate talk between specialists on the nature of the drug and the stages of treatment, ending with Clotaldo's disapproval of the methodology. And well he might disapprove, for there is an air of jiggery-pokery about the proceedings; Basilio's trick has a venerable lineage in the world's storytelling; it is usually played on drunken tinkers or blacksmiths for the diversion of kings. Clotaldo's considered apologia on the confection of soporifics (ll. 990–1024) serves only to underline the impropriety, as if the adviser recognized his old master's failing touch and felt obliged to dignify trickery with science. But the image of the laboratory is not wholly accurate; the model for this phase of the play is the theater itself. After being returned to the Tower from the palace, Segismundo dreams that he has been playing his part in a play:

> SEGISMUNDO (*en sueños*)
> Salga a la anchurosa plaza
> del gran teatro del mundo . . .
>
> (ll. 2072–2073)

For Calderón's audience, the analogy between the events on stage and the theater did not require the constant prompting of a text; it infused the very soul of the performance. No only did Antonio de Prado the father and Lorenzo de Prado the son face each other through their parts as they played the confrontation of stage-father and stage-son (the

game of theater must on this level alone have come into uncanny
contact with life); it was also Antonio de Prado the *autor,* the director
of the troupe, who played the King who hovers in the wings like a
solicitous director, instructing Clotaldo and the court as to their next
move, erupting indignantly from time to time to remonstrate with the
principal player when he gets out of hand. As he played the King, Prado
was recreating in similar terms the relationship he bore to the individuals
who were on stage acting in Calderón's play, that of the director to his
cast. These creative relationships between the stage and real life have been
eroded by time; they are hard to revive in criticism based on published
texts, but they were surely the very essence of the acted theater. In addition, the tale of the "Sleeper Awakes" is in itself eminently theatrical;
it involves a deception in which everyone pretends to be who they are.
Identities become self-conscious. The courtier is called on to play the
courtier. The servants who enter dressing Segismundo do not do so because he is the Prince but so that he may look and feel like one. The
office becomes a part, the court a stage.[17] In brief, a large part of
Act II is a play within a play, a point not missed by Clarín on
his entry to the court and reinforced by his glancing allusion to the
one-day prince (ll. 2243–2248), an allusion which could still have recalled in Calderón's day the appointment of the mock Twelfth Night
King during Epiphany revels.[18] But Basilio's play is altered by Segismundo in unexpected ways.

If he is not reduced to the part which Basilio would have him
play in the palace, Segismundo recreates another which in all proba-

17. This point has been clearly expressed by E. Orozco Díaz: "Observemos . . .
que la forma en que en *La vida es sueño* se hace aparecer a Segismundo en palacio, ya vestido de príncipe, supone hacerle vivir con sentido de representación
teatral. Su padre, el rey Basilio, diríamos que le otorga el papel de príncipe para
ver cómo lo representa. Cuando éste, despojado de sus ricas vestiduras, y otra
vez cubierto con sus antiguas pieles, despierte en su torre prisión, considerará lo
vivido en palacio como un sueño; esto es, como una ficción, aunque tan sensible
y real como la materialidad de una representación teatral." *El teatro y la teatralidad
del Barroco* (Barcelona, 1969), pp. 229–230.

18. There were many variations on the burlesque figure of authority who appeared at various festivals throughout the year. Julio Caro Baroja in *El Carnaval*
(Madrid, 1965) has demonstrated the importance of these folk games in Spain;
see especially Part III, chaps. I–VII.

bility stimulated audience memory. One feature of the palace scene led Menéndez y Pelayo to another source; he related Segismundo's new-world monologue (ll. 1224–1247),

> ¡Válgame el cielo, qué veo!
> ¡Válgame el cielo, qué miro! . . .
>
> (ll. 1224–1225)

to one of Orlando's in the anonymous *Un pastoral albergue,* after the mad paladin's senses have been restored by a magic potion flown down by Astolfo from the Mountains of the Moon (such, incidentally, is the background that offers perspective to Clotaldo's rigmarole about drugs).[19] The imitation was, I think, deeper and more immediate, a matter not so much of studied plagiarism as of acting virtuosity. From the rambling burlesque of *Un pastoral albergue,* an acting style was carried forward into *La vida es sueño.* Orlando was a virtuoso part; it may lack coherence in cold print, but under the conditions of performance it could not have failed to hold an audience. Whoever romped through the part of the inconsistent paladin must have, like a stage chameleon, changed at every turn the color of his style. At one moment, Orlando wears the mantle of dignity befitting Charlemagne's warrior; at another, he radiates sentimental warmth as Doña Alda's lover; at the next, he is an antic rogue, louder in his threats than playground champions as he prepares to kick Reinaldos into the middle of the next century or fixes his rival with a look which will dissolve him there and then into atoms. *Furioso,* he is a giant clown who leaves comic havoc in his wake. Peyrón, the *gracioso* shepherd, is plucked from the trunk of an oak which the paladin has just felled and booted away to the stars (a large doll was substituted for the actor). Later, tricked by rustics into believing that he is kissing

19. Morley and Bruerton do not think that *Un pastoral albergue* was the work of Lope de Vega, though his name has been invoked (*Cronología de las comedias de Lope de Vega* [Madrid, 1968], p. 528). For Menéndez y Pelayo's observations, see *Obras de Lope de Vega,* Biblioteca de autores españoles, CCXXXIII (Madrid, 1970), 116–122; the text of the play can be found in CCXXXIV, pp. 195–252. Chevalier suggests a date of roughly 1615–1620 (*L'Arioste en Espagne,* p. 431). The drug from the Mountains of the Moon puts in an appearance in several of Calderón's *autos;* see *La cena de Baltasar,* ed. A. Valbuena Prat (Madrid, 1957), ll. 984–985, and notes to p. 42; the image clearly pleased him.

Angélica's hand, Orlando accidentally pulls off Peyrón's arm (at the end, the shepherd receives a silver replacement from Charlemagne himself). Mutability is the essence of the part. It needs little imagination to add the laughter and the shudder that the actor's transitions were designed to arouse. The part played by Segismundo in the King's play is too close to such a medley role for resemblance to be fortuitous. There is the opening mood of wonder (borrowed directly from *Un pastoral albergue,* as Menéndez y Pelayo noted), then the rampage through court etiquette which ends with the courtier's ejection from the balcony to his death; Segismundo returns triumphant:

¡Vive Dios, que pudo ser!

For Rosaura, past experience is repeated with only slight variation; she is the object at one moment of the most polished of amorous addresses and at the next of a violent attempted rape (Rosaura's attractions always awake basic male reactions—first, Astolfo, now Segismundo; her identification with Astraea, the virgin, is wishful). Old Clotaldo finds himself wrestling ignobly on the throne-room floor for his life, with the Prince, whose words recall the Wild Man's threats from Act I:

o será desta suerte
el darte agora entre mis brazos muerte. [*Luchan*]

The interlude closes with Segismundo's sharp intimation of revenge on Basilio himself. Thus the mixture of unpredictable delight and violence concocted in *Un pastoral albergue* has been raised to a new level of wonder and terror; perhaps fifteen or twenty years after the part was written, Orlando re-emerges within Segismundo, in a version of the Wild Man transferred to the court of King Basilio. Today, we could restate the content of these scenes as follows: frail restraints of hierarchy and decorum are fractured by the perverse fury of an anarchic spirit. Calderón's audience may have reached a similar conclusion, but their thoughts will have been moved and colored by circumstances which we can only partially restate: they saw the obedient actors in the King's performance scattered and confused by a "quick-change" actor who had stepped into their midst from out of a burlesqued romance.

There are long moments in this play in which the forward course

of action is arrested and characters focus upon themselves, gathering
together the broken fragments of experience from which they try to
relate the inner world of self to the outer world of acts and conse-
quences which defy their knowing—as if the moving frames of some
(imagined) film gave way from time to time to a motionless portrait
which we slowly scan to resolve the identity of its subject before
renewed movement catches him up in time and the contingency of
action. Monologue in *La vida es sueño* is an interior exploration, a
momentary grappling with the past before self is moved on once more
into an unpredictable future. It is perhaps at such moments that we
feel most strongly the modern voice of the play, as the individual
penetrates hitherto unseen areas of his own being. The greatest of
such moments occurs at the end of Act II. Alone with the memory
of having been Prince, and deceived by Basilio's lie, Segismundo
reaches out for the protection of controlled despair contained by the
phrase "la vida es sueño." Whatever the origins of the analogy,
whether in lyric poetry or in the preachers' admonitions against world-
liness, here it acquires new meaning to which neither source does
justice.[20] At bottom, the monologue maintains a strange paradox, yet
not a foolish one: "I exist, but life itself is illusory":

> . . . el hombre que vive sueña
> lo que es hasta despertar.
>
> (ll. 2156–2157)

At once, both the reality of existence and the unreality bred of living
it are asserted. The content of the monologue had been prefigured in
what went before, in the pervasive sense that at the court parts had
been acted; *that* stage, the invention of Basilio, bore a resemblance
to the very theater in which the Madrid audience was gathered,
where Prado's players conjured up fantasy roles compounded from
past theatrical art. Segismundo's first illustrative figure not only resumes
a particular judgment against Basilio and a general one on kings;
it embraces, too, the player-King (El Rey) who has lived his illusion

20. For antecedents in lyric poetry, see E. M. Wilson and J. Sage, *Poesías líricas
en las obras dramáticas de Calderón* (London, 1964), 135–136. For the use of the
analogy in sermons, see F. G. Olmedo, S.J., *Las fuentes de La vida es sueño* (Madrid,
1928), chap. I.

of power on the stage, courting our applause ("este aplauso"; the demonstrative suggests localization: this present acclaim from *this* audience). From there the monologue opens out toward the audience; Segismundo is addressing us, so many individuals intent upon dreaming the illusion of a public identity. Then it closes upon himself, pronouncing emphatically the "I" of the dreamer while denouncing the chained figure as a fiction that is dreamed. In a dazzling assertion of the autonomy of his own thought, the character has destroyed the very part he plays,

> Yo sueño que estoy aquí
> destas prisiones cargado . . .
>
>   (ll. 2179–2180)

The popular *estribillo* that closes the monologue reiterates the bleak assurance that Death will bring release to the dreamer; such dreams are dreams, they have an ending which is the sleeper's awakening in death. The primitive desire for self-annihilation in Act I has advanced to a subtler homicide, the extinction within the mind of all that is outside it.

Accompanying the spoken language of *La vida es sueño,* there is an unspoken language of gesture and sign; a series of numinous stage icons, such as the Prince in chains, operates in conjunction with the flow of poetry. Lope de Vega, publishing his thirteenth *parte* in 1620, sensed how print removed the visual dimension to a play's existence; the book offered the reader only a body, to which the actors' actions had once given a soul; now, Lope urges, let the reader restore movement to these depleted *figuras,* infusing grace into them as he recalls the performance itself. But the effects wrought by performance are not altogether lost to us. They may be impressed upon the surrounding characters; tragic empathy between audience and play is implemented, after all, by the convincing sympathies that run from mind to mind within the play. When, for example, the hooded surgeon enters in Act III, line 601, of *El médico de su honra,* his appearance arrests and confounds King Peter: the formless face swims under the feeble moonlight like a white jasper. What horror has the King seen if it is not pallid and sightless Death? Without disruption to the natural fluency of action, a chilling mystery has been evoked. Similarly, Clarín's death has an iconographical effect. As he falls bleeding on the stage ("en sangre todo teñido"), he not only moves the King by a sermon on fate; he dumbly accuses Basilio, speaking "por la boca de una herida." It is slaughter and sedition that the King confesses when confronted by the bleeding corpse, a token figure of the carnage of war. The climactic moment of the play is itself built around an emblem, prophesied beforehand and even rehearsed between Segismundo and Clotaldo in Act II. I refer to Segismundo's triumph, when he asserts his newly gained power by standing over the prostrate monarch. For it is clear that as Segismundo discredits his father's policy before the assembled people, clause by clause, Basilio lies supine on the ground, his snow-white hair forming the carpet on which the Prince treads his way to supremacy. Here, we are in the presence of a traditional iconographical image. Upon it attends meaning that derives from the age's political commonplaces and their visual representation. Such an icon would show the mutability of kingship and Fortune's rule over the affairs of men. In Lope's *El gran duque de Moscovia,* there is an impressive list of ten such trampled sovereigns, including Bajazet reduced to Tamburlaine's mounting block.[21] The tyrant Boris Gudonov admits to being humbled in such a wise, but escapes the ultimate insult of being trampled by taking his own life. As the just, exiled Demetrio sweeps a monastery floor, his attendant muses on the fate that Time holds in store for kings:

> Barreré,
> consolado en que las leyes
> del mundo a los altos reyes
> ponen en el cuello el pie.
>
> (p. 369b)

Segismundo lingers over his scene of triumph, drawing the court's attention to its horrendous significance:

> Sirva de ejemplo este raro
> espectáculo, esta extraña
> admiración, este horror,
> este prodigio; . . .
>
> (ll. 3228–3231)

21. *Obras de Lope de Vega,* Biblioteca de autores españoles, CXCI (Madrid, 1966), p. 388b.

The Prince's timing is faultless; having thus gathered suspense around his next action, he lifts his father up and thus proves that Basilio's prophesy was only partial. Thereupon, he reverses the tableau, and falls at his father's feet. Prudence and Temperance have overcome Injustice and Inclemency; Humility bows its head—and receives the crown.[22] It is easy for us to listen only for the voice of virtue. And yet, at the same time, Act III deals with the dangerous crossing of great men, of opposing armies, of strategies on which a crown depends. Just as Basilio managed the palace drama, ultimately controlling its outcome by a bluff, is there not the suspicion that Segismundo is now replying in kind, staging his own heroic triumph, manipulating the old image of virtue's triumph over fortune and error while secure in the knowledge of his own mastery? A blurring of moral certitude has been seen by T. E. May; general principles of just conduct dissolve into the flux of events and the existential interplay of individual against individual. Contradiction is presented and perceived, he says, in a manner that is characteristically baroque.[23] Such a reading suggests a significant break with an orthodox presentation of moral and political order. I do not wish to make a debate of critical attitudes, but to examine further the master image of Act III—The Rise and Fall of Princes.

The fall of princes from off Fortune's tumbling wheel was the informing medieval idea of tragedy. In the Spanish translation of Boccaccio's *De casibus illustrium virorum*—a key text for the transmission of Fortune's tragedies—a large wood block dramatically illustrates Fortune at her work of moving the wheel; two kings rise up and two fall down, uttering the famous "formula of four": "Reinaré," "Reino," "Reiné," "Sin Reino so." [24] How much this image contributed

22. The traditional icon could be used to illustrate concepts other than the fate of kings; it could show the triumphs of virtue over evil. For a discussion and illustrations of Fortune trampling kings, see S. C. Chew, *The Pilgrimage of Life* (New Haven and London, 1962), chap. 3, "The World of Fortune"; for virtue trampling vice, see chap. 5, "The Spiritual Guardians of Man."

23. "Segismundo y el soldado rebelde," in *Hacia Calderón: Coloquio anglogermano, Exeter, 1969* (Berlin, 1970), pp. 71–75.

24. Frontispiece to *Cayda de principes* (Toledo, 1511), trans. Pero López de Ayala, Juan García, and Juan Alfonso de Zamora. For the medieval idea of tragedy

to the tragic concept in the seventeenth century is too general a topic
for me to treat with any confidence; but there is abundant evidence
of the theme's attraction. Doubtless under the pressure of contemporary
events, the fall of princes seems to have yielded a popular variation,
the rise and fall of the court *privado*. Don Alvaro de Luna provided
one of the favorite historical figures through whom the mutability of
power could be impressed; the tragic rhythm of *La próspera fortuna
de don Alvaro de Luna* and its companion play, *La adversa fortuna,*
is medieval, but the issue, one suspects, was contemporary.[25] Among
those Calderón plays which can confidently be assigned to the later
1620s (a decade that began with spectacular reverses and advances at
the Hapsburg court), several re-enact the old formulation of Fortune's
tragedy. *La gran Cenobia* (1625)[26] takes its plot material from no
less than Boccaccio's *De casibus*. The proud rise and bloody fall of
Aureliano (accompanied contrapuntally by the fall and restoration of
Queen Cenobia) follow the scheme set down in the formula of four:
traditional topics give the scheme verbal clothing (e.g., Fortune's wheel,
the tragedy of Fortune played out on the world's stage). In *La cisma
de Inglaterra,* Wolsey is Fortune's slave, for whom, on the summit of
her hill, glitters the throne of Peter.[27] In *Saber del mal y del bien,*
one densely packed speech parades again the characteristics of fickle
Fortune, above all the image of her tragic stage on which we act our
parts until Death receives us in the wings.[28] The pattern of events in
Act III of *La vida es sueño* bears a rough correspondence to such
familiar spectacles of mutability, but there is also a distancing, a creative

and Fortune, see H. R. Patch, *The Goddess Fortune in Medieval Literature* (Cambridge, Mass., 1927), p. 68; for the "formula of four," see p. 164.

25. First published in Tirso de Molina's *Segunda parte* of 1635, so authorship is
open to question. The two parts are edited by Blanca de los Ríos in *Tirso de
Molina: Obras dramáticas completas* (Madrid, 1946), II, 1960–2039. Doña Blanca
observed a parallel between the two plays and *La vida es sueño* ("obrar bien es lo
que importa," pp. 1969b and 1987a) that may well argue for Calderón's acquaintance with them.

26. Payment for a performance before the King and Queen was made on 23 June
1625; see N. D. Shergold and J. E. Varey, "Some Early Calderón Dates," *BHS,*
XXXVIII (1961), 278.

27. Performed before 31 March 1627; see *ibid.,* p. 277.

28. Performed before 28 March 1628; see *ibid.,* p. 284.

reworking that breaks free from didactic statement and gains a response that is no longer tied to Fortune's tragedy.

When the liberated Segismundo declares his intent to reign, he invokes Fortune:

> A reinar, Fortuna, vamos;
>
> (l. 2420)

The first move has been given to her wheel; between this moment and that of the Prince's triumph, the full revolution will be completed through Basilio. Just as the major identities of the mythographers' Prometheus are held together in opposition within Segismundo and Basilio, so now the two sides of Fortune's wheel, the prosperous and the adverse, are presented within the opposition of son and father, youth and age. The leisurely traditional rhythm of mutability, which would span a whole play, or even two, has been contracted into a tense, simultaneous spectacle of the rising and waning of power. The contrapuntal organization of *La gran Cenobia* has become chiasmal. But by whose hand has the wheel been turned full round? Orthodox limitations to the power of the capricious goddess influenced all the plays I have mentioned, and probably many more. Close to the spirit of Boccaccio's vision of mutability, *La gran Cenobia* identifies the motive force of chance with Aureliano's deadly sin of pride; Fortune's hostility is a providential response to tyranny, and the omens of downfall come significantly from one Astrea, whose voice we identify with truth and justice. In *La adversa fortuna de don Alvaro de Luna,* it is the envy of the grandees that demands Alvaro's execution; and countering Don Alvaro's grim indictment of mankind, the accomplice of Fortune,

> Alerta, humanos, alerta,
> no confiéis en el hombre.
>
> (p. 2037b)

there is Juana's remedy in Stoic apathy and her promise of a virtuous glory that will outlive humiliation. In Act III of *La vida es sueño,* the catalyst of chance has not disappeared, but it is no longer a scrutable force, receiving definition from morality. It is the mob, the personification of wild fury and caprice, that, split by factionalism, alters the course of individual destinies. There was no rigid framework of history to this play that required respect for a known outcome. Events are happenings in an autonomous flow of action; uncertainty is written into every part as the gathering momentum of revolution and counterrevolution drives the characters forward on its arbitrary course. The image of the rebel army awaiting on a lofty hill recalls menacing Fortune on her traditional hilltop, though the emblem is unobtrusively accommodated to the natural setting.[29] To the sound of the trumpets of war, images of unleashed disorder flare across the poetry of Basilio and his followers as they witness the replacement of their past order by the anarchy of mob rule. Basilio's three examples of the unbridled horse, of the river falling to the sea, of the toppling boulder are picked up by Estrella and extended into a hysterical *accumulatio:* the unbridled tumult occupies streets and squares, waves of scarlet blood engulf the kingdom that is now in ruins. Under a darkened sun (Basilio had once compared such an eclipse to the cosmic upheaval at Christ's death) and the sough of wind, the city becomes a landscape of death through which skeleton soldiers move:

> cada piedra un pirámide levanta
> y cada flor construye un monumento;
> cada edificio es un sepulcro altivo,
> cada soldado un esqueleto vivo.

(ll. 2472–2475)

This is the dramatic restoration, in all her baleful magnificence, of mutable Fortune, translated into the fury of the mob. She becomes incarnate in the enraged clash of opinion and in the lethal struggling for power; she *is* the flux and arbitrariness of human affairs.

Like threads in a labyrinth, images and their nexus of associations cross over from Act II into Act III, and thus insinuate continuity within the evolution of individual character. The Prince's metaphor spans the act; it prefaces and guides each advance towards self-control and the control he acquires over others. And as successive possibilities of fulfillment offer themselves to the Prince, so he modifies and mitigates the bleak pessimism once epitomized in his metaphor. In the end, it is laid to rest as a touch of mild rhetorical coloring to Segismundo's

29. For Fortune on a hilltop, see Chew, *Pilgrimage of Life,* p. 53; and Patch, *Goddess Fortune,* pp. 132–136.

final affirmation of intention and self-acclaim; man's happiness passes away as does a dream, so one must take advantage of it, today:

> pues así llegué a saber
> que toda la dicha humana,
> en fin, pasa como un sueño.
> Y quiero hoy aprovecharla . . .
>
> (ll. 3312–3315)

It appears that metaphors, too, decline on Fortune's wheel. Indeed, the fate of "la vida es sueño" mirrors the shifts and developments of its inventor; for as Segismundo proclaims his new identity as Poland's Prince, he commits himself to that realm of public act and utterance from the very insubstantial nature of which the metaphor had once been engendered.[30] Segismundo's progressive scrutiny and modification of "la vida es sueño" is the outward expression of an inner accommodation to the new realities of role, power, and acclaim, which had been arraigned in that first fierce revelation of life's vain show. In two guises, the image of the theater reappears. Basilio and his followers remorsefully see themselves as actors on Fortune's tragic stage; Segismundo rapturously imagines himself on a grander stage, in a triumph through Rome, with himself as the victorious general. One function of both images is to contrast the variable dispositions of Fortune. But another is to retrieve and carry forward that perception grasped by the banished Prince and wrought into his metaphor: that our acts are parts compounded of illusions, analogous to the counterfeit roles conjured and sustained by the actor on the stage. It is this background, revived in the dying echoes of the metaphor and its associated imagery,

---

30. E. M. Wilson's reading of the play would seem to contradict this point. He sees Segismundo renouncing power at the end: "he restores his conquered father to the throne of Poland" ("On *La vida es sueño*," in *Critical Essays on the Theatre of Calderón*, ed. B. W. Wardropper [New York, 1965], 78). I cannot find the textual justification for such a reading, whereas the transfer of power from Basilio to Segismundo seems unequivocal. The new Prince assumes command over the court. Basilio's admission of defeat

> Tú venciste;
> corónente tus hazañas.
>
> (ll. 3252–3253)

offers a cue for the literal transference of the crown; or at least expresses such an act through metaphor.

that I feel we should allow to color our reading of Act III, as a brilliant ground upon which fresh action is impasted and at the same time subtly altered. For deep contradictions are contained and shaped out in the part of Segismundo as he emerges from the turmoil of events. True, he appeals strongly for our assent to his moral regeneration; yet where we see conversion we witness also the advance of self-interest. The old Segismundo is exorcised at the same time that the Prince discovers stability in the very accouterments of power which he had ruthlessly abjured as evanescent. The mutation of thought is bound in with the hazardous contingency of action; moral certitude is transmitted into flickering possibilities generated, but not objectively confirmed, by the dynamic interaction of individual and individual, of individual and that part of self divided against him, of individual and event. Thus while some have seen the final Segismundo as a type of Stoic-Christian hero, who maintains order and banishes the dark world of unreason, others have recognized him as a tyrant who renews a cycle of injustice in the name of political expediency.[31] In readings as diverse as these there is a lesson: ambiguity is all. To weight interpretation toward a systematic belief, providential or Machiavellian, is to upset the quivering balance of uncertainty.

There is, one could say, a "moment of truth," not to be overlooked, when Segismundo berates his father's policy before the assembled court. But does his reasoning in any way clear away the enigma of the stars? If an exchange of views were possible, it could be pointed out that the Prince's arguments are mutually exclusive and neither is definitive. The first position (that Basilio brought disaster upon himself) is a piece of judicial rhetoric that simplifies in order to condemn, while the second (that here we see the working out of heaven's decree) is a well-prepared cue for the Prince to win universal *admiratio*:

> Sentencia del cielo fue;
> por más que quiso estorbarlo
> él, no pudo. ¿Y podré yo,
> que soy menor en las canas,

31. See, for example, the debate between A. A. Parker, "Calderón's Rebel Soldier and Poetic Justice," *BHS*, XLVI (1969), 120–127, and H. B. Hall, "Poetic Justice in *La vida es sueño*, a Further Comment," *BHS*, XLVI (1969), 128–131.

en el valor y en la ciencia,
vencerla?

(ll. 3236–3241)

The area of mystery against which the characters have acted is still preserved. What we follow is the course of individual thought as it asserts itself over uncertainty in the exercise of the newly gained art of power. But Calderón's audience was moved by more than words. For those closing scenes, Lorenzo de Prado had once more donned the skins, and thus costume recovered the lineage of the triumphant Prince in the Wild Man, the embodiment of a Protean might coupled with unpredictability. The royal image is still, at the end, confronted by its rival; but both roles now subsist within the same character, fused in a paradoxical symbiosis that Machiavelli himself had similarly imaged in his analysis of political man as a Chiron, semihuman and semianimal, sustained by law and also by force.

In Act III the movement toward meaning is a progress from the familiar to the new; the creative imagination concentrated on the traditional dramatic form of the Rise and Fall of Princes and upon it bestowed a new spirit. For some readers, the renewal takes place within Segismundo himself, in an act of spiritual regeneration that liberates him from the irrational. T. E. May touches upon a different and fascinating level of meaning, the "optimistic" possibility that there can be continuity of order that overrules the uncertainties of individual knowledge and decision.[32] We can look still further. Far beneath the acts of individuals and the fate of institutions, another conflict is traced out; it is the war of generations, the eclipse of age by youth. Act III can be read as a study of the ceaseless rhythm of human extinction and renewal, as deep and irresistible as the succession of day upon night, of spring upon winter. It is through poetry that this ordering is reached; it is felt rather than stated as a seasonal pageant in which Basilio is white-haired winter, overcome by advancing spring, who seeks him out on the mountainside, trunk by trunk, branch by branch. Segismundo is the rising sun that

32. *"La vida es sueño* es 'optimista' porque muestra que el orden puede predominar en el estado, si lo quieren bien los gobernantes," "Segismundo y el soldado rebelde," p. 75.

buries the black shadows of night beneath the ocean (ll. 2293–2297);
as the Solar Prince, cradled in the arms of dawn, he brings new light and
life to the twilight kingdom of the Winter King:

> Generoso Segismundo,
> cuya majestad heroica
> sale al día de sus hechos
> de la noche de sus sombras;
> y como el mayor planeta
> que en los brazos de la aurora
> se restituye luciente
> a las flores y a las rosas,
> y sobre mares y montes,
> cuando coronado asoma,
> luz esparce, rayos brilla,
> cumbres baña, espumas borda;
> así amanezcas al mundo,
> luciente sol de Polonia.
>
> (ll. 2690–2703)

This attempt to bring to the reading of *La vida es sueño* the play's
complex affiliations with living theater and specifically theatrical spectacle
may appear to some to disorganize the clean thematic lines which have
been traced out in other studies. It is inevitable that it has turned out so,
for to consider the artist's reshaping of elements drawn from a prolific
and developing dramatic genre is to turn away from general prescriptions
about theme or lesson. Instead, the "hereness and nowness" of action,
poetry, and character suggests itself; transformation means for an
audience a surprising confrontation with the unforeseen, with which
meaning itself is simultaneous. *La vida es sueño* is a succession of spectacular breakthroughs into new perceptions of consciousness and states
of being, dependent nonetheless on traditional frameworks of dramatic
presentation. Thus the sentimental magic of the romantic epic that opens
the play leads us forward through its charms into subtler mysteries of
human knowledge and human dereliction. Calderón's self-consciousness
as a dramatist is fundamental. I do not refer only to the *gracioso*'s humor
that is shaped so deftly from out of his own art, or to the renovation of
an antique stage myth, or to the play within a play in Act II. The game
of theater is played on many fronts (the romance epic, *la mujer vestida
de hombre,* the Wild Man and Pageant King, the mad Orlando, to

recapitulate a few); but as familiar moves were integrated and transcended, so the actors' game entered into eloquent contact with the perilous uncertainties of reality itself.[33]

33. I acknowledge a general debt to T. E. May and a particular one to G. G. Brown, who pointed out faults in presentation and recommended improvements.

Circumstance and Setting in the Earliest Italian Productions of Comedy

BONNER MITCHELL

BEGINNING STUDENTS armed with a definition of the Renaissance are often much surprised to discover that the literary movement in Italy was more than a century old before the three grand classical genres —epic, tragedy, and comedy—were cultivated in a large way. They are soon told about the late diffusion of Aristotle's *Poetics,* after 1500, and the equally late—and incomplete—resolution of the *Questione della lingua* in favor of the Tuscan vernacular in the domain of belles-lettres. In the case of the two dramatic genres, however, there is an additional explanation. A different sort of condition, such as often escapes the attention of literary scholars, had to be fulfilled. The presentation of classical drama was a difficult and elaborate affair that required, besides enlightened sponsors, a considerable apprenticeship of directors, actors, and public. We may say that in the case of classical tragedy this condition was never realized in the sixteenth century. Neoclassical comedy, on the other hand, enjoyed one of its periods of greatest vitality and highest quality. The *commedia erudita* found its proper milieu in sixteenth-century Italy (as it did not in France). Its triumph was made possible by a rather long early period of experimentation and initiation. This period, which may be taken to run from about 1485 to 1520, embraced what art historians call—or used to call—the High Renaissance. I propose here not to survey the period, a task which merits undertaking on a much larger scale,[1] but to recapture some of the atmosphere of early comedy performances by referring to details of several specific productions.

First, however, we must look briefly at the main lines of development. It is not meaningful, for the purposes of theatrical history, to make a basic division between productions of Latin comedy and those of the first original comedies in Italian. There was much chronological overlapping, and the distinction was not yet clear in the minds of some contemporaries. Thus in telling about the performance of Ariosto's *I Suppositi* in Rome in 1519, a Venetian reporter says that the play is "taken partly from the *Suppositi* [*Menaechmi* ?] of Plautus and partly from Terence's *Eunuch*," and does not mention Ariosto's name at all.[2] A more useful division can be made into two main traditions of production associated mainly with different cities. One, academic and often patriotically oriented, is tied principally to Rome. Another, more courtly and light-hearted, belongs to Ferrara and to two cities with which it had close dynastic and cultural relations, Mantua and Urbino. The two traditions do not of course embrace the whole of activity in the comedy of time,[3] and they are not, either, totally distinct. The Ferrara tradition is imported into Rome soon after the native one has achieved its greatest production.

Rome had not had a distinguished part in the early Italian Renais-

1. There is no systematic history of the early productions. The principal books touching upon them in a general way are Alessandro D'Ancona's old *Origini del teatro italiano* (Turin, 1891), Vol. II (hereafter cited as "D'Ancona"); Wilhelm Creizenach, *Geschichte des neueren Dramas* (Halle, 1911–1923), Vol. II; Ireneo Sanesi, *La Commedia* (Milan, 1954), Vol. I; Mario Apollonio, *Storia del teatro italiano* (Florence, 1940), Vol. II; and Marvin T. Herrick, *Italian Comedy in the Renaissance* (Urbana, Ill., 1960).

2. "La comedia è stà trata, parte de li Supositi di Plauto e di l'Eunuco di Terenzio. . . ." Letter published in *I Diarii di Marino Sanuto*, MCCCXLVI–MDXXXII, . . . ed. Renaldo Fulin et al. (Venice, 1879–1903), XXVII, 72–74. All translations from Italian are mine.

3. The omission of Florence requires some explanation. While there were some productions of comedies in the city during the period, they seem to have been rather few and information about them is scanty. This despite the fact that about 1518 the Florentine Machiavelli wrote the masterpiece of sixteenth-century comedy, *La Mandragola*.

sance, but after the re-establishment of a settled papal court in the middle of the *quattrocento,* humanists came to live in the city and the new ideas took hold among the native élite. Around 1465 Pomponius Laetus, successor to Lorenzo Valla in the Chair of Latin and Rhetoric at the Studio, or University, formed a sort of literary club devoted to the study of ancient Rome. Its members indulged in some half-serious pagan rites (causing a frightened Pomponius to spend a short time in jail) and also began to do productions in Latin of plays by Plautus and Seneca. These productions, like similar ones in other European universities, had a pedagogical function. Doing the role of a Plautus character was a pleasant way of working on one's Latin pronunciation and also on one's rhetorical gestures and tones. In Rome, particularly, the study of Latin letters was inseparable from the study of rhetoric. Both were dominated by the Ciceronian movement, one of the most pedantic and least "liberal" intellectual phenomena of the Renaissance.[4] In the Eternal City these studies also had patriotic content. Young Romans were taught that they alone had inherited the faculty of correct Latin pronunciation and that the purity of their Latin was the city's most valuable intellectual distinction. (It was a distinction to be clung to all the more because Romans had not done themselves honor in vernacular literature.) The city's élite were formed in this rhetorical school, and a number of young men had experience in the recitation of Latin plays. Tommaso Inghirami, Pomponius' successor at the Studio, had so distinguished himself at a public production of Seneca's *Hippolytus* about 1486 that he retained ever after the nickname of "Fedra," after the tragic heroine's role he had played.

The Roman academic tradition found a perfect expression and climax in a grand 1513 production of Plautus' *Poenulus.* Fortunately for history, several detailed descriptions of this production have survived.[5] Romans were extremely proud of what they had done and wished the accomplishment to be recorded. The circumstances of this production, also thoroughly documented, are essential to an understanding of its details. Leo

4. See Izora Scott, *Controversies over the Imitation of Cicero* . . . (New York, 1910), which contains a translation of Erasmus' satirical dialogue the *Ciceronianus,* aimed primarily at Roman Ciceronians.

5. The principal accounts have been reproduced and studied by Fabrizio Cruciani in *Il Teatro del Campidoglio e le feste romane del 1513* (Milan, 1968) (hereafter cited as "Cruciani").

X, son of Lorenzo the Magnificent, had become pope on 12 March of the same year, amid perhaps the greatest enthusiasm Romans and other Italians have ever shown on the election of a new pontiff. The joy of the Romans, more surprising than that of the Florentines, was based on hopes that Leo would bring prosperity to the city and would grant its local government more political and economic rights. This government, seated on the glorious hill of the Campidoglio, ancient Capitolium, retained the form of a republican *comune* but was in fact weak—and destined to grow weaker—in a city ruled by the Church. Its officers were largely members of the local élite who had been educated by Pomponius and his friends. In their minds' pride in Latin culture and *romanitas* was tied to republican ideals. Leo X, who wished to have the good will of this government, asked it during the summer of 1513 to grant Roman citizenship to his brother Giuliano de' Medici and his nephew Lorenzo. No concession of privileges could have pleased the Roman vanity so much as this superficially humble request for a favor. The Roman patricians were seized with a sort of fever of pride and industry. They decided to make the ceremonies and celebrations for this granting of citizenship a demonstration of the material resources and superior culture of their city, a proof of the survival of the S.P.Q.R.

The development of comic productions in Ferrara, an independent princely state, was due to the patronage of the Este family. Duke Ercole I, who ruled from 1471 to 1505, took an almost professional interest in theatrical productions. His daughter Isabella, who in 1490 married Francesco Gonzaga and became Marchioness of Mantua, was even more devoted to the theater. After her marriage she promoted its development in Mantua and also returned often to Ferrara to see productions. Through friendly influence on her sister-in-law Elisabetta Gonzaga, Duchess of Urbino, she also encouraged interest in drama in that refined little court.[6] She was a beautiful and charming lady, and her influence in cultural matters was easy. When she visited Rome in 1514, Bibbiena's *La Calandria* was staged in her honor (and to the great pleasure of pope and cardinals).

6. Numerous documents concerning Isabella's relations with the courts of Ferrara and Urbino are cited in Alessandro Luzio and Rodolfo Renier, *Mantova e Urbino; Isabella d'Este ed Elisabetta Gonzaga nelle relationi famigliari e nelle vicende politiche* (Turin-Rome, 1893).

Comedies of Plautus and Terence were staged in Ferrara beginning in the 1480s. There were some productions in Latin, but translations soon seem to have prevailed. It was necessary at first to commission these translations, and Duke Ercole seems to have guarded his copies with some jealousy. Isabella was reduced at least once to asking her agent to get her some without her father's knowledge![7] Plautus and Terence were at first translated into verse, primarily, it seems, *terza rima*. The result was often unhappy since the rapid give-and-take of Latin dialogue was lost. Isabella, free of pedantry, had the good sense to write in 1498 that she preferred translations in prose, and her translator Niccolo Cosmico notes that she had asked him not to translate "in an exquisite way" but "according to the common speech of these parts."[8] How far this sensible point of view was from the Ciceronianism of Rome! Isabella was, however, ahead of her time, and the battle for natural dialogue in comedies was to be a long one.

Plays in Ferrara, Mantua, and Urbino were, of course, given for special occasions, the day of the commercial theater being far into the future. The occasions were of three main kinds: (1) carnival, (2) visits of distinguished guests, and (3) marriages. The specific productions to which we shall refer are the following:

(1) A series of Plautus comedies given in Ferrara in 1502 for carnival and in honor of the marriage of Alfonso d'Este and Lucrezia Borgia;

(2) Bibbiena's *La Calandria* in Urbino for the carnival of 1513;

(3) *I Suppositi* of Ariosto for the carnival of 1519 in Rome.

The descriptions of these productions are less detailed than the accounts of the Roman celebrations. They are found, as we shall indicate, in private letters and diaries.

Let us look first at the physical setting, stage scenery, and costumes of the productions and then at the other entertainments by which the plays were accompanied. The *comune* of Rome had in 1513 commissioned the construction of an enormous temporary theater on the Campidoglio. It was of course to be in the classical style. The city was the European

7. Letter quoted by D'Ancona, II, 372–373.
8. "[La Vostra Eccellenza mi aveva raccomandato] ch'io non cercasse parlare exquisito, ma ch'io mi regiesse secondo il comune dire di queste parte." Letter of Cosmico quoted, along with that of Isabella, by D'Ancona, II, 372–374.

center for studies of classical archaeology, and numerous artists, among
them Raphael, were actively engaged in measuring and studying ancient
buildings. Moreover the humanist Sulpizio da Veroli, director of some
productions of Latin plays in Pomponius' time, had done the first edition
of Vitruvius' *De Architectura* in 1486, showing in his preface particular
interest in the structure of theaters. Revival of ancient drama and ancient
architecture seemed then to go together. Every attempt was made to
construct a building of genuine ancient inspiration, though not, as it
turned out, an authentic theater.[9] The structure was placed on a vast open
space of the Campidoglio, which did not yet have the magnificent piazza
designed by Michelangelo that we know today. Reports of the building's
measurements differ, but it seems to have been at least thirty-five meters
long by twenty-nine meters wide and at least seventeen meters high. It
was constructed of wood made to look like marble. There was no roof
but a "ceiling" of blue and white cloth. The entrance, which could be
seen from the foot of the hill, resembled an arch of triumph. All interior
walls were divided by classical orders, probably Doric, of pilasters. Within
the divisions was a very heavy decoration of paintings. The paintings
showed historical or mythological scenes but often constituted contemporary allusions. They were meant, first, to flatter the Medici and,
secondly, to impress them with the grandeur of Rome. Some were de-
pictions of ancient events on the Capitolium. Another series, the product
of unusual imagination, showed important moments or aspects of relations between ancient Romans and Etruscans. An Etruscan king was
shown reigning in Rome to the great satisfaction of the population! The
Etruscans were seen teaching the willing Romans various useful arts,
including that of priesthood and, appropriately, that of the theater. The
Etruscans were taken by polite convention to be the racial and cultural
ancestors of the Florentines, who were thereby permitted to pretend to
an ancient distinction they had not possessed as a minor Roman colony.
Such a delicate and scholarly compliment could come only from a
humanist, and all the paintings had in fact been "ideati," or conceived,

9. See Arnaldo Bruschi, "Riconstruzione e nota critica sull'architettura del
teatro capitolino," published as an appendix in Cruciani. Much information about
Renaissance attempts to reconstruct ancient theaters is found in *Le Lieu théâtral de
la Renaissance,* ed. Jean Jacquot (Paris, 1964).

by Tommaso Inghirami, alias "Fedra," who was also the director of the play.

The end of the building containing the stage was, like the other sides, decorated with paintings between pilasters. While, however, on the other sides the lower walls were hidden by grandstand seats for spectators, here on the stage there were five doors through which actors could enter and exit. Despite Vasari's statement to the contrary in his life of Baldassare Peruzzi, there seems to have been *no* special stage scenery. The audience had to use its imagination in this respect, having before its eyes only the unchanging general decoration for the celebration.

The contemporary reporters were ecstatic about the magnificence of the theater. The following remarks of Paolo Palliolo may serve as an example of the general reaction:

I can't believe that Apelles, Zeuxis or Parhassius or any . . . celebrated painter ever surpassed in elegance this noble work, which not only the people of Rome but a great multitude of foreigners rushed to see. It was examined by some old men who had not been out of their houses for a long time and who may never come out of them again alive. Those who couldn't walk had themselves carried.[10]

Palliolo goes on to remark rather pitifully that if the theater was not quite so grand as that of Marcus Scaurus in the first century B.C. one has to take into account the "disheartened and reduced" state of the Roman people ("posteritate, exaninita et . . . attenuata"), who are no longer even masters of themselves, much less of an empire. The Romans in fact numbered only about 50,000 in 1513.

The costumes of the actors in *Poenulus* are described by Palliolo in great (and difficult) detail. Fedra's training had led him to attempt some

---

10. "Non posso persuadermi che Apelle, Zeusi, Parrhasio, né altro. . . . famigerato pittore havesse di elegantia superata questa nobile opera, al cui spettacolo è concorso non solo il populo di Roma, ma copiosa moltitudine di forestieri. Sono venuti a vederla alcuni vecchi, quali per buono spatio di tempo non sonno altre volte usciti de casa e Dio sa si più ne usciranno vivi. . . . / (quelli che non hanno potuto venire se sonno fatti portare). . . . De Paulo Palliolo Fanese narratione delli spectacoli celebrati in Campidoglio da Romani nel ricevere lo Magnifico Juliano et Laurentio di Medici per suoi patritii," in Cruciani, p. 33.

historical accuracy. Thus the young men who played men's roles—others, of course, played women's—wore flesh-colored stockings to resemble the bare legs of the ancients. But many aspects of costumes were inappropriate not only for period but also for social class. The two poor girls being exploited by a *leno* "appeared . . . not in the dress of courtesans, but with such pomp and gravity that in their appearance they represented two great queens." [11] Their copious garments glittered with gold and even with precious stones. After some hesitation Palliolo approves of this inaccuracy on the grounds that for such a grand occasion as the Capitoline celebrations nothing mean could be tolerated.

In the courtly Ferrara tradition one did not build whole theaters, but the decoration related strictly to the plays was much richer. Just before going to Ferrara to meet her new husband in January 1502, Lucrezia Borgia had been honored by a performance of the *Menaechmi* in the bedroom of her father Pope Alexander VI in the Vatican. Este representatives who were present reported to their duke with scorn that there had been no stage scenery at all. [12] In Ferrara the very next month Lucrezia was able to see how much more advanced the court of her new family was in this regard. The room for the staging of the five Plautus comedies is described by Isabella in a letter to her husband in Mantua. [13] A large hall in the present Palazzo della Ragione had been prepared. At one end there was a grandstand, divided into three sections so that ladies could sit in the middle and gentlemen on each side. (The most distinguished guests were, however, to sit nearer the stage.) The stage was raised over a simulated city wall with battlements. It contained six houses "not more luxurious than the usual" ("non avantegiate del consueto"). The scene was thus a practical and realistic one for the street-corner action of Plautus comedies.

Baldassare Castiglione, who was soon to immortalize the little court of Urbino in *The Courtier,* directed the 1513 production of *La Calandria,*

---

11. "Comparsero. . . . non in habito di meretricule, ma con tanta pompa et gravitate che con la loro apparentia due gran Reine rappresentavano. . . ." Palliolo, in Cruciani, p. 62.

12. Letter published by Ferdinand Gregorovius in *Lucrèce Borgia,* trans. Paul Régnaud (Paris, 1876), II, 371–374.

13. Letter quoted by D'Ancona, II, 383.

and we have a letter of his describing the setting and performance.[14] A large room, presumably in the magnificent Palazzo Ducale, had been prepared. The back wall bore an appropriate Latin inscription reminding the people that Caesar himself had enjoyed theatrical entertainment while home from war. The stage at the other end was in this case also sitting upon an apparent city wall. It "was designed to look like a very beautiful city, with streets, palaces, houses, towers, and real streets, and everything in relief, but helped by excellent painting expert in perspective." [15] The modern discovery of perspective had thus by 1513 been put to work in stage scenery. The most imposing "building" of the scenery was an octagonal temple. There was also an arch of triumph. Castiglione's description reminds one very closely of a series of well-known architectural perspectives painted precisely in Urbino about 1475 (and of uncertain attribution). This stage showed an ideal classical city rather than a bourgeois neighborhood, as had been done in Ferrara in 1502, or a real city, as would be done in Rome in 1519.

The production of Ariosto's *I Suppositi* in Rome in 1519 was sponsored by the Florentine Cardinal Cybò (who had, however, reportedly been given a thousand ducats for that purpose by Pope Leo). Having expressed an interest in comedies while passing through Ferrara, he had been offered the text of this play, one of the earliest *commedie erudite*. The production took place in the Vatican Palace. The room, unidentified, had been decorated by the hand or under the directions of Raphael! Most of the decorations were directly related to the comedy, but the curtain had a local and topical subject, the "Caprices of Fra Mariano." This monk was the principal court buffoon and often amused the pope and his guests by such dainty tricks as running down the table and knocking off dishes and silverware. The curtain, presumably also done by Raphael, was much appreciated by the pontiff and the rest of the audience. The stage itself was a reproduction of the real city of Ferrara. In the marveling words of a Venetian correspondent, "In that room was

14. Undated letter to Count Ludovico di Canossa in *Lettere di Conte Baldassar Castiglione . . .* , ed. Pier Antonio Serassi (Padua, 1769), I, 156–159.

15. "La scena poi era finta una città bellissima con le strade, palazzi, case, torri, strade vere, e ogni cosa di rilievo, ma aiutata ancora da bonissima pittura con prospettiva ben intesa. . . ." *Ibid.,* I, 158.

made Ferrara exactly as it is." [16] With the writing in Italian of new comedies set in contemporary cities, it had become possible to provide a new
sort of realistic stage setting.

The descriptions of costumes for these productions are not so full as
for those used in the *Poenulus,* but it seems clear that courtly circles
were also very fond of richness in this regard, and they may have been
as little concerned for appropriateness. In Ferrara, at the beginning of the
1502 celebrations, Duke Ercole had taken his most distinguished guests
to see the costumes prepared for the five comedies. [17] There were one
hundred and thirty of them. In a gesture worthy of a *nouveau riche*
(which he was not), the duke seems to have been eager to impress upon
the guests that not one costume would have to be used twice! Evidence
of expenditure, as well as of culture, added to his glory.

None of the plays we have mentioned was presented entirely as an
independent spectacle. All were part of a series of entertainments, and
most had independent *intermedii* between their acts. *Poenulus* was the
last of a two-day series of ceremonies and entertainments, all of which
had utilized the theater and the stage. There had been (1) a solemn
mass, (2) the actual conferring of citizenship, with elegant Ciceronian
orations, (3) a banquet of incredible splendor, length, and copiousness,
and (4) a dramatic pageant. The pageant, consisting of several allegorical
skits and an eclogue, had been directed by another professor of the
Studio, Camillo Porzio, and written by several clever young Latinists.
For the spoken parts of the skits were also in Latin, as was the eclogue
featuring two illiterate farmers of the Roman countryside! The skits and
the eclogue were closely related to the occasion. Characters representing
Rome and Florence argued over the possession of Giuliano and Lorenzo
as citizens. Clarice Orsini, the dead Roman mother of Giuliano and
Pope Leo, was brought down from a Heaven more pagan than Christian
to appear with the river gods Arno and Tiber and rejoice in the grand
occasion. The farmers of the eclogue had many good things to say
about the new pope. At last came the play itself, which was not interrupted by *intermedii.* This respect for dramatic unity, unusual for the
time, was probably due to the academic purism of Fedra.

16. ". . . . in dita sala fu fata Ferara precise come la è. . . ." *Diarii di Marino
Sanuto,* XXVII, 74.

17. Letter of Isabella quoted by D'Ancona, II, 384.

In courtly milieus comedies were often given within a tight schedule of dancing, jousts, and banquets. And there were nearly always elaborate *intermedii,* which afforded a kind of "relief" from the unified action of the play. The need for these breaks must have been felt particularly in the case of Plautus comedies recited in Latin or in *terza rima* translations. In writing to her husband about the Ferrara plays of 1502, Isabella complained that the recitation of the *Bacchides* was "so long and dull and without intermezzo dances that several times I wished myself [at home] in Mantua." [18] And we sense the relief of the Ferrarese diarist Bernardo Zambotti when he says that after the "ornate and dignified speeches" of the first act of *Asinaria* "there appeared fourteen satyrs." [19] Some of the *intermedii* were simply dances or pantomimes, generally called "moresche." Others were dramatic skits whose subjects were most often allegorical. Their intellectual content was usually trite, the most common theme being, perhaps, that of *Omnia vincit amor.* But costumes were magnificent, and there was nearly always music, for skits as well as for dances. Modern sociological critics who deplore this sort of light entertainment would have appreciated by exception the first *intermedio* of the 1513 production of *La Calandria* in Urbino, an episode from the story of Jason which showed the evils of war between friends and neighbors. At the end of *La Calandria,* a Cupid recited *stanze* written by Castiglione that explained the meaning of all the *intermedii* that had gone before. In this rare case they had formed a whole.

What of the public who saw these early productions of comedy? The general educational level may have been higher than for performances of Plautus in ancient Rome,[20] since the plays were not put on primarily for the common people. For the Roman production of 1513 the intellectual level—or at least pretension—of the audience was unusually high. Roman

18. ". . . . la comedia de la Bachide. . . . fu tanto longa et fastidiosa et senza balli intramezzi che più volte m'augurai a Mantova. . . ." Letter quoted by D'Ancona, II, 385.

19. ". . . . facti li acti de la comedia, cioè de la prima parte con parlamenti ornati et digni, comparse quatordeci satiri. . . ." *Diario Ferrarese dal anno 1476 sino al 1504,* ed. Giuseppe Pardi, in *Rerum Italicarum Scriptores di L. A. Muratori,* Vol. XXIV, Part VII (Bologna, 1935), p. 329.

20. Interesting speculations about the original Roman audiences of Plautus are found in Barthélémy-A. Taladoire, *Essai sur le comique de Plaute* (Imprimerie Nationale de Monaco, 1956), pp. 7–34.

patricians were proud to renew contact with their "native" academic training. Ordinary people did, however, try to see as much of the festival as they could. We are told that the door of the theater had guards who "did not allow to enter just any artisan or vile plebeian but only those whom they judged from their looks to be worthy of such entertainment." [21] Some artisans and vile plebeians scaled the walls, however, and watched the proceedings from the top or through windows. One cannot resist speculating about how many people actually followed the Latin of the pageant and the play. Palliolo reports that everyone much appreciated the Latin pronunciation of the actors, who could only "have been born and nourished in the fountain of Latium." [22] The audience was, however, very large and heterogeneous. There were many *letterati,* and some eager persons had doubtless read or reread the play for the occasion, but it seems unlikely that more than half of the spectators knew the text or that many more, for all the Latin culture of High Renaissance Rome, were capable of following unfamiliar Latin recitations in detail. Did some people pretend to understand when they did not, like American college students at a French play? In a sense, to be sure, an understanding of the words at this spectacular performance was no more necessary than at the opera in our own day.

The courts of Ferrara and Mantua probably allowed uninvited guests to see comedies when there was room. That of Urbino, in a small city, may have been more exclusive. For the Roman production of *I Suppositi* we learn with astonishment that Pope Leo himself took a hand in deciding who should be allowed into the room (there being no difficulty, apparently, in gaining access to the Vatican Palace). The Este ambassador reported: "Our Master stationed himself at the door and quietly, with his benediction, allowed to enter whom he pleased." [23] It may well be that the pontiff was more interested in excluding severe

21. ". . . . non lassavano intrare ogni mecanico et vile plebeio, ma solo quelli che in lo aspetto giudicavano degni di tali spettacoli." Palliolo, in Cruciani, p. 51.

22. "La loro lingua et pronuntia meravigliosamente dilettava a tutti gli auditori et chiaramente dimostrava esse essere nati et nudriti nel fonte di Latio. . . ." *Ibid.,* p. 61.

23. ". . . . il. . . . Nostro Signore si pose a la porta, e senza strepito con la sua benedizione permesse entrare chi li parea. . . ." Quoted by D'Ancona, II, 88.

churchmen who might be shocked by the comedy than in keeping away commoners.

It would be the nature of the perfected *commedia erudita,* despite its name, to appeal to a very wide section of society. These early productions of comedy already had that sort of appeal, though it was based less often on a genuine "literary" appreciation of the plays. Even in the case of Plautus comedies recited in half-understood Latin or in stilted *terza rima,* the pleasures afforded by rich costumes and decorations and by music and dancing nearly always sufficed to make the production a success. Moreover these secondary elements added greatly to the prestige of sponsoring princes or governments. That alone was enough to justify their costliness (and to insure their continued presence in many productions later in the century). They made the director's task more difficult, calling upon a truly Renaissance variety of talents. Castiglione reported that he had had to "fight with painters and with carpenters and actors and musicians and morris dancers,"[24] as well as write *stanze* and a prologue. When *La Calandria*'s author, Bibbiena, set about producing it in Rome the next year, he asked the Duke of Urbino for details of Castiglione's production so that he could copy them.[25] The various arts of the director, like those of the playwright, were being learned and passed on.

24. "[Le stanze] furon fatte molto in fretta e da chi avea da combattere e con pittori, e con maestri di legnami, e recitatori e musici, e moreschieri." *Lettere di Castiglione,* I, 59.
25. D'Ancona, II, 88.

The Stage in the Time
of Shakespeare:
A Survey of Major Scholarship

Review Article

T. J. KING

T HE CONFLICTING THEORIES about the way Shakespeare's plays were first acted are of perennial interest, not only to scholars attempting authentic reconstructions of the Globe and other playhouses of the period, but also to actors trying to approximate the original theatrical values in this astonishing body of dramatic literature. This review article evaluates the various theories advanced since 1909 and attempts to show why valid conclusions about pre-Restoration staging can be drawn only from a study of all the available pictorial and architectural evidence as well as the stage directions in texts that may reflect actual performances.[1]

1. Reprinted in part, by permission of the publishers, from T. J. King, *Shakespearean Staging, 1599–1642,* © 1971 by the President and Fellows of Harvard College. Six books of related interest deserve mention here, but they provide only limited discussion of pictorial and textual evidence concerning staging: William Poel, *Shakespeare in the Theatre* (London, 1913); T. S. Graves, *The Court and the London Theaters during the Reign of Elizabeth* (Menasha, Wis., 1913); Joseph Quincy Adams, Jr., *Shakespearean Playhouses* (Boston, 1917); Muriel C. Bradbrook, *Elizabethan Stage Conditions* (Cambridge, Eng., 1932); Cécile de Banke, *Shakespearean Stage Production: Then and Now* (New York, 1953); J. L. Styan, *Shakespeare's Stagecraft* (Cambridge, Eng., 1967). The authoritative reference

Perhaps the most pervasive misunderstanding about the Elizabethan theater is the notion that the stage, or parts of it, was used to represent a specific place such as "A Street," or "A Room at the Castle," or "Another Part of the Forest." Although Nicholas Rowe (1709) and most subsequent editors add designations of locale to the stage directions at the start of every scene, these sophistications based on eighteenth-century stage conditions have no authority. In Shakespeare's day, professional actors performed on an essentially *placeless* stage for which designations of locale were usually unnecessary. For example, the First Folio *Twelfth Night*—which, according to W. W. Greg, was printed from the company "prompt-book or a transcript of it"[2]—includes the stage direction *Enter Viola and Malvolio, at severall doores* (II.ii), "several" being used here in the sense of "distinct or apart" rather than "more than two" and "door" used in the early sense of "a passage into a building or room, a doorway." There is no reference to fictional locale in this scene other than Viola's vague comment that she has "since arrived but hither" (l.4). The stage may gain temporary localization by functional properties brought on, such as a bed or banquet, but when the stage is cleared of actors and properties, any designation of place that may have been suggested by the preceding scene is nullified.

Although the preservation of early performance records is largely a matter of historical accident, it is clear that in the years before the closing of the theaters in 1642 Shakespeare's plays were acted not only at the first and second Globe but also at a minimum of seven other places in the London area: Blackfriars, Gray's Inn, the Middle Temple, the Great Hall in Whitehall, St. James, Hampton Court, and the Cockpit-in-Court. For Shakespeare's company—first known as the Lord Chamberlain's Men, which in 1603 became the King's Men—court performances

---

work, Gerald Eades Bentley, *The Jacobean and Caroline Stage*, 7 vols. (Oxford, 1941–1968), states: "Since these volumes are intended for reference, I have tried to reduce to a minimum the amount of conjecture about theatres and their facilities for the staging of plays" (VI, v). References to Bentley are given within parentheses in my text, as are references to E. K. Chambers, *The Elizabethan Stage*, 4 vols. (Oxford, 1923), and Alfred Harbage, *Annals of English Drama: 975–1700*, 2d ed., revised by S. Schoenbaum (Philadelphia, 1964).

2. W. W. Greg, *The Shakespeare First Folio* (Oxford, 1955), p. 427. Citations from the First Folio in my text are to the Norton Facsimile prepared by Charlton Hinman (New York, 1968).

were prestigious and lucrative engagements, especially in the reign of James I. It therefore seems likely that when Shakespeare wrote his plays, he had in mind not only the Globe but also the several royal entertainment halls. While some recent investigations have offered hypothetical reconstructions of the Globe stage, the obstinate fact remains that we have no authentic picture of the inside of this playhouse. Instead, we must rely on the Swan drawing—our only picture of the interior of an open-air Elizabethan playhouse comparable to the Globe—and the available architectural evidence from places where Shakespeare's plays are known to have been performed, such as the Middle Temple, where, according to the *Diary* of John Manningham, *Twelfth Night* was acted on 2 February 1601/2.[3]

Described below are nine façades providing pictorial and architectural evidence about the English pre-Restoration stage. Despite their apparent diversity, the façades share the essential characteristic of being *placeless* and are of two basic designs: (A) to (E) have doorways and an open space above; (F) to (I) have a gallery above from which curtains are, or could be, hung. Either of these basic designs can, with minor adjustments, provide a suitable façade in front of which to act any and all of Shakespeare's plays.

(A) The so-called De Witt sketch of the Swan, which is in fact Arend van Buchell's pen-and-ink copy of De Witt's original, ca. 1596. According to a contemporary reference, this structure was still standing in 1632. The drawing—held by the University Library, Utrecht—shows a platform stage, a nonrepresentational façade with two double doors hinged to open on stage, and a gallery above where actors, or audience, or both are observing actors on stage. A sound and thorough survey of scholarly opinion about this drawing is given by D. F. Rowan, who observes that Middleton's *A Chaste Maid in Cheapside* (Chambers, III,

3. E. K. Chambers, *William Shakespeare: A Study of Facts and Problems* (Oxford, 1930), II, 327–328. As part of the quatercentenary celebration of the opening of Middle Temple Hall, the Inn invited the Oxford and Cambridge Shakespeare Company to perform *Twelfth Night* there for three nights, 4–6 March 1970. *The Law Guardian* (London), May 1970, reports: "H. M. Queen Elizabeth the Queen Mother, a Master of the Bench, who as Treasurer in 1949 had reopened the Hall after its repair from war damage, came to the first night." The play was reportedly acted in front of the hall screen, with the audience seated on scaffolding at the upper end of the hall.

441)—the only extant play for which there is conclusive evidence of performance at the Swan—is compatible with the stage depicted in this drawing.[4]

(B) The hall screen at Hampton Court, built 1531–1536, where the King's Men acted *Othello* on 8 December 1636, and *Hamlet* on 24 January 1636/7 (Bentley, I, 128–129). The screen has two open doorways and a gallery above. In an excellent analysis of the hall screens here and at the Middle Temple, Richard Hosley points to the structural similarities between these screens and the façade shown in the Swan drawing.[5]

(C) The hall screen at the Middle Temple, originally built in 1574, damaged by enemy action during World War II, and reconstructed exactly according to the original design. The screen is a placeless façade with two doorways and a gallery above.

(D) Inigo Jones's drawings for the remodeled Cockpit-in-Court at Whitehall. These form part of the so-called Jones/Webb Collection at Worcester College Library, Oxford. The renovated building was first used by the King's Men on 5 November 1630, when they offered "An Induction for the House" and Fletcher's play *The Mad Lover* (Bentley, I, 28). Court records for 1638 indicate that among the plays performed there were "ould Castel" on 29 May, "Ceaser" on 13 November, and "The mery wifes of winsor" on 15 November.[6] The drawing shows a placeless façade with five open entrances and an observation post above.

(E) Drawings for an unidentified pre-Restoration playhouse recently found by D. F. Rowan in the same collection as the Cockpit-in-Court drawings.[7] This stage has an unlocalized façade with three entrances and an observation post above.

4. "The 'Swan' Revisited," *RORD*, X (1967), 33–48. All nine façades are reproduced by King, *Shakespearean Staging*, Plates I–IX.

5. "The Origins of the Shakespearian Playhouse," in *Shakespeare 400*, ed. James G. McManaway (New York, 1964), pp. 29–39.

6. Chambers, *William Shakespeare*, II, 353. See also D. F. Rowan, "The Cockpit-in-Court," in *The Elizabethan Theatre* [I], ed. David Galloway (Toronto, 1969), pp. 89–102; Glynne Wickham, "The Cockpit Reconstructed," *NTM*, VII, no. 2 (1967), 26–36; reprinted in *Shakespeare's Dramatic Heritage* (London, 1969), pp. 151–162.

7. "A Neglected Jones/Webb Theatre Project: 'Barber-Surgeons' Hall Writ Large,'" *NTM*, IX, no. 3 (1969), 6–15; "A Neglected Jones/Webb Theatre Project: 'Barber-Surgeons' Hall Writ Large,'" *ShS*, XXIII, (1970), 125–129.

(F) A scale drawing of Trinity Hall, Aldersgate Street, London, reproduced by Charles T. Prouty.[8] The drawing is dated 1782, when the hall was in use as a nonconformist chapel, but Prouty maintains that it must have been built before 1446. Accounts of the Churchwardens of St. Botolph without Aldersgate show receipts from the rental of Trinity Hall to "diverse players" or "for players" in seven of the years between 1557 and 1567. Prouty suggests that a curtain or arras was hung from the lower edge of the gallery at the western end of the hall, thus providing a tiring house or space *within*. This gives an unlocalized façade through which actors may enter by parting the curtain at either end or at the center. The gallery above provides an observation post

(G) A small engraving of a stage with actors on it from the title page of *Roxana* (1632), a Latin play by William Alabaster, probably performed at Trinity College, Cambridge, ca. 1592. The play was first printed in London, however, about forty years after production, and the engraving may therefore furnish evidence about the professional theater at the time of printing. Curtains are hung from the downstage edge of the gallery above, from which actors, or audience, or both, are watching actors on the stage.[9]

(H) A small engraving of a stage from the title page of *Messalina* (1640) by Nathanael Richards. The play was probably acted by the King's Revels company sometime between July 1634 and May 1636, during which time the company was acting at Salisbury Court (Bentley, V, 1002–1004). Curtains are hung from what appears to be a gallery with a curtained window above.

(I) The frontispiece of *The Wits or Sport Upon Sport* (1672), a collection of drolls probably acted in the Commonwealth or early Restoration period. On stage are Falstaff, "The Changeling," and other characters from pre-Restoration plays. A curtain is hung from a gallery with a curtained window above. Actors, or audience, or both, are in the gallery watching actors on the stage below, where an actor is seen stepping from between the hangings.

From these nine pieces of evidence it can be seen that the stage equipment used by English pre-Restoration actors was not so elaborate or

8. "An Early Elizabethan Playhouse," *ShS*, VI, (1953), 64–74.

9. See Joseph Quincy Adams, Jr., "The Four Pictorial Representations of the Elizabethan Stage," *JEGP*, X (1911), 329–333.

standardized as some theories of Shakespearean stagecraft suggest. Furthermore, textual evidence indicates that acting companies improvised procedures according to the auditorium and stage properties available to them. This is shown by a collation of two variant texts of John Fletcher's *The Woman's Prize*, first acted by the King's Men about 1611 and revived in 1633 (Chambers, III, 222). According to R. C. Bald, the manuscript of the play in the Lambarde Collection of the Folger Shakespeare Library gives a transcript of the promptbook as the play was acted before 1623, when Sir Henry Herbert became Master of the Revels. A second version printed in the Beaumont and Fletcher Folio of 1647 is probably closer to the author's original text.[10] Bald notes one difference in stage directions that seems significant: where the folio reads *Enter Livia discovered abed, and Moroso by her* (V.i), the manuscript reads "Enter Livia sick carryed in a chair by servants: Moroso by her." If Bald's inferences concerning the provenance of these texts are correct, the Folio stage directions indicate the author's original intentions, but the manuscript acting version shows how the exigencies of the theater compelled a change in staging procedures.

If a play requires hangings and is to be acted in a hall with doorways and a bare façade, hangings can be fitted over one or more of the doorways, perhaps for special scenes only. Evidence for this procedure is found in Philip Massinger's *The City Madam*, a play first acted by the King's Men in 1632 and printed with variant title pages, some dated 1658, others 1659. This text was apparently printed from prompt copy.[11] Notations appear in the margins of the printed text just as they appear in the margins of some playhouse documents: *Whil'st the Act Plays, the Footstep, little Table, and Arras hung up for the Musicians* (IV.iv) and *Musicians come down to make ready for the song at Arras* (V.i).

No door frames are shown in the stage façades of the Trinity Hall, *Roxana, Messalina,* and *The Wits* drawings, but a "door" in the sense of a "passage into a building or room; a doorway," can be provided by parting the hangings at the center opening or at either end. One stage

10. *Bibliographical Studies in the Beaumont and Fletcher Folio of 1647*, Supplement to the Bibliographical Society's Transactions, no. 13, 1938 (for 1937), 77–78.

11. "Copy for the quarto of *The City Madam* was very clearly a manuscript that had been used as a theatrical promptbook." *The City Madam*, ed. Cyrus Hoy, Regents Renaissance Drama Series (Lincoln, Nebr., 1964), p. xix.

direction suggests that a movable door can be represented figuratively and need not be a literal part of the stage setting. The 1640 Quarto of *Love's Cruelty* by James Shirley—licensed for the Queen's Men in 1631 —carries the direction *Hippolito seemes to open a chamber doore and brings forth Eubella* (IV).[12]

Given these indications of flexibility in staging procedures, no authentic item of pictorial evidence should be discounted without careful consideration of its suitability for the performance of Shakespeare's plays. For example, the *Roxana* drawing is sometimes rejected for the study of Shakespearean staging because it appears on the title page of a play probably performed at Cambridge. This drawing is significant, however, because the title page of Shakespeare's *Hamlet* (Q1–1603) states that it is as "acted by his Highnesse servants in the Cittie of London: as also in the two Universities of Cambridge and Oxford, and else-where."[13] There is no reason to assume that *Hamlet* cannot be acted on a stage such as that shown in the *Roxana* drawing.

The appraisal offered here of major scholarship by nineteen authors is not intended to discredit what are often useful and illuminating studies. Instead, I hope to show how the failure of some scholars to apply consistent criteria for the evaluation of evidence has led to widely divergent and sometimes mutually contradictory theories.

(1) The earliest of the important books on staging is Victor E. Albright, *The Shakespearean Stage* (New York, 1909), which advances a highly conjectural reconstruction of a "Typical Elizabethan Stage."[14] Be-

---

12. The National Library of Scotland copy of this quarto has manuscript markings to indicate that it was used as a promptbook. See G. Blakemore Evans, "New Evidence on the Provenance of the Padua Prompt-Books of Shakespeare's *Macbeth, Measure for Measure,* and *Winter's Tale," Studies in Bibliography,* XX (1967), 239–242.

13. Greg, *First Folio,* describes this quarto as "a version of the play acted by a company touring in the country," p. 300. The need for flexibility in staging procedures, especially on tour, is well documented by W. F. Rothwell, "Was There a Typical Elizabethan Stage?," *ShS,* XII (1959), 15–21.

14. (Repr., New York, 1965). In reviewing previous scholarship Albright observes (p. 151): "Among the articles mentioned in the Bibliography there are three doctors' dissertations on the Elizabethan stage: Cecil Brodmeier, *Die Shakespeare-Bühne nach den alten Bühnenanweisungen* (Weimar, 1904); George F. Reynolds, *Some Principles of Elizabethan Staging* (Chicago, 1905); Richard

cause his theories have been so influential for so many years, I have given more discussion to Albright's work than I have given to later studies that accept his theories without questioning the unreliable evidence he adduces. Perhaps the most significant flaw in his line of argument is that he accepts pictorial evidence tending to support his theories, yet rejects other equally valid evidence contradicting them. For example, he notes that the Swan drawing shows no curtains and discounts it as "hearsay evidence by a man unacquainted with the art of acting, and, as a result, is impracticable, self-contradictory, and lacks some necessary parts" (p. 40); he rejects *The Wits* drawing because it "in no sense represents an Elizabethan stage. . . . Perhaps it was drawn partly from imagination and partly from the actual performance of plays on hastily constructed platforms for the nonce in the ruined theaters, private houses, halls, inn-yards, anywhere and at any time [during the Commonwealth period] the law-defying actors could get a stand" (p. 43). He accepts the *Roxana* and *Messalina* drawings as authentic because they show hangings needed for his hypothetical "inner stage."

Another obvious deficiency in Albright's scholarship is his un-warranted assumption that evidence for his reconstruction can be derived from "a study of the origin and form of the Restoration stage" (p. 45). As his principal illustration he reproduces a picture from the 1673 edition of Elkanah Settle's *The Empress of Morocco* showing the stage of the Duke's Theater—also known as Dorset Garden—built in 1671. Harbage describes this as "an elaborate theatre (possibly designed by Christopher Wren) on the model of Lisle's Tennis Court . . . it was the first modern theatre with a 'picture frame' stage" (*Annals*, p. 306). The title page describes the work as "A Tragedy with Sculptures." Each scene is precisely localized by stage directions describing representational settings and spectacular effects, e.g., Act I, scene i: "The scene opened, is represented the Prospect of a large River, with a glorious Fleet of Ships,

---

Wegener, *Die Bühneneinrichtung des Shakespeareschen Theaters nach den zeit-genössichen Dramen* (Halle, 1907)." Albright refutes the theories advanced by these three scholars but acknowledges his debt to William Archer, "The Eliza-bethan Stage," *QR*, April 1908, pp. 442–471: "His conception of the material stage is so nearly like my own that it would be useless to point out the slight differences" (Albright, p. 162).

supposed to be the Navy of Muly Hamet, after the Sound of Trumpets and the Discharging of Guns." Albright reproduces the drawing of a dungeon setting with "A Wall set with spikes of iron" (Plate 6), but this is of questionable validity for the study of pre-Restoration staging. Although masques and plays at court provided occasional scenic innovations before 1642, plays written for public performance by professionals did not use scenery.[15]

From *The Empress of Morocco* drawing, Albright infers that the Restoration stage had five distinct parts: "inner stage and outer stage with a curtain between them, proscenium doors leading to the outer stage, and balcony windows over the doors. . . . The setting is all on the inner stage . . . the outer is entirely bare" (p. 47). Albright asserts that the *Messalina* drawing shows "an outer stage with a curtain, perhaps 25 feet wide, across the rear, and evidences of a space behind the curtain, which corresponds to the Restoration inner stage" (p. 47). Although this title-page engraving shows no doors, Albright asserts: "the sides of the stage, up even with the ends of the gallery, are covered with the encroaching pictures [on the title page]" (p. 48), and "on both sides of the outer stage in the cut-off corners there were proscenium doors, arranged much the same as we find them in the Duke's Theater" (p. 49). This highly questionable evidence is used to construct a "perspective view" (Frontispiece, Plate 4) and a ground plan (Plate 8) of a "Typical Elizabethan Stage."

As evidence for "an outer stage approached by two proscenium doors, and an inner stage at the rear separated from the outer by a curtain," Albright cites stage directions from several plays, only two of which are attributed to Shakespeare. Neither of these stage directions requires an "inner stage": *First Part of the Contention* (1594), *Exet Salisbury, Warwick drawes the curtaines and showes Duke Humphrey in his bed* (III.ii.146); *Henry VIII* (1623), *Exit Lord Chamberlaine, and the King drawes the Curtaine and sits reading pensively* (II.ii.62). The curtains in the *Contention* stage directions, however, may be those on a curtained bedstead thrust on stage for this scene. The direction *Bed put forth* is found at this point in the 1623 Folio text of this play. Greg contends that

15. See Kenneth R. Richards, "Changeable Scenery for Plays on the Caroline Stage," *TN*, XXIII (Autumn 1968), 6–20.

there seems to be "no escape from the conclusion that the manuscript behind Folio [*Henry the Sixth, Part Two*] had at some time been used as a prompt-book." [16] The scene in *Henry VIII* can be staged by hanging curtains over an open doorway.

Albright's acceptance of evidence from precisely localized settings on the Restoration stage leads to his mistaken notion that most of Shakespeare's plays were first acted with settings that represented specific places. His chapter "The Shakespearian Method of Stage Presentation," suggests three kinds of settings: "First, those in which properties are used, as room scenes, forest scenes, etc.; second, those in which no properties are needed in the action or mentioned in the lines, as street scenes, battle scenes, wall scenes, and the like; third, those in which no properties are needed, and which could be played either with or without a setting, as the many conversational scenes" (p. 114). To illustrate this procedure, Albright gives a synopsis of *The Merchant of Venice;* he describes the settings for Act I as follows: "Scene 1. *A street.* Outer scene. The meeting of the Venetians; Bassanio reveals his secret need to Antonio. The action before the closed curtains without properties. Scene 2. *A room* in Portia's house. Inner scene. Portia and Nerissa talking over the various suitors. The curtains drawn and the action on both stages with room properties on the inner. Scene 3. A *street.* Outer scene. The Jew and Bassanio meet and a loan is effected. The action before the closed curtains without properties" (p. 104). Albright's localization as "A Street" was first suggested by Theobald (1733), while "A Room in Portia's House" was first suggested by Capell (1767/68). The stage directions in the earliest authoritative text, the Quarto of 1600, give no indication of fictional locale. The dialogue of the opening scene makes two references to "Venice" (ll. 115, 180), but a street is not mentioned, nor does the text indicate whether the action supposedly takes place indoors or out-of-doors. Bassanio speaks of Portia being at "Belmont" (ll. 161, 171, 182), but the stage direction at the start of the second scene states only *Enter Portia with her waiting woman Nerissa.* No room properties are indicated by the dialogue, other than "these three chests of gold, silver, and lead" (ll. 29–30). There is no reason to assume that the

16. *First Folio,* p. 183.

stage was decorated to represent a fully furnished room; the chests can be placed on a portable stand hung with curtains and carried on and off stage by servants.

Albright's conclusion that the "Shakespearean Method of Stage Presentation" utilized an "inner stage" thus relies on evidence of questionable validity: pictorial evidence from the 1673 edition of *The Empress of Morocco,* written for production with spectacular effects in the Duke's Theater built in 1671, and—for the localization of Shakespeare's scenes—emendations by eighteenth-century editors. Other features of his reconstruction also require close examination, especially his "upper stage," and "machinery for ascending and descending."

In "The Uses of the Upper Stage," Albright contends: "In the early part of the Elizabethan period the many historical plays, with their scenes of besieging cities, storming forts, and scaling walls, called this member of the stage into frequent service. After 1600 . . . the gallery was used less and less, and in the Restoration it disappeared altogether as a permanent fixture" (p. 133). But this conjecture is contradicted by textual evidence indicating that an acting place "above"—sometimes described fictionally as "a window" or "the walls"—was required in several Jacobean and Caroline plays. For example, in three scenes of John Ford's *'Tis Pity She's a Whore* (1633), acted at the Phoenix, characters appear "above" to speak with, or observe, others on the main stage. This acting place should not be considered as an "upper stage," however, because entire scenes are not played within its confines. Furthermore, it was only after the Restoration and the gradual adoption of the "picture frame" stage with representational settings that the acting space "above" fell into disuse.

Evidence of "machinery for ascending and descending" on the pre-Restoration English stage is meager. Albright's strongest piece of textual evidence (p. 72) is from the Prologue to Greene's *Alphonsus of Aragon: After you have sounded thrise, let Venus be let downe, from the top of the Stage.* Chambers (III, 327) dates the play ca. 1587 without much evidence concerning company or playhouse; whatever device Greene may have had in mind when he wrote these directions, he probably did not expect to have standardized equipment available. The concluding direction—not cited by Albright—states: *If you can conveniently, let a chair*

downe from the top of the stage and draw her up. This stage practice
may have been outmoded when Ben Jonson wrote his Prologue for
Every Man in His Humour (1616 Folio) stating that in this play,

> Neither Chorus wafts you ore the seas
> Nor creaking throne comes down the boys to please.

Although court records indicate equipment to lower a throne to the
stage in the Cockpit-in-Court, such machinery was not required in the
vast majority of plays, and it seems reasonable to assume that it was not
necessarily available in most of the places where Shakespeare's plays
were acted.[17]

Furthermore, when stage directions require an actor to "ascend" or
"descend" from the acting place above, e.g., *Juno descends* in *The
Tempest* (Folio, IV.i.73), he could do so by means of a movable staircase set in place for special scenes only. *The Knight of Malta,* given by the
King's Men ca. 1616 (Bentley, III, 351), contains a notation apparently
printed from prompt copy: *The Scaffold set out and the staires* (II.v).
These are also mentioned in Henslowe's inventory of properties for the
Lord Admiral's Men dated 10 March 1598, at which time the company
was playing at the Rose: "i payer of stayers for Fayeton." [18]

(2) Among the prominent scholars apparently misled by Albright's
tenuous, sometimes invalid, evidence is Ashley H. Thorndike, whose
Shakespeare's Theater (New York, 1916) acknowledges indebtedness to
Albright for showing that "the theaters of the Restoration period were
manifestly modeled on the Elizabethan" (p. 77). Thorndike reproduces
Albright's "Typical Elizabethan Stage" (p. 90) and the illustration from
Settle's *The Empress of Morocco* (p. 110), but rejects the Swan and
The Wits drawings. The *Messalina* drawing is accepted as "the best
representation we have of a typical stage" (p. 71). Although he notes
that proponents of the "inner stage" have "tended to exaggerate the
usefulness of this part of the stage and its properties" (p. 101), Thorn-

17. The accounts of the Office of the Works record payment for work at the
Cockpit-in-Court in the year 1 October 1631/30 September 1632: "John Walker
Property maker viz:t for hanging the Throne and Chaire in the Cockpit wth cloth
bound about wth whalebone packthred and wyer for the better foulding of the same
to come downe from the cloude[es] to the Stage" (Bentley, VI, 273).

18. *Henslowe's Diary,* ed. R. A. Foakes and R. T. Rickert (Cambridge, Eng.,
1961), p. 319.

dike's analysis of the staging of *Antony and Cleopatra* follows Albright's theory that Shakespeare used the stage façade as a background to represent specific places: "with its forty-two scenes in Europe, Asia, and Africa, [it is] perhaps the most difficult of Shakespeare's plays for us to imagine as designed for a theater" (p. 124).

Thorndike provides a "list of stage directions illustrating the use of the curtains and the inner stage in plays acted 1576–1642" (pp. 433–444), including stage directions from *The Contention* and *Henry VIII* cited by Albright, as well as three other uses of the "inner stage" in plays of Shakespeare: *Romeo and Juliet* (1597), *She falls upon her bed, within the curtains* (IV.iii.59); *The Tempest* (1623), *Here Prospero discovers Ferdinand and Miranda, playing at Chesse* (V.i.172); and the dialogue references to "curtains" in *The Winter's Tale* (1623) when Hermione "like a statue" is discovered (V.iii.20). Again, the bed in *Romeo and Juliet* may have curtains of its own; the other scenes can be played with curtains hung over an open doorway. Thus, while Thorndike attempts a more thorough survey of textual evidence than Albright, his uncritical acceptance of Albright's theories make his study of limited value.

(3) For historical evidence about play production during this period, most scholarship is heavily indebted to the authoritative reference work, E. K. Chambers, *The Elizabethan Stage,* 4 vols. (Oxford, 1923), which devotes three chapters to staging. In Chapter XIX, "Staging at Court," Chambers asserts that Elizabethan court performances can only be understood in the perspective given by a survey of the "development" of scenic representation at other Renaissance courts, most notably Sebastiano Serlio's drawings (1551) of tragic, comic, and pastoral settings for the Italian stage (IV, 359–362), and designs for scenery at the Hôtel de Bourgogne (ca. 1633) by Laurent Mahelot (III, 16–17). Concerning performances at the early English court, however, Chambers notes: "The copious Revels Accounts of Edward and of Mary are silent about play settings. . . . The first and most salient fact which emerges is that a very large number of [plays] need practically no setting at all. . . . The action proceeds continuously in a locality, which is either wholly undefined, or at the most vaguely defined" (III, 21–22).

Although all the extant pictorial evidence indicates that English actors continued to perform on an essentially *placeless* stage, Chambers suggests "the possibility of a considerable evolution in the capacities of stage management between 1558 and 1642" (III, 2). He points to the "houses" used for amateur court performances of the precisely localized plays of Plautus and Terence or their Renaissance imitators (III, 42); he asserts that this practice was carried over to the professional playhouses where stages were furnished to represent a wide variety of places. In his Chapter XX, "Staging in the Theatres: Sixteenth Century," Chambers follows Albright's theories by suggesting that the manager of an Elizabethan theater provided settings, "not necessarily so elaborate or decorative as those of the Court, but at least intelligible, for open country scenes, battle and siege scenes, garden scenes, street and threshold scenes, hall scenes, chamber scenes" (III, 70).[19] Chambers offers hypothetical floor plans for "Square Theatre (Proportions of Fortune)" and "Octagonal Theatre (e.g., Globe, size of Fortune)." These are remarkably similar in design to plans proposed by Albright and Thorndike. Two doors lead to the tiring-house or backstage area; between the doors is a curtained alcove labeled "Place behind Stage," but it is similar in function to Albright's "inner stage" (III, 84–85).

Chambers defends the authenticity of the Swan drawing as "our one contemporary picture of the interior of a public play-house, and it is a dangerous business to explain away its evidence by an assumption of inaccurate observation on the part of De Witt" (II, 526). He attempts to reconcile the Swan drawing with his theory about a curtained alcove: "we cannot, on the evidence before us, assert that the Swan had an alcove at all; and if it had not, it was probably driven to provide for chamber scenes by means of some curtained structure on the stage itself" (III, 86). But neither can we, on the basis of the evidence before us, assert that "chamber scenes" were played within the confines of a "curtained structure." More likely, necessary properties were put forth on the main stage in full view of the audience. As noted, *Henry the Sixth, Part Two* (1623) has the direction *Bed put forth* (III.ii.146).

Chambers reproduces the Jones drawings for the Cockpit-in-Court

19. Harley Granville-Barker cites this passage and sharply criticizes Chambers in "A Note upon Chapters XX. and XXI. of *The Elizabethan Stage*," *RES*, I (1925), 60–71. Skepticism about Chambers' assumption that there was an "evolution" in theatrical practice is expressed by A. H. Scouten, "Some Assumptions behind Accounts of the Elizabethan Stage," in *On Stage and Off* (Pullman, Wash., 1968), pp. 4–11.

(Frontispiece, IV), but gives them only limited discussion (I, 216, 234). Three other drawings are relegated to a bibliographical note: *"Roxana* (1632) may be taken as representing a type of academic stage. . . . *Messalina* (1640), if it represents a specific stage at all, is likely to represent . . . Salisbury Court . . . *The Wits* . . . (1672) . . . shows the type of stage on which the 'drolls' contained in the book were given when the publique Theatres were shut up" (II, 519–520).

In Chapter XXI, "Staging in the Theatres: Seventeenth Century," Chambers notes: "At the Globe, then, the types of scene presented are much the same as those with which we have become familiar in the sixteenth century; the old categories of open-country scenes, battle scenes, garden scenes, street scenes, threshold scenes, hall scenes, and chamber scenes" (III, 106). In assembling textual evidence for this chapter, Chambers states that he relies primarily on plays acted by Shakespeare's company at the Globe and Blackfriars in the years 1599–1613, but he also considers "any evidence which may seem to point to specific development in one or more particular directions" (III, 104). He goes far afield, however, to support his theory about the use of representational settings. For example, he cites the manuscript plays *Cuckqueens and Cuckolds Errant* (1601) and *The Faery Pastorall* (1603) by William Percy, who "alone of the dramatists, prefixes to his books, for the guidance of the producer, a note of the equipment required to set them forth" (III, 136). In suggesting the date and provenance of these texts, Chambers observes that the MSS have "elaborate stage-directions, which contain several references to Paul's, for which the plays, whether in fact acted or not, were evidently intended. . . . It seems to me just conceivable [the plays] were originally produced by the Paul's boys before 1590, and revised by Percy after 1599 in hopes of a revival" (III, 464). Other than this slim evidence, there is no link between William Percy and the professional theater. He was third son of Henry Percy, eighth Earl of Northumberland, and was educated at Oxford. Chambers notes: "His life is obscure, but in 1638 he was living in Oxford and 'drinking nothing but ale' and here he died in 1648" (III, 464).

Only two stage directions from Shakespeare are cited by Chambers to show the use of "some kind of recess on the level of the main stage" (III, 110): *The Tempest* (1623), *Here Prospero discovers Ferdinand and Miranda, playing at Cheese* (V.i.172); and *The Merry Wives of Windsor*

(1602), *He steps into the Counting-house* (I.iv.40). Perhaps because in Shakespeare's plays the evidence for an alcove is so meager, Chambers qualifies his earlier statements and suggests the alcove may have "proved too dark and too cramped for the convenient handling of chamber scenes and . . . the tendency of the early seventeenth century was to confine its use to action which could be kept shallow" (III, 120). Nevertheless, this suggestion immediately brings to mind important questions: if the hypothetical alcove was "too dark and too cramped" in the early seventeenth century, why was not this also true in the late sixteenth century? And, if so, why were plays not acted at the public playhouse *without* an alcove as the Swan drawing indicates? While Chambers remains an eminent authority for his monumental literary and historical scholarship, in theatrical matters he appears to have been misled by Albright's theories about a "Typical Elizabethan Stage."

(4) In a series of significant articles, W. J. Lawrence did much to spur interest in the study of Elizabethan theaters. In *The Physical Conditions of the Elizabethan Public Playhouse* (Cambridge, Mass., 1927) he provides a "fusion of several lectures" given at Harvard during the academic year 1925/26; the author notes that the book represents his "maturer conclusions on a complex subject which has held me in willing bondage . . . for more than a quarter of a century" (p. vii).[20] His opening remarks seem to offer a refreshing departure from previous scholarship: "The first step toward a sound comprehension of the characteristics of Shakespeare's stage is to rid one's mind of prejudices and preconceptions born of familiarity with the magnified peep-show of today. . . . The appeal [of Shakespeare's stage] was largely to the imagination, and to that appeal there was vivid response. . . . The players, having no background, had every background" (p. 4). Nevertheless, by his selection of evidence Lawrence reveals prejudices and preconceptions of his own. He reproduces the *Roxana* and *Messalina* title pages, but not *The Wits* drawing, presumably because it "depicts the old [Red Bull] theatre as it was in Commonwealth days, after it had been dismantled by the Puritans"

20. Lawrence published four collections of his essays: *The Elizabethan Playhouse and Other Studies* (Stratford-upon-Avon, 1912); *The Elizabethan Playhouse and Other Studies,* Second Series (Stratford-upon-Avon, 1913); *Pre-Restoration Stage Studies* (Cambridge, Mass., 1927); *Those Nut-Cracking Elizabethans* (London, 1935).

(p. 9). The Swan drawing is reproduced, but dismissed as "a very primitive sort of arrangement . . . followed only where the stage had to be in whole or part removable" (p. 5).

The central argument of the book supports a posthumously published diagram for a "conjectural Elizabethan Stage with Oblique Doors" (facing p. 22) by William Archer (1856–1924). The ground plan is remarkably close to those of Albright, Thorndike, and Chambers, showing "curtains separating inner and outer stage" and "oblique doors surmounted by boxes or balconies." Archer's major addition to the earlier ground plans is a "middle, or third, entering door, leading from the tyring-house to the inner stage." As Lawrence's principal evidence for a third door at the back of the "inner stage," he cites (p. 17) *The Second Maiden's Tragedy,* an anonymous manuscript carrying a Revels license for the King's Men dated 31 October 1611 (Chambers, IV, 45): "Enter the Tyrant agen at a farder dore, which opened, bringes hym to the tombe, wher the Lady lies buried. The tomb here discovered, ritchly set forthe." But these stage directions provide no proof of a curtained "inner stage" with a back door. This action could be performed on a stage like that of the Swan by having the Tyrant exit through one door, cross over backstage, and open the other door through which the tomb can be "ritchly set forth." Plays acted at the Globe and elsewhere frequently use the wording *at one door and . . . at the other,* which strongly suggests that professional playwrights thought of the stage as having two entrances.[21] Apparently Lawrence's views about the public playhouse did not change substantially after this book. In a later collection of essays, *Those Nut-Cracking Elizabethans,* the Frontispiece depicts "A Typical Public Theatre" remarkably like that first published by Albright.

(5) Theatrical documents used in original productions of pre-Restoration plays are described and reproduced by W. W. Greg, *Dra-*

---

21. Plays could, of course, be acted in front of a façade with more than two entrances. The Cockpit-in-Court drawing, for instance, shows five doorways. Only one text that may depend on prompt copy carries directions to suggest the need for a third entrance. *Patient Grissil* (1603) has *Enter Urcenze and Onophrio at severall doores, Farnezie in the midst* (G3). The dialogue, however, suggests that Farnezie enters first and observes the meeting of Urcenze and Onophrio. *In the mid'st* may therefore mean that he enters from one of two doorways and stands center stage while he comments on their entrances.

matic Documents from the Elizabethan Playhouses, 2 vols. (Oxford, 1931). The author's statement about the significance of these stage plots, actors' parts, and promptbooks deserves quotation at length:

But though it is desirable to point out the caution needed in arguing from a restricted number of extant documents, it would be a serious error not to recognize their great importance for criticism. Every item of historical evidence performs a twofold function: positively it enlarges the basis we have to build on, and enables us to extend the structure of valid inference; negatively it is often of even greater service in limiting the field of admissible conjecture. That is why to a certain type of mind all fresh evidence is so extremely distasteful. In the present case, when we have made reasonable allowance for individual variation, the documents we are considering afford a very considerable and very valuable body of evidence (I, x–xi).

The stage directions in these playhouse documents not only provide authentic information about actual performance procedures but also enable scholars to make educated guesses about the extent to which a given text may depend on playhouse copy.[22] Although editors attempting to determine the substantive text of a play usually regard playhouse emendations as nonauthorial corruptions, these markings are a valuable source of evidence for the stage historian. Only by analyzing the staging requirements of texts probably dependent on playhouse copy can we make valid inferences about the extent to which the stages shown in the contemporary pictorial evidence are suitable for performances of Elizabethan plays. Unfortunately, Greg does not include the contemporary pictures in these volumes, and most later stage studies do not systematically take into account Greg's compilation of authentic textual evidence from the playhouses.

(6) Serious objections to the theories of Albright, Thorndike, Chambers, and Lawrence are offered by George F. Reynolds, *The Staging of Elizabethan Plays at the Red Bull Theater, 1605–1625* (New York, 1940). With cautious skepticism Reynolds observes: "One book and article after another accepts without question the same general ideas of the stage, and each new model and pictured reconstruction closely resembles its predecessor except perhaps in minor details. . . . This unanimity is in contradiction in some items to probability and in others to the evidence

---

22. See R. B. McKerrow, "The Elizabethan Printer and Dramatic Manuscripts," *Library,* 4th ser., XII (1931), 253–275.

on which we can feel most certain" (p. 1). Reynolds does not, however, address himself directly to the question of how Shakespeare's plays were performed. Instead, he studies those acted at the Red Bull, a circular, open-air theater used by the Queen Anne's Men (ca. 1605–1617), the Red Bull (Revels) company (1619–1623), and Prince Charles's Men (1623–1625) (Bentley, VI, 214–247). Although Reynolds acknowledges that plays acted at the Globe and Blackfriars "are more important as litera-ture, and more interesting because of their more immediate bearing on Shakespeare" (pp. 2–3), he chooses the Red Bull repertory for study because fewer plays need be taken into account and because "it is practically impossible to determine which among the King's men's plays represent a Globe and which a Blackfriars production, [while] most of these Red Bull plays were given only in a public theater" (p. 3).

As textual evidence he cites forty-six plays, including two playhouse documents: *The Two Noble Ladies* and *The Welsh Ambassador*. Reynolds carefully cites stage directions in these important manuscripts, but his analysis gives equal weight to several other texts of questionable value for the study of staging at the Red Bull. For example, he cites Thomas Heywood's *The Silver Age* thirty-one times, but this classical legend with elaborate effects is not a play in the sense that Shakespeare's works are plays. Chambers states that the 1613 text of *The Silver Age* presumably represents the work as "given at Court, apparently by the King's and Queen's men together" (III, 345) Instead of citing original quartos of plays by Dekker, Reynolds uses the Pearson text (1873), about which Fredson Bowers later observed: "The slovenly Pearson reprint can scarcely qualify as an edited text, and in all collations and notes it has been consistently ignored." [23]

In evaluating contemporary pictures of Elizabethan stages, Reynolds notes that the Swan "represents more or less truly a public theater of about 1596, and it shows more of the theater building than do the others." The frontispiece of *The Wits* shows chandeliers which "imply a theater illuminated by artificial light. The small curtain conceals the only entrance, an impossible arrangement for most Elizabethan plays." The title-page drawing for *Roxana* "shows a Caroline academic setting," and that of *Messalina* "is probably of a similar type" (p. 30). Reynolds

23. *The Dramatic Works of Thomas Dekker* (Cambridge, Eng., 1953–1961), I, x.

suggests that Red Bull plays "could be given on a stage structurally like that of the Swan, with the single important addition of a third stage door" (p. 188). In offering evidence for this statement, however, he admits: "Proof that the Red Bull had at least three doors leading from the tiring-house to the stage is not as plentiful as one might expect" (p. 109). He cites only one stage direction from a Red Bull play specifically requiring three doors: *The Four Prentices of London* (Chambers, III, 340–341) has *Enter three in blacke clokes, at three doores* (Prologue). Also cited is the moral masque *The World Tossed at Tennis* (Bentley, IV, 907–911): *Enter at the three severall doores the nine Worthies, three after three.* This work cannot be considered as typical of plays performed at the Red Bull, however; the Induction states that the masque was "prepar'd for his Majesties Entertainment at Denmarke-House."

Despite these shortcomings in his evaluation of evidence, Reynolds' work provides important correctives to dogmatic assertions by earlier scholars. He notes there are no significant differences in staging procedures "between plays given surely and only at the Red Bull and those given elsewhere, nor between plays of early and of late date" (p. 187). He also questions whether the stage equipment needed was so elaborate or standardized as some theories suggest:

Examination of all the plays given in a definite period at a single theater shows—not what one might expect, a series of customary stagings for similar scenes, but rather the opposite—that similar scenes were often staged differently. . . . "Studies" were, it appears, usually discovered, but prison and temple scenes and various interiors, banqueting scenes for instance, permit no sure generalization as to their staging. Unsatisfactory as such a conclusion is for guidance, it at least guards one against dogmatism (p. 188).

Although Reynolds' work provides an important landmark, several subsequent studies continue to propose misguided theories about a typical Elizabethan stage.

(7) Evidence for a hypothetical scale model reconstruction of the Globe is offered by John Cranford Adams, *The Globe Playhouse: Its Design and Equipment* (Cambridge, Mass., 1942). Adams finds the Swan drawing "abounds in . . . contradictions, omissions, and obvious errors" (p. 49), the most conspicuous being the lack of curtains (p. 136). With some reservations he accepts the *Roxana* and *Messalina* drawings and suggests that they are intended to "represent the public, unroofed type

of stage" (p. 94). He therefore uses these drawings as evidence for a curtained "rear stage" in his scale model (Frontispiece) having several structural features remarkably similar to those suggested by Albright: a platform stage with two entrance doors between which is a wide curtain closing off a "rear stage"; a curtained "upper stage" between "window stages" set above each of the entrance doors; a superstructure with machinery for raising and lowering actors, or properties, or both. Each of these features is presumably needed for the performance of Shakespeare's plays.

In Chapter VI, "The Tiring-House, First Level," Adams apparently follows Albright's ideas about Shakespearean staging and suggests that Elizabethan actors needed a "supplementary, shallow rear stage suitable for use (1) as a three-dimensional backdrop when the two stages were merged into one large interior (examples: the Capulet ballroom, a court of justice . . .); (2) as an interior logically connected with a larger exterior (examples: the Capulet burial vault . . . a cave near a lime-grove in Bermuda [sic] . . .); and (3) as in itself an interior (examples: Friar Laurence's cell, a room in Olivia's house . . .)" (p. 173).

As noted, designations of fictional locale are not included in the stage directions of Shakespeare's authoritative texts, but are emendations first suggested by eighteenth-century editors. Adams directly cites only two plays of Shakespeare as evidence for a "rear stage" at the Globe; the discovery of Ferdinand and Miranda in *The Tempest* (V.i.172) and the dialogue references to a "curtain" when Hermione is discovered in *The Winter's Tale* (V.iii). Among the other plays cited as evidence for the supposed "rear stage" are at least four works probably never acted: *The Jews' Tragedy* (Bentley, IV, 546–547), *Andromana* (Bentley, V, 1034–1035), *Albovine* (Bentley, III, 197–199), and *Orgula* (Harbage, *Annals,* p. 155). This eclectic choice of texts could perhaps be defended on the grounds that all the evidence should be taken into account, if, in fact, Adams did give all the evidence. This is not the case, however. He does not cite Greg, *Dramatic Documents,* nor does he attempt to show whether or not any of his evidence from printed texts may be derived from actual performance. A study of the titles listed in Adams' index shows that he does not make even passing reference to fifty-nine plays for which there is reliable evidence of performance before 1642 but whose texts do not require or even suggest the use of a "rear stage." All fifty-nine plays can be acted in any hall or auditorium with an unlocalized façade such as that shown in the Swan drawing. It is therefore highly unlikely that Shakespeare wrote his plays for a stage so elaborate as that suggested by Adams' reconstruction.

(8) According to George R. Kernodle, *From Art to Theatre* (Chicago, 1944), "The Elizabethan Stage was not an isolated invention but was, on the contrary, a logical result of the patterns and conventions of the visual arts of the Renaissance" (p. 2). From a study of early *tableaux vivants,* triumphal arches, and municipal theaters in England and on the Continent, he offers "a reconstruction of a composite façade with the basic pattern of the Elizabethan stage." This includes the following main features: a pair of heavy doors that swing open center-stage to provide a discovery space, two smaller entrance doors on either side of the center door, a small window above each of the small entrance doors, a curtained upper stage above the center doors, and a "heavenly throne . . . in a canopy at the top." He states: "Every detail of decoration here is known to have been used on either a theatre or a tableau façade in England or Flanders" (Fig. 47, p. 152).

Unfortunately, Kernodle's preoccupation with "the visual arts of the Renaissance" leads him to neglect authentic evidence concerning English pre-Restoration playhouses. He gives passing notice to the Swan drawing (p. 151), *The Wits* drawing, (p. 151), and the stage designs by Inigo Jones for the Cockpit-in-Court (p. 134), but he does not reproduce these, nor the *Roxana* and *Messalina* drawings, which are not even mentioned in his text. None of these English pictures shows a façade nearly so elaborate as the one he suggests.

(9) Richard Southern published his series of four lectures given at the University of Bristol (1951/2) in *The Open Stage* (London, 1953); he states his study is derived from "a conviction that had been borne in upon me recently that whenever you put on any sort of theatrical show the thing which matters most (on the material side) is not the scenery but the *stage*—its shape, its nature, and its relation to the audience" (p. 9). After tracing the development of the classical Greek stage through the Greco-Roman and the Renaissance theaters, he finds: "One form of stage could be tangibly traced at any period and reasonably shown to have an unbroken development . . . a fairly high platform with some sort of curtained booth at the back from which the players came, and with

possibly a canopy above. . . . It is because of this players' room behind that I [call this] the 'booth' stage" (p. 16).

In his discussion of the Elizabethan stage, Southern credits C. Walter Hodges with giving considerable advance to the "simple theory of the booth stage" by suggesting that "Burbage's first English playhouse was made by erecting a galleried auditorium round just this familiar type of stage, but retaining the effect of the free-standing platform and its booth behind . . . as the most vital part and core of the whole structure" (p. 21). Southern offers eloquent arguments for acting the plays of Shakespeare and his contemporaries on an "open stage" rather than with representational settings on the "picture frame" stage found in most conventional modern theaters: "The open stage is placeless. . . . It is never Caesar's House. Maybe at a pinch it might be said to be 'Rome,' but that's as close as one should go" (p. 106). This idea, of course, sharply contradicts theories advanced by Albright, Thorndike, Chambers, Lawrence, and John Cranford Adams. Southern supports his case by reference to the unlocalized façade of the Swan drawing, but makes only limited use of textual evidence.

(10) In his abundant compilation of pictorial evidence, C. Walter Hodges, *The Globe Restored* (London, 1953), offers a series of reconstructions showing how the trestle stage and portable booth described by Southern were supposedly developed into the stage equipment for the Globe.[24] The eighth and last drawing in this line of development, "The Second Globe, 1614," shows a complex façade having a stage with a railing, at least four entrance doors, a curtained acting space center-stage, and a curtained space above flanked by open archways. Hodges observes: "It may have been at this stage of theatre development that the traditional flat façade of the tiring-house began to give way to new influences, and I show a curved façade somewhat resembling the Cockpit drawing by Inigo Jones" (p. 177).

Although the Swan drawing shows no curtains or booth, Hodges supports its authenticity and attempts to reconcile this bare stage with

24. Hodges' work has been revised and enlarged in its second edition (1968), which includes a detailed drawing of "The Globe Playhouse, 1599–1613: A Conjectural Reconstruction" (between pp. 90–91). This drawing shows basically the same stage equipment as the drawing in the first edition entitled "The Second Globe, 1614."

theories requiring a "curtained recess." He suggests that there was in "most if not all" Elizabethan stages "a part of the rear wall which was either permanently hung with curtain or arras, or where a curtain or arras could be put up when required" for the discovery of "a specially arranged group or set-piece." But he also notes: "There was an established practice of bringing large properties forward on to the stage in preference to having a scene take place within a curtained recess" (p. 54). The hangings shown in the *Roxana* and *Messalina* drawings could probably serve the dramatic function of concealing and revealing a tableau or set-piece, but Hodges is skeptical about accepting these drawings as evidence: "We do not know what sort of stages, whether indoor or outdoor, permanent or temporary, public or private, these are meant to represent. We only know that in spite of their particular convenience in some respects, they are not typical of stages of the period as a whole" (p. 36). Hodges reproduces these title pages (Plates 44 and 45), and *The Wits* drawing (p. 39), but makes only passing reference to the latter as "a popular performance in Restoration times, evidently indoors" (p. 26). As noted, Hodges accepts some features of the Cockpit-in-Court drawing, which he reproduces (Plate 50), but states "Whether the design was ever in fact used, or whether it was only a project is . . . a question. However, . . . it is a good example of theatre architecture at the period of indecision before the proscenium theatre became the established form" (p. 113).

Although there is only meager textual evidence for machinery to raise and lower actors, or large properties, or both, on the English stage of Shakespeare's day, Hodges reproduces a sketch showing elaborate machinery for the Italian stage and states: "This drawing shows a system of winding drums, counterweights and escapements for a flying throne, and for the free flight of Mercury and Cupids . . . which may have been copied from the work of the famous Giacomo Torelli at a theatre in Venice between 1640 and 1645" (p. 117). Hodges follows Albright in accepting the evidence of stage directions in *Alphonsus of Aragon* (p. 117) and the allusion to a "creaking throne" in Ben Jonson's *Every Man in His Humour* (p. 31). He also observes: "There are two instances in Shakespeare of the use of the flying machine—though both of these are almost certainly interpolations by another hand, catering to popular taste. The first is in *Macbeth*, III, v, where Hecate flies aloft seated in a 'foggy cloud'; and the second is in *Cymbeline,* V, iv, where Jupiter descends mounted on an eagle" (p. 77). The stage directions in the 1623 Folio—the authoritative text for both plays—do not require flying machines, however. Hecate's exit line indicates that she leaves the stage by following voices *within:*

> Hearke, I am call'd: my little Spirit see
> Sits in a Foggy cloud, and stayes for me.
> *Sing within. Come away, come away, &c.*

(III.v.34–35)

The descent of Jupiter *sitting upon an Eagle* (V.iv.92) requires an elaborate costume, but can be staged on a staircase such as that used in other plays. Although Hodges provides an admirable survey of pictorial evidence to support the "open stage" concept of Elizabethan theater, he does not offer a systematic analysis of the available textual evidence.

(11) Leslie Hotson, *The First Night of Twelfth Night* (London, 1954), contends that Shakespeare's plays were performed with the audience surrounding the stage on four sides and the players making their entrances from individual "houses" or "mansions" set about the stage. As noted, references are found to "houses" for performances at court, where they were used for precisely localized Roman comedies (Chambers, III, 42), but such equipment is neither required nor desirable in Shakespeare's plays, where most scenes are only vaguely localized.

Hotson claims to describe the staging of *Twelfth Night* at Whitehall on 6 January 1600/1, but this assignment of place and date of performance is highly conjectural, and scholars have raised serious objections to Hotson's interpretation of contemporary documents.[25] Furthermore, Hotson does not mention that the earliest external evidence for performance of this play is an entry in the *Diary* of John Manningham, who saw it acted at the Middle Temple on 2 February 1601/2. Nor does Hotson mention that the play was not printed until 1623, probably from a manuscript dependent on prompt copy. The First Folio text of *Twelfth Night* makes no mention of houses, and it can be staged in any hall or playhouse with at least two unlocalized entrances to the stage.

An extension of Leslie Hotson's earlier theory about production "in the round" is given by his *Shakespeare's Wooden O* (New York, 1960).

---

25. Alois M. Nagler, *Shakespeare's Stage* (New Haven, Conn., 1958), p. 39.

The author suggests that the "audience [was] stationed on both sides by an oblong stage" with a "tiring-house or dressing room underneath, inside the hollow stage" and " 'houses' stood facing each other from the stage-ends" (p. 281), but this theory relies on textual evidence not clearly identified. His leading illustrative example is Middleton's *A Game at Chess,* performed at the Globe on nine consecutive days in August 1624. Although Bentley (IV, 870–879) lists nine variant texts of the play, Hotson does not specify which text he cites. There is thus no way of determining the source for statements such as "Act 4 presents the dumb show of the 'wrong bedrooms' . . . with four separate places convincingly represented" (p. 44). Of all nine texts, the one probably closest to prompt copy—but not mentioned by Hotson—is the Archdale manuscript (Folger 410924), dated 13 August 1624 in the hand of Ralph Crane, scrivener for the King's Men at the Globe (Bentley, IV, 879). In this text the action of the dumb show is described as follows: "Musick. Dumb shew (brackets) Enter Black Queens Pawn with Lights, conducting White Queens Pawne to a Chamber: and then ye Black Bishops Pawne to an other & exit." The opening stage direction for Act I in this manuscript also reads: "Enter (from ye Black-house) a Woman-Pawne (in Black) & (from the White-house) a Woman-Pawne (in White)." The exchange described in the dumb show can be staged with two doorways as follows: black queen's pawn enters from the white doorway with white queen's pawn, who is led across stage to the black doorway, from which black bishop's pawn is led across the stage to the white doorway and *exeunt.* There is no textual evidence that "four separate places are convincingly represented."

Hotson's conjectures about the De Witt sketch are in keeping with his "in the round" theory. He interprets the vertical lines beneath the stage as representing "alleys . . . to give light to the end-windows of the under-stage tiring-house or cellarage" (p. 91) and further contends: "Trained to the one-side or façade stage of the Rederijkers, De Witt is struck by the Roman form of the *amphiteatra,* and, neglecting the rest of the house, comments pointedly and graphically by showing the audience in the lords' room on the other side of the Swan stage" (p. 111). His index shows no references to the other graphic or architectural evidence.

(12) Alfred Harbage published his Alexander Lectures given at the University of Toronto in 1954/55 in *Theatre for Shakespeare* (Toronto,

1955). Although the author states "the lectures are printed precisely as they were delivered, and their tone is not always polite" (p. x), they demonstrate once more his rare combination of erudition and theatrical sense. In Chapter II, "Elizabethan Guidance in the Staging," he observes that "no subject in theatrical history has been more militantly disputed" than "how Shakespeare's plays were staged in the first place," and he points to "two mutually contradictory theories . . . locked in a death grip" (p. 19). Harbage does not identify the scholars, but he describes the two opposing views as the "multiple stage" theory—presumably that advocated by Albright, Thorndike, Chambers, Lawrence, and John Cranford Adams—and the "new theory"—presumably that of Hotson— dismissing "the 'inner' and almost the 'upper' stage, proposing in their stead a number of practicable scenic structures of frame and canvas scattered about the platform and serving as the locales of a play" (p. 19). Harbage does not immediately refute either theory, however, and notes: "Neither the curtained enclosure nor the practicable scenic structure is a figment of the imagination—they both existed—but to let our mind dwell on them is to misconstrue the essential nature of Elizabethan staging" (p. 19).

In evaluating the pictorial evidence, Harbage observes that to reject the Swan drawing would be "perilous" and that "two additional pictures of open stages in use [the *Roxana* and *The Wits* drawings], although later and less authoritative than the drawing of the Swan, agree with it in showing actors upon a bare platform accessible only from the rear and overlooked by a rear gallery. . . . Both show . . . as the means of access a split curtain instead of doors. The pictorial evidence suggests that the only entrances to some Shakespearean stages were made through two rear doors, to others through a split rear curtain" (pp. 22-23). Harbage then cites the stage plots in Greg, *Dramatic Documents,* as evidence for the following analysis:

Entrances to most stages were made through both doors and curtain, with the curtain covering a central aperture into a backstage area occasionally opened to view for theatrical purposes. This curtained area cannot be considered a stage *per se,* no more can its existence be denied. For most of the purposes to which it was put, either of the broad rear doors of the Swan would have served, and in view of our certain knowledge that tents, tombs, and similar structures were occasionally set up on the great platform itself, any Elizabethan play could have been staged at the Swan theatre as shown (p. 23).

Harbage further documents his case by summarizing the "stage directions and implied action in eighty-six plays, including seventeen by Shakespeare—all those known to have been staged by particular companies using London amphitheatres between 1576, when the first was built, and 1608, when Shakespeare's company ceased using such structures exclusively, barring only such plays as were not printed within the same period" (p. 24). From this large body of evidence Harbage can generalize about rules rather than exceptions in Elizabethan staging procedures:

The suburbs of the Elizabethan stage have received more emphasis than the stage itself. The extent of the over-emphasis is suggested by the following figures. In the eighty-six plays . . . forty-eight require no use of the gallery, thirty-nine no use of enclosure whether on or at the rear of the stage, and twenty-five no use of either gallery or enclosure. . . . In 1312 scenes [of a total of 1463], the staging consisted of actors entering upon and leaving an open platform, either totally bare or equipped incidentally with a few seats, a table, a bed, a gibbet, a judgement bar, a raised throne, or the like. The exigencies of the fable dictated departures from the norm of simple platform playing (pp. 31–32).

In this brief lecture Harbage not only raises important questions about the preconceptions that appear to have guided so many earlier studies, but also brings together authentic textual evidence that should serve as a firmly fixed point of departure for later investigations.

(13) Indebtedness to earlier work by John Cranford Adams is acknowledged by Irwin Smith, *Shakespeare's Globe Playhouse: A Modern Reconstruction* (New York, 1956), who observes that Adams' reconstruction of the Globe is "as nearly complete and accurate as present-day scholarship is likely to produce" (p. xv), and follows Adams' evaluation of pictorial evidence, as well as the latter's theories about the "rear stage" (p. 106).[26] Smith provides fifteen meticulously detailed scale drawings for his reconstruction, but the stage equipment shown is derived ultimately from Albright's "Typical Elizabethan Stage."

As in his study of the Globe, Irwin Smith, *Shakespeare's Blackfriars Playhouse: Its History and Its Design* (New York, 1964), follows closely

26. Cf. John Cranford Adams, *The Globe Playhouse: Its Design and Equipment* (Cambridge, Mass., 1942), p. 173.

the theories of John Cranford Adams. What Smith describes as "an imaginative reconstruction of the Blackfriars auditorium and stage" (p. 307) is identical in almost every respect with the reconstructions he and Adams offer for the Globe, and both men rely on much the same textual evidence. Among the plays cited by Smith as evidence for a "curtained rear stage" at Blackfriars are two texts not printed until after they had been performed on the Restoration stage: *The Parson's Wedding* by Thomas Killigrew, manager of the King's Company at the time the play was first printed in 1663 (Bentley, IV, 701–705), and *News from Plymouth* by William Davenant, manager of the Duke's Company before the play was first printed in 1673 (Bentley, III, 209–211). The index to Smith's book shows that *The Parson's Wedding* and *News from Plymouth* are cited a total of twenty-five times to support his theories about the stage at Blackfriars. In contrast to his reliance on these texts, Smith gives only passing notice to four of the extant manuscript promptbooks from the repertory of the King's Men: *Believe As You List, The Honest Man's Fortune, The Second Maiden's Tragedy,* and *Sir John van Olden Barnavelt;* these four texts are cited a total of twenty-two times. Smith lists these plays in the repertory of the King's Men, but he does not identify them as playhouse manuscripts, nor does he discuss their textual characteristics. Yet these contemporary documents clearly provide a higher order of evidence than plays surviving only in late printed texts.

(14) Two of Richard Hosley's many valuable articles on the subject of staging deserve special mention here because they provide useful correctives to the conjectures of Hotson, as well as those of Albright and his followers.[27] "The Gallery over the Stage in the Public Playhouse of Shakespeare's Time," *Shakespeare Quarterly,* VIII (1957), 15–31, gives a

27. See also "The Use of the Upper Stage in *Romeo and Juliet,*" *SQ,* V (1954), 371–379; "Shakespeare's Use of a Gallery over the Stage," *ShS,* X (1957), 77–89; "Was There a Music-Room in Shakespeare's Globe?," *ShS,* XIII (1960), 113–123; "The Staging of Desdemona's Bed," *SQ,* XIV (1963), 57–65; "The Staging of the Monument Scenes in *Antony and Cleopatra,*" *The Library Chronicle,* XXX (1964), 62–71; "Reconstitution du théâtre du Swan," in *Le lieu théâtral à la Renaissance,* ed. Jean Jacquot (Paris, 1964), pp. 295–316; "The Origins of the So-called Elizabethan Multiple Stage," *TDR,* XII (1968), 28–50; "A Reconstruction of the Second Blackfriars," in *Elizabethan Theatre* [I], ed. Galloway, pp. 74–88; "The Playhouse and the Stage," in *A New Companion to Shakespeare Studies,* ed. Kenneth Muir and S. Schoenbaum (Cambridge, Eng., 1971), pp. 15–34.

careful analysis of the stage directions in 127 Elizabethan and Jacobean plays—including thirty-eight by Shakespeare—and concludes that the gallery shown in the Swan drawing is suitable for the limited action in scenes requiring a raised production area. Some stage directions describe this in the theatrical terms *above* or *aloft;* others use fictional terms such as *at a window* or *on the walls.* This space is required infrequently, however. Of the 127 plays examined, fifty-nine make no use of this acting space; the remaining sixty-eight require it on the average of 1.7 scenes per play (p. 31). This evidence contradicts the theory of John Cranford Adams that an "upper stage" was frequently used for "such scenes as would in reality have taken place in some room on the second level of an Elizabethan dwelling, tavern, prison, or palace." [28] Furthermore, Hosley argues convincingly that the gallery over the stage in the public play-house of Shakespeare's time "functioned primarily and constantly as the Lord's room, and only secondarily, occasionally, and then for relatively short periods as a raised production area; and that during such periods it exercised both functions simultaneously" (p. 31).

In "The Discovery-Space in Shakespeare's Globe," *ShS,* XII (1959), 35–46, Hosley sharply contradicts conjectures about an "inner stage" fitted up to represent various fictional locales. He notes that the term "inner stage" apparently never occurs in Elizabethan documents, and he asserts that there is "no unambiguous [pictorial] evidence whatsoever for an Elizabethan 'inner stage'" (p. 36). Instead, Hosley proposes that the tiring house of the first Globe was "essentially similar to that of the Swan as pictured in the De Witt drawing of 1596," which shows two double doors hinged to open on stage. When fully opened, either door "would have discovered a considerable space within the tiring-house; and this space might have been discovered by drawing aside curtains instead of opening a door, if we accept the expedient of fitting up hangings in front of an open doorway" (p. 35). For textual evidence, Hosley cites stage directions in thirty plays—including twelve by Shakespeare— "first performed by the Chamberlain-King's Men between the spring of 1599, when the first Globe was built, and the autumn of 1608, when the King's men may have begun using Blackfriars as well as the Globe" (p. 36). Hosley notes that twenty-one of these plays were produced without

28. Adams, *The Globe Playhouse,* p. 275.

a single discovery or concealment. In the remaining nine plays, the discoveries are few and infrequent, "essentially for shows or disclosure," and do not involve any appreciable movement within the discovery space. Occasionally the space may be localized temporarily as a "study" or a "shop," but for most scenes major properties such as beds or banquets are brought on in full view of the audience by servants or stage-keepers. Hosley's investigations are based on valid, verifiable evidence and make important contributions to our understanding of the Shakespearean stage.

(15) A. M. Nagler, *Shakespeare's Stage* (New Haven, Conn., 1958), asserts that the Globe has received "too much attention," especially since "the plays were also performed 'on the road,' in provincial towns where the strolling players (and Shakespeare was one of them) had to content themselves with halls and yards that certainly bore no resemblance to the permanent theatres in London" (pp. 18–19). He accepts the Swan drawing as authentic and reconstructs a "Shakespearean stage" by adding to the Swan façade curtains and a pavilion or "tent" such as that seen by Thomas Platter in his visit to a London playhouse in 1599: "The two doors of the tiring house cannot be seen during the perform ance: they are covered by a curtain, which hangs from the gallery and has three openings. Before both doors there are slits in the curtain; the third opening is not visible, for in front of it stands the pavilion which extends up to the gallery. The tent itself is closed off with curtains" (p. 53).

Nagler then describes how *Romeo and Juliet*—the First and Second Quartos, 1597 and 1598, serve as the basis of textual evidence—may have been acted with this stage equipment. However, neither quarto mentions a "tent" added to the stage façade for use as "Friar Laurence's cell" and for an entrance way in other scenes, e.g., "Mercutio and his friends enter from the left, Tybalt and his men from the right. Romeo comes in from the tent to stop the quarrel" (p. 56). Though it is true that the play could be acted with this equipment, questions remain as to how much was required or actually used by Shakespeare's company. Nagler's book concludes with a reconstruction of a performance of *The Tempest* at Blackfriars, probably under essentially the same conditions as *Romeo and Juliet*.

(16) Fifteen Shakespearean and fourteen non-Shakespearean plays pre-

sumably first performed at the Globe playhouse provide the basic textual
evidence for Bernard Beckerman, *Shakespeare at the Globe, 1599–1609*
(New York, 1962). This valuable study of the repertory of the Chamberlain-King's Men in the most important decade in the history of this playhouse concludes: "The actual production of a drama relied upon specific
parts of this stage much less than we have thought. Style in staging was
inherent in the dramatic form, not the stage structure" (p. 214). Nevertheless, Beckerman asserts that among the principal parts of the stage
needed to perform the Globe plays were "at the rear of the platform, two
doors and a curtained recess between them [providing] access to the
stage" (p. 106). This "curtained recess" is not shown in the Swan drawing, which leads him to suggest: "The Swan, as it is depicted in the
drawing, unaltered, could not have accommodated the Globe plays" (p.
100). He does not point out, however, that most of the Globe plays *can*
be acted on the stage of the Swan "unaltered"; the others can be acted if
hangings are added for the very few scenes in which they are required.
As noted, Richard Hosley's analysis of thirty texts of essentially the same
Globe repertory indicates that the stage there was "similar to that of the
Swan as depicted in the De Witt drawing of 1596." [29]

Furthermore, Beckerman's discussion of an important sequence in
Macbeth indicates that he does not entirely subscribe to the idea of an
essentially placeless stage. In assessing the possibility that the stage at the
Globe had a third entry, he notes: "No stage direction specifying an
entry from a middle door, such as can be found in non-Globe plays,[30]
appears. However, certain scenes do suggest the use of a third entrance.
In *Macbeth* (V.vii) Malcolm, who has presumably come through one
door (A), is invited into the castle of Dunsinane by Siward. At his exit
(through B presumably) Macbeth enters. Either he can come from the
door (A) through which Malcolm entered, which is dramatically unconvincing, or from the door (B) of Dunsinane, which is awkward, or
from a third entrance, evidence for which is not conclusive" (p. 70).
However, Macbeth's entrance through door (A) after the exit of Malcolm through (B) would be "dramatically unconvincing" only if one
does not accept the Elizabethan convention that when the stage is

29. "The Discovery-Space in Shakespeare's Globe," *ShS*, XII (1959), 35.
30. Cf. George F. Reynolds, *The Staging of Elizabethan Plays at the Red Bull
Theater, 1605–1625* (New York, 1940), p. 109.

cleared of actors and properties, any designation of place suggested by the preceding scene is nullified. In watching pursuits and killings, and in hearing loud *alarums,* the audience is much more concerned with the action than with its exact fictional locale.

(17) Glynne Wickham offers a comprehensive survey of valuable source material relating to stage practice in his *Early English Stages: 1300 to 1660.* Volume I (New York, 1959) covers the period from the Middle Ages to the building of The Theater in 1576; Volume II, Part i, (New York, 1963) concludes with a study of the Swan, built in 1596. Among Wickham's many important contributions to an understanding of theatrical conditions are his cogent arguments that the basic con ventions for English professional troupes were established in perform- ances at the banquet halls of Tudor palaces and manor houses. Plays successfully performed for nobility were later given in London and provincial towns in whatever kind of hall a paying audience could be assembled. He argues against the "Inn Yard" theory about Elizabethan performances and suggests that "a hall or gallery within the inn was in fact the theatre" (II,pt.i,188).

After a survey of architectural precedents for Elizabethan playhouse design, Wickham accepts De Witt's sketch of the Swan "at its face value without modification, interpolation or any other unwarranted change. . . . The whole of this stage, with its screen, gallery and dress- ing-room, indistinguishable from the Tudor Hall, is set down, put, placed, dumped in the conventional three-tiered Tudor game-house in a man- ner which will admit the maximum number of spectators consistent with box-office capacity and a reasonable view of the action on the stage" (II,pt.i,204). Wickham points to the difficulties in drawing inferences about staging from printed playbooks (II,pt.i,154), but this volume of his study does not take into account the dramatic documents from Eliza- bethan playhouses.

Volume II, Part ii (New York, 1972), analyzes and amply illustrates the available pictorial and architectural evidence concerning places of entertainment in the period after the building of the Swan in 1596. This part begins with an account of theatrical events in the year 1597 which led to the Swan's being abandoned as a playhouse, the dismantling of the Theater, the renovation of the Boar's Head Inn, and the construction of the first Globe and the first Fortune. Wickham then cites evidence con-

cerning buildings that served for nontheatrical entertainments—the Bear
Garden and the Tiltyard and Royal Cockpit in Westminster, and other
cockpits in London and the provinces—in order to show how these
structures influenced important playhouses of the period: the Curtain,
the Rose, the Swan, the Hope, the Amphitheatre, the Riding Academy,
and the Cockpit (or Phoenix) in Drury Lane. Inigo Jones's drawings
for the renovation of the Cockpit-in-Court and for an unidentified private playhouse—possibly the Salisbury Court—are also examined closely.

After a study of the Red Lion, the Cross Keys, the Boar's Head, and
the Red Bull—all places of performance associated with buildings that
had been at one time inns or taverns—Wickham analyzes the evidence
about playhouses built primarily for the performance of stage plays: the
first and second Globe, the first and second Fortune, the Blackfriars,
the Whitefriars, Salisbury Court, the Phoenix, Porter's Hall, William
Davenant's plans for a playhouse not built, and buildings used for banquets and masques where plays were also performed. The final books of
Volume II, Part ii, discuss the information available concerning stages
and tiring houses in playhouses built or adapted in the period between
1598 and the outbreak of Civil War. The third and concluding volume of
Wickham's work will offer a comprehensive survey of play production
techniques during the entire period 1300 to 1600.

(18) The central subjects of Frances A. Yates, *Theatre of the World*
(Chicago, 1969), are John Dee, mathematician and astrologer (1527–
1608), and Robert Fludd, physician and mystical philosopher (1574–
1637), studied as "representatives of Renaissance philosophy in England, with particular reference to the evidence in their works of the influence of the Renaissance revival of Vitruvius" (p. xi). To support her
contention for a Vitruvian influence on Elizabethan public playhouses—
including the Globe—Miss Yates offers as her primary evidence a picture of the interior of a theater from Fludd's Latin tract *De Naturali,
Supernaturali, Praeternaturali, et Contranaturali Microcosmi Historia*
(Oppenheim, 1619) (Plate 16). She describes this stage façade as having
"what is so notoriously lacking in the Swan stage wall, namely facilities
of a kind requisite for the production of Shakespeare's plays on a stage
with a fixed architectural background. Here [is] . . . a large central
opening flanked by two other entrances. Here can be seen a terrace on
the upper level. And here also is an upper chamber with windows. . . .

We now see that the upper chamber with its windows was in the centre of the terrace, and that there were two entrances on to this terrace, symmetrically placed directly above the two side entrances to the main stage below" (pp. 137–138). But nowhere in her book does Miss Yates describe why or how these elaborate facilities are "requisite to the production of Shakespeare's plays," nor does she cite the stage directions of even one play.

The Fludd drawing was first brought to the attention of stage historians by Richard Bernheimer, who suggests that the inscription *Theatrum Orbi* above the bay window on the upper level of the stage in the drawing may allude to Shakespeare's Globe.[31] But in comparing the print with "what is known about the characteristics of the Shakespearean stage," Bernheimer relies heavily on the work of John Cranford Adams. For example, as evidence for "two doors on the terrace above" at the Globe, Bernheimer cites a reference by Adams[32] to stage directions in the anonymous *Claudius Tiberius Nero*, which Bernheimer describes as "performed at the Globe in 1607" (p. 21). Although this play was first printed in 1607, there is nothing to suggest that it was acted at the Globe or anywhere else. Harbage lists the play as "Closet?" (*Annals*, p. 95), and Chambers notes: "The epistle, apparently not by the author, says the play's 'Father was an Academician'" (IV, 5). The evidence linking the Fludd drawing to the English stage is tenuous at best, and, as Bentley observes, "it is not at all clear what the tennis-court-like interior really depicts" (VI, 86, n. 1).

(19) Andrew Gurr describes his *The Shakespearean Stage: 1574–1642* (Cambridge, Eng., 1970) as a "conspectus of the material background to Shakespearean drama, a picture of the society in which the drama flourished, of the acting companies, their theatres, and their acting and staging" (p. vii). The work provides a succinct and useful summary of such scholarly works as E. K. Chambers, *The Elizabethan Stage,* and G. E. Bentley, *The Jacobean and Caroline Stage.* In evaluating scholar-

---

31. "Another Globe Theatre," *SQ,* IX (1958), 19–29. See also Frances A. Yates, *The Art of Memory* (Oxford, 1966); "New Light on the Globe Theatre," *New York Review of Books,* 26 May 1966, pp. 16–21; and "The Stage in Robert Fludd's Memory System," *ShakS,* III (1967), 138–166; I. A. Shapiro, "Robert Fludd's Stage-Illustration," *ShakS,* II (1966), 192–209.

32. Adams, *The Globe Playhouse,* p. 246.

ship about playhouses and staging, Gurr notes that Reynolds' study of the Red Bull is "the first book which made a properly restricted use of the available evidence" (p. 177). Gurr reprints the Swan drawing (Plate V) and accepts it as accurate and authentic. Two of the three drawings by Inigo Jones for the Cockpit-in-Court playhouse are included (Figure 4) with the suggestion that "the small, shallow stage would prohibit anything at all elaborate in the way of spectacle. It is clearly designed purely for playing" (p. 109). Gurr does not, however, cite the available court records about performances of Shakespeare's plays at this theater. He reproduces the Fludd drawing, but not other more reliable evidence concerning the pre-Restoration stage.

This survey has shown how the lack of consistent criteria for the evaluation of evidence has led to conflicting theories about the way Shakespeare's plays were first acted. Ten authors place primary emphasis on selected pictorial evidence but make no systematic study of the stage directions in the plays acted by professionals in this period: Albright (1909), Thorndike (1916), Lawrence (1927), Kernodle (1944), Southern (1953), Hodges (1953), Nagler (1958), Wickham (1963, 1972), Yates (1969), and Gurr (1970). Five other scholars—Chambers (1923), John Cranford Adams (1942), Hotson (1954, 1960), Smith (1956, 1964), and Beckerman (1962)—set aside the pictorial evidence wholly or in part and place primary emphasis on arbitrary selections of textual evidence, which in some cases is of questionable validity for the study of staging.

As shown, Greg (1931) argues cogently that documents from the Elizabethan playhouses—promptbooks, stage plots, and actors' parts—be used as evidence to "extend the structure of valid inference" and "limit the field of admissible conjecture" about Elizabethan stage conditions. In a systematic study of plays acted at the Red Bull, Reynolds (1940) takes into account two promptbooks of the period and shows a healthy skepticism about reconstructing a "Typical Elizabethan Stage." Harbage (1955) surveys the staging requirements for eighty-six plays first acted in the years between 1576 and 1608, and finds that in the vast majority of scenes "staging consisted of actors entering upon and leaving an open platform" either totally bare, or with large properties *brought on* or *thrust out*. Two important articles by Richard Hosley (1957, 1959) analyze the staging requirements of Elizabethan plays and show how these needs have been served by the façade shown in the Swan drawing, our only picture of the interior of an Elizabethan public playhouse.

It is hoped that future studies of stage conditions will take into account significant evidence from the contemporary playhouse documents as well as important bibliographical and textual studies which attempt to discriminate between texts that may depend on playhouse copy and those that probably do not. Only by a careful examination of texts that may reflect actual performances can we gain a clearer picture than has heretofore been available of how the plays of Shakespeare were acted by his contemporaries.

Review

King, T. J. *Shakespearean Staging, 1599–1642*. Cambridge, Mass.: Harvard University Press, 1971. Pp. 163. $6.75.

The title, *Shakespearean Staging, 1599–1642*, does not quite express the author's ambitions. In a book of modest length he endeavors to encompass the subject not merely of the staging of Shakespeare's plays but of all the plays "first performed by professional actors" between 1599 and 1642. Noting the wide divergence in theories of Elizabethan staging, Mr. King attributes it to the failure by scholars to apply "consistent criteria" in the evaluation of evidence. This he intends to remedy, first, by treating the works of the forty-three year period as a uniform body of material, and secondly, by seeking "positive correlations between the external evidence, as provided by contemporary architecture and pictures of early English stages, and the internal evidence, as provided by the texts of plays first performed in the years 1599–1642." He divides the 276 plays which constitute his internal evidence into three categories, according to likelihood of playhouse origin. The smallest number of plays, eighteen in all, are given the greatest

237

weight. They consist of works "dependent on prompt copy." The second
category, 42 plays, includes works "that may depend wholly or in part
on prompt copy." The texts of the remaining 216 plays purportedly lack
a playhouse source. By distinguishing between the primary evidence of
the prompt copy and the subsidiary evidence of non-playhouse copy,
King hopes to arrive at an authoritative description of staging.

In presenting his findings, however, King employs an arrangement
based not on the foregoing textual categories, but on playhouse features. Succeeding the Introduction are chapters entitled: Entrances and
Large Properties, Above the Stage, Doors or Hangings, Below the Stage,
and Twelfth Night at the Middle Temple. Several appendixes follow, including a critique of major scholarship on Elizabethan theatrical practice
since 1940. The effect of this arrangement is to study staging in terms
of the physical parts of the stage. For each of the parts, King culls the
evidence for its use, first from the plays based on prompt and probable
prompt copies, and then from the remaining plays. He attempts a synthe-
sis in a conjectural recreation of the original staging of *Twelfth Night*.
Through this scheme, essentially a catalogue or handlist method, King
manages to supply the reader with a considerable amount of information,
both about the provenance of the plays as well as their use of the stage.
It is in this respect that the book is most effective and should prove
valuable to students of late Tudor and Stuart drama.

To assess the results of this study properly, however, necessitates a
discrimination between its more conventional aspect, namely, an examination of how plays use the stage, and its more original contribution, the
division of evidence according to copy source. From the first it is apparent that King is using the term "staging" in a limited way. He
deals only with the actor's relation to stage furniture—doors, scaffolds,
properties, etc.—rather than the actor's relation to other actors and the
audience. This method is perfectly justified as long as the reader
understands that the title *Shakespearean Staging* treats only one element
of Renaissance staging, and perhaps not the most significant one. Unfortunately, there has been and continues to be a tendency to treat the
actor's use of properties and stage equipment as the whole substance of
mounting a play, and I suspect that King's title will reinforce this assumption among Shakespearean scholars and students.

In general, his findings as to the use of the stage support rather than revise current thinking. True, King does not resolve one of the knottier problems concerning the number of entries, to which I will refer later, but he does show how slight was the dependence of the plays upon the physical playhouse. Regrettably, King has a bent toward presenting his results as more unusual than they are. Early in his Introduction, he writes, for example, that the 276 plays he has examined show "that the stage equipment needed was much simpler than has been thought." Thought? By whom? At what time? It is true that in his appendix on previous scholarship he points out that Alfred Harbage has anticipated him and he also gives credit to Richard Hosley, but he does not make clear how conclusively Harbage, Hosley, and I have illustrated the independence of most Renaissance scenes from stage equipment and structure. In its amassing of evidence, *Shakespearean Staging* is a welcome reference work on stage usage, but it is hardly pioneering.

The second feature of the book, the distinction between prompt and non-prompt copy, is quite another matter. Here King introduces a question of methodology that is of considerable importance. Surprisingly enough, no one has sufficiently explored what prompt copy can reveal about theatrical presentation. Instead, concern with prompt copy has focused principally upon issues of textual authenticity. But using bibliographical evidence of playhouse origin as a guide for establishing the provenance of a text, which has occupied most scholarly attention, is not the same thing as using prompt copy to illuminate staging practice. King himself does not distinguish between these uses, but merely assumes that demonstration of playhouse origin automatically endows a text with theatrical authority greater than that of all other texts.

There are many difficulties in utilizing prompt copies, however. Of the eighteen plays listed by King as indubitably of playhouse origin, half reflect staging after 1630; and of the remaining nine, five date from 1620–1629, three from 1615–1619, and one from 1611. King assumes, as others do, that staging practice did not change between 1600 and 1642, and therefore the lateness of these prompt copies does not reduce their authority for the entire period. The matter is not easily settled though. For instance, intermissions became increasingly prevalent in public theaters during the first half of the seventeenth century. To what extent this change affected staging is uncertain. Does the direction in *The City Madam* bidding stagehands to hang up the arras for the musicians

"Whil'st the Act Plays" reflect Stuart staging only or staging from 1599 onwards? The chronological issue is further complicated if staging is thought to embrace a broader range of elements than mere use of stage equipment. It is then necessary to examine not only entries, exits, and properties, but also actor relationships and scene development. Admittedly, there is insufficient evidence to show that staging in this larger sense did indeed change over the course of the years. On the other hand, there is not sufficient evidence to assume that it did not.

The first text King cites as primary evidence is the Padua copy of the Folio edition of *Measure for Measure,* which contains seventeenth-century prompt markings. The text for the Folio edition itself, according to Greg, depended upon rough foul papers,[1] so that it must be the manuscript additions which have special importance for the study of staging. Yet a glance shows that these additions tell very little about some of the more controversial issues governing stage usage. Besides indications of intermissions, there are a few actor warnings, anticipated entries, and several redundant stage directions. Nothing in the copy clarifies the use of the façade or stage machinery. The very paucity of the markings suggests one of two possibilities. Either the prompter did not complete his work, in which case the supposed prompt copy loses its force as primary evidence, or these few markings were all that were needed for the staging of the text, in which case the author's rough foul papers supply the bulk of the clues for staging. Either supposition undermines King's contention about prompt copy primacy.

In claiming greater authority for the Padua *Measure for Measure* rather than, say, *Timon,* King fails to pose another question. Does not an experienced dramatist embody in his manuscript the actual practices of his stage? The fact that so many authorial stage directions remain standing in prompt copies indicates that this is the case. Moreover, is not the text of a mature Shakespearean play, whether or not of playhouse origin, likely to reflect staging practice more accurately than the prompt manuscript of a relatively inexperienced author such as Henry Glapthorne? Unfortunately, Mr. King does not come to grips with issues such as these.

The problems found in the Padua *Measure for Measure* beset more

1. *Shakespeare's First Folio* (Oxford, 1955), pp. 354–356.

prompt copies. The earliest prompt text that King uses is the manuscript copy of *The Second Maiden's Tragedy* (1611). Although there is some doubt as to whether the play was ever produced, it does contain evidence of playhouse preparation. King in any case places it in the first category as prime evidence. Yet in treating this play, which poses some interesting problems of staging, King ignores some of the most provocative matters. He makes no attempt, for example, to resolve the relationship between authorial and prompt directions. In fact, he does not seem to make an accurate distinction between the two. Citing Greg's edition of the play, he refers to the stage direction for Anselmus, "Locks him self in," as a prompter's note, although Greg reads the hand as that of the original scribe and thus of the author (King, p. 52; Greg, Malone Society Reprint [Oxford, 1909], p. x). According to Greg, the prompter made sixteen additions to the manuscript. Eleven were for sound and music cues, and five for entries, of which two supply the names of actors. In contrast, there are numerous, rather full, authorial stage directions. Together, the author's and prompter's directions should resolve all questions of staging. Yet they do not. There are some instances where exits are not marked (for a Page, line 1918; for Bellarius, between lines 2022 and 2120). No entry is marked for Anselmus before he speaks (about line 2021). Even more puzzling, stage business is not fully marked. At line 2210 Govianus exits, leaving behind the bodies of Bellarius, Anselmus, and Anselmus' Wife. The Tyrant and attendants enter at line 2211. No provision is made for the disposal of the corpses. Why? What is the significance of this omission? Does it mean that the prompt copy was unfinished and therefore the play was not presented? Or does it suggest that the copy was not actually employed for the performance but may possibly have served in the preparation of the running plot?

What is curious about *Shakespearean Staging* is that the author has seized upon a vital and potentially rich mode of investigation, but has made so little of it. Of all his curiosities, his selection of *Twelfth Night* for comprehensive reconstruction is most odd. His own assessment is that *Twelfth Night* probably depended upon prompt copy. Textual markings are few, and clear evidence of the prompter's hand does not exist. Yet King devotes eighteen pages of this brief book to the play's staging, while he neglects manuscripts that indubitably show the prompter at work and, in addition, require imaginative analysis.

Ultimately, if prompt copy is to receive principal authority, its evidence should be either conclusive or singular. As King uses the material, this is not the case. Not that his analysis of the stage is necessarily incorrect. But his conclusions do not differ in any significant way from those of Hosley, for instance, and they fail to settle controversial issues that have beset Elizabethan stage history. One of the more tantalizing questions, for example, concerns the number of entries to an Elizabethan public stage. Were there only two doors or entries? Or were there three entries, two of which may have been doors and one an enclosed recess between the doors? King follows Wickham, Hodges, and Hosley in giving pre-eminence to the Swan drawing, and therefore argues for two entries. He attempts to correlate this evidence with other visual representations, such as the Frontispiece of *The Wits* and the drawings by Inigo Jones for the Cockpit-in-Court. Of the nine prints he reproduces— including hall screens and the drawings for an unidentified pre-Restoration playhouse newly discovered by D. F. Rowan[2]—three show what may possibly be one entry (hangings are used), three indicate two entries, one has no entries proper, one represents three entries, and one five entries. Of course, the Swan drawing is the only representation of a public playhouse, and although King treats all his evidence, visual and textual alike, without reference to chronology, it is natural for him as well as for any other scholar arguing for two entries to concentrate on the Swan. In doing so, the problem of reconciling the Swan façade with textual evidence once again arises.

It is sufficiently established that a curtained area was required regularly, if infrequently, in most public playhouses. What then was the nature of that area? Was it located behind one of two entries? Was it temporarily erected on stage? Or was it a permanent part of the stage façade, serving for both entry and discovery? It is not my intention to reargue this issue here, for it is intricate and elusive. But in connection with the book under discussion I wish to observe that resort to prompt copy does not resolve the controversy. Two of King's prime pieces of evidence, *The Second Maiden's Tragedy* of 1611 and Massinger's *The City Madam* printed in 1658, contain complicated sequences of action

2. "A Neglected Jones/Webb Theatre Project: 'Barber-Surgeons' Hall Writ Large,'" *ShS*, XXIII (1970), 125–129. See also pp. 37–51 of this volume.

that King cites as evidence of a two-entry theory. In the scenes from *The Second Maiden's Tragedy,* mentioned above, his argument requires that one entry serve first as a tomb and then as a closet for Anselmus. In the space of three hundred lines (1702–2003) the other entry would be employed thirteen times over four scenes. At three changes of scene the actors entering the stage would have to await the exits of the actors clearing the stage. None of this is impossible, but it does produce a different flow of movement from one based upon exit at one door and entry at another. *The City Madam* is equally complicated, its staging directions indicating discovery at one point, and temporary hangings at another. An elaborate finale, involving the discovery of living "statues" and the entrance of more than fourteen actors, can be staged with two doors only in the most awkward manner. Both plays illustrate the elusiveness of the evidence as well as the indefiniteness of prompt copy. For an understanding of stage practice, it is not sufficient to prove that scenes could be physically accommodated by two entries. One must also consider the consequence of the theatrical effect produced by two entries.

But though prompt copy may not help to resolve questions of staging in the narrow sense, it may offer insight for staging in its broadest meaning. To gain such insight, we may have to ask new questions about prompt copies. Why, for example, is there redundancy in these copies? Frequently, the prompter will repeat in the margin of a printed or written text a direction already specified by the dramatist. One assumption is that such repetition is for the purpose of clarity, so that the prompter could see the stage direction more easily and thus prompt the performance more effectively. In the Padua copy of *Measure for Measure,* however, where such redundancy occurs, only a few directions are repeated; most are not. Why those particular repetitions?

And how should we weigh authorial intent? Is the staging projected by an experienced dramatist less reliable a guide to playhouse practice than actual prompt copy? A certain assumption exists that it is, but in only a few instances, those involving non- or semi-professional writers, can such inferiority be definitely demonstrated. This question requires further examination in light of another question.

Why are there so few markings in so-called prompt copy? As one examines both manuscript and printed examples, one is struck by the absence of expected stage directions. Necessary entries or exits are left unmarked. Required stage business is not noted. Even without having made a systematic study of prompt copies, I know that a number of them could not serve as guides for actual production unless the prompter's book was incidental to the performance. In reading King's book, I came to the conclusion that few scholars have asked the right questions of prompt copy. Without being certain that the "right" questions would yield more illuminating results, I suspect that we should ask not "why is this stage direction in this copy?" so much as "why is that necessary direction missing?" To puzzle over what is omitted may yield more meaningful results than merely to know what is included. Mr. King has performed a signal service in directing our attention to matters of prompt copy even if he has not fully exploited his own premise.

BERNARD BECKERMAN

Notes on Contributors

Bernard Beckerman, Dean of the School of Arts of Columbia University, is well known for his many studies of the drama, including *Shakespeare at the Globe: 1599–1609* and *The Dynamics of Drama*.

Werner Habicht is Professor of English at the University of Bonn. He is the author of *Studien zur Dramenform vor Shakespeare* (1968) and has previously contributed to *Renaissance Drama*.

David J. Houser, an Assistant Professor of English at Kansas State University, is currently investigating the disguised authority figure in the plays of Marston and Jonson.

William Ingram, who teaches at the University of Michigan, has published several articles on the Elizabethan theater and is now working on the manuscript of *Sir Thomas More*.

T. J. King, who teaches at the City University of New York, is the author of *Shakespearean Staging, 1599–1642* and has previously contributed to *Renaissance Drama*.

Nancy T. Leslie is a doctoral candidate at Emory University and is writing a dissertation on Marlowe in the theater.

Bonner Mitchell, Professor of French and Italian at the University of

Missouri, has published a critical edition of French literary manifestoes and, more recently, *A Renaissance Entertainment.*

STEPHEN ORGEL of the University of California at Berkeley is best known for his work on Jonson, both his edition of the masques and his critical study, *The Jonsonian Masque.*

ALAN K. G. PATERSON is Lecturer in Spanish at Queen Mary College, University of London. He is the author of several articles on the Spanish comedia and has edited Tirso de Molina's *La Venganza de Tamar.*

D. F. ROWAN, Professor of English at the University of New Brunswick, has written several articles on early playhouses and is best known for his work on the Jones / Webb theater drawings which he brought to light.

J. L. SIMMONS is an Associate Professor of English at Tulane University and has written essays on several Shakespearean plays, including a recent one on *Antony and Cleopatra* in *ELH.*

MARION TROUSDALE, who teaches at the University of Maryland, is interested in modern as well as Elizabethan drama and has contributed to *The Review of English Literature.*

Books Received

The listing of a book does not preclude its subsequent review in *Renaissance Drama*.

BERGERON, DAVID. *English Civic Pageantry 1558–1642*. Columbia: University of South Carolina Press, 1971. Pp. x + 325. $9.95.

BORN, HANSPETER. *The Rare Wit and the Rude Groom: The Authorship of A Knack to Know a Knave in Relation to Greene, Nashe, & Shakespeare*. Bern: Francke Verlag. Pp. ix + 176.

BRAEKMAN, W. *Shakespeare's* Titus Andronicus: *Its Relationship to the German Play of 1620 and to Jan Vos's Aran en Titus*. Ghent, 1968. From the seminar of English and American literature of the University of Ghent. Pp. 173.

BROMLEY, JOHN C. *The Shakespearean Kings*. Boulder: Colorado Associated University Press, 1971. Pp. xiii + 138. $7.95.

Calderón de la Barca Studies, 1951–1968: A Critical Survey and Annotated Bibliography, ed. JACK H. PARKER and ARTHUR M. FOX. Toronto, Ont.: University of Toronto Press, 1971. Pp. xiii + 247. $12.50.

CALDWELL, HARRY B., and MIDDLETON, DAVID L. *English Tragedy, 1370–1600: Fifty Years of Criticism*. San Antonio: Trinity University Press, 1971. Pp. xii + 89. $6.00.

Coleridge on Shakespeare: The Text of the Lectures of 1811–1812, ed. R. A. FOAKES. Charlottesville: University Press of Virginia, 1971. Pp. x + 171. $5.75.

DESSEN, ALAN C. *Jonson's Moral Comedy.* Evanston: Northwestern University Press, 1971. Pp. ix + 256. $7.95.

GURR, ANDREW. *The Shakespearean Stage, 1574–1642.* Cambridge, Eng.: Cambridge University Press, 1970. Pp. ix + 192. $9.50 (paper, $2.75).

Erasmus: Praise of Folly, ed. BETTY RADICE and ROBERT BALDICK. Baltimore: Penguin Books, Inc., 1971. Pp. 265. $1.95 (paper).

JONSON, BEN. *Every Man in His Humour,* ed. J. W. LEVER. Regents Renaissance Drama. Lincoln: University of Nebraska Press, 1971. Pp. xxviii + 296.

LEVIN, RICHARD. *The Multiple Plot in English Renaissance Drama.* Chicago and London: University of Chicago Press, 1971. Pp. xiv + 277. $9.50.

LOPE DE VEGA, attributed author. *La fianza satisfecha,* ed. WILLIAM M. WHITBY and ROBERT R. ANDERSON. Cambridge, Eng.: Cambridge University Press, 1971. Pp. xi + 208. $10.50.

LUDWIG, WALTHER. *Ioannis Harmonii Marsi Comoedia Stephanium.* Munich: Wilhelm Fink Verlag, 1971. Pp. 189.

A New Companion to Shakespeare Studies, ed. KENNETH MUIR and S. SCHOENBAUM. Cambridge, Eng.: Cambridge University Press, 1971. Pp. v + 298. $12.50 (paper, $3.95).

PIERCE, ROBERT B. *Shakespeare's History Plays: The Family and the State.* Columbus: Ohio State University Press, 1971. Pp. xii + 261. $8.95.

SACKVILLE, THOMAS, and NORTON, THOMAS. *Gorboduc, or Ferrex and Porrex,* ed. IRBY B. CAUTHEN, JR. Regents Renaissance Drama. Lincoln: University of Nebraska Press, 1970. Pp. xxx + 88. $4.75 (paper, $1.65).

Shakespeare Survey 24, ed. KENNETH MUIR. Cambridge, Eng.: Cambridge University Press, 1972. Pp. viii + 184. $10.00.

Shakespeare's Later Comedies: An Anthology of Modern Criticism, ed. D. J. PALMER. Baltimore: Penguin Books, Inc., 1971. Pp. 459. $3.95 (paper).

WEBSTER, JOHN. *The Devil's Law-Case,* ed. FRANCES A. SHIRLEY. Regents Renaissance Drama. Lincoln: University of Nebraska Press, 1972.

WILLEFORD, WILLIAM. *The Fool and His Scepter.* Evanston: Northwestern University Press, 1969. Pp. xxii + 265. $8.50.